TEXTUAL BODIES

SUNY Series,
The Body in Culture, History, and Religion

Howard Eilberg-Schwartz, Editor

TEXTUAL BODIES

Changing Boundaries of Literary Representation

Edited by
Lori Hope Lefkovitz

STATE UNIVERSITY OF NEW YORK PRESS

Chapter two is reprinted from *The Paternal Romance* by Robert Con Davis, copyright 1993 by the Board of Trustees of the University of Illinois Press and used with permission of the author and of the University of Illinois Press.

Chapter seven is reprinted by permission from *The Proceedings of the Second International Lewis Carroll Conference* (Winston Salem: Lewis Carroll Society of North America, 1995).

Production by Ruth Fisher
Marketing by Nancy Farrell

Published by
State University of New York Press, Albany

© 1997 State University of New York

For information, address the State University of New York Press, State University Plaza, Albany, NY 12246

Library of Congress Cataloging-in-Publication Data
Textual bodies : changing boundaries of literary representation /
    edited by Lori Hope Lefkovitz.
        p.   cm. — (SUNY series, the body in culture, history, and
    religion)
        Includes bibliographical references and index.
        ISBN 0-7914-3161-4 (hardcover : acid-free). — ISBN 0-7914-3162-2
(pbk. : acid-free)
        I. Lefkovitz, Lori Hope, 1956– . II. Series.
PN56.B62T49   1997
809'.9336—dc20   96-21758
                                                             CIP

10 9 8 7 6 5 4 3 2 1

For
the bodies closest to my own:
Leonard David Gordon,
and our daughters,
Ronya Heleni and Samara Esther

CONTENTS

ACKNOWLEDGMENTS

My work on the body in literature began with an earlier book, *The Character of Beauty in the Victorian Novel,* a study of the role that physical description plays in characterization. The idea for this collection began with a panel on "Literary Allusions to the Body" that I chaired at the 1988 NEMLA convention. The interest in that topic was so surprisingly large, as measured by the number of proposals I received and by the bodies packed in the room, that there seemed to be a place waiting for a collection like this one. I am especially grateful to those contributors and to the SUNY Press, who have been patiently waiting these years. Thanks to a Mellon grant to Kenyon College, I was on an interdisciplinary steering committee in 1986–87 preparing a faculty summer seminar on "The Human Body and the Human Being." We read literature from Sappho through Kafka, and the faculty participants represented all of the disciplines. I am grateful to the members of that group for extending my view of the body and increasing my interdisciplinary vocabulary on the subject. My engagement with this subject led to several courses, and I want to thank my students, especially the group of seniors who participated in my seminar on literary theory that had "the body" as its subject. Nancy Comley and Denise Witzig read the manuscript and gave useful advice and support for which I am very grateful. I team taught, with Leonard Gordon, a course on "Treatments of the Human Body in Classical Judaism," at the National Havurah Committee Summer Institute in 1987 and later at the Community College for Adult Jewish Studies in Columbus, Ohio, and I learned from both groups. In 1988, I participated in a Midwest Faculty Seminar at the University of Chicago on "The Body as Social Text," and the diversity of approaches to the body impressed me yet again. One of the speakers pointed out at that conference that there are cultures in which the body has more permeable boundaries than it does in our culture. As individuals, we tend to think of ourselves as having or being a single body, defined by the limits of what we call our own parts, having a singular, independent existence and integrity; there are cultures, however, in which the body's limits extend into what we think of as the bodies of others, into the bodies of our lovers, parents, children, and so on. At the time, I was a nursing mother away from my infant for the first time since her birth, and I fully felt—in my body—the point that he was making. And that is why this book is for the bodies that have been part of my own, with special recognition of Leonard Gordon's attention to my textual bodies.

Lori Hope Lefkovitz

Introduction

Textual Bodies: Changing Boundaries of Literary Representation

The body's history in Western discourse intersects, of course, with the history of many artifacts and phenomena, but in compiling the essays for this collection, I have been impressed with the recurrence of a particular set of connections: The body's history in literature is also the history of bodily violation; as the body acquires new definition, what it means to transgress its boundaries changes accordingly. In one way or another, each of the contributions here illustrates the connection between the body and transgression. In our culture, the body alternately insists on its own integrity or relinquishes that integrity to intimacy, duty, or violation (for example, in the forms of sex acts, pregnancy, self-sacrifice, or various expressions of asceticism); the body is alternately inviolate, vulnerable, and violated, a construct never fully itself.

The eleven essays in this collection are deliberately rereadings of major texts in the Western canon, and as such, they collectively demonstrate both how interpretations change when read for a particular theme—in this case, the body—and how the body, as read through literature over time and in light of recent theory, has itself changed. The essays contained here share an emphasis on the situation and treatment of the human body in particular texts. Each is a work of practical criticism informed by recent efforts to theorize the body and construct its social history, and each illuminates literature through the figure of the body. The essays are arranged chronologically according to the texts that are interpreted, though sets of recurrent themes suggested other organizational possibilities: Fragmentation of the body, metamorphosis, illness and bodily negation, and male rendering of female bodies are among the echoing concerns. The essays range in subject matter from Page duBois' analysis of the fragmented body of Sappho's poetry as analogous to the fragmented body within the Greek classical tradition through themes of mutilation as analyzed first by Richard Rambuss in his reading of Chaucer's *The Prioress's Tale,* then by Sheila Delany in her reading of a medieval hagiography, and finally by Martina Sciolino in her reading of Kathy Acker's relatively recent novel *Great Expectations;* we also find cross-dressing as metamorphosis in medieval literature treated in Roberta Davidson's reading of romance, a subject itself transformed in Deborah Laycock's reading of shape-shifting and fashion in eighteenth-century literature; Robert Con Davis demonstrates how woman's body, figured as illness in ancient gynecological literature, structures the gendering of the human subject in Aristotelian doctrine, and woman's ill body recurs in Miriam Bailin's reading of the body ironically negated in that famous medical woman's, Florence Nightingale's, work; the negation of body as Victorian phenomenon finds further resonance in Donald Rackin's new reading of Lewis Carroll's *Alices.* Freddie Rokem's "Slapping Women," an analysis of female characters who enact a scene with a slap that throws bodies off balance in comparable "dramas" by Ibsen, Strindberg, and Freud, raises among its questions the articulation of the female body by the male voice, and cross-gendered ventriloquism is a question also fundamental to Gita Rajan's reading of Walter Pater and Antoine Watteau.

DuBois on Sappho and Sciolino on Kathy Acker's novel *Great Expectations* frame the collection and share a concern with the incomplete body, asking us to recognize its importance in our personal and historical memories. DuBois poses a startling question: Why do we pursue a dream of wholeness? Like much ancient Greek sculpture, the body of Sappho's poetry, Sappho's individual poems, and the body represented in Sappho's poems are necessarily fragments, and we have relentlessly re-membered this fragmented past by refusing the disturbances of dismemberment. DuBois argues that this impulse, a problem of historiography, has consequences for bodies of poetry, bodies in poetry, and bodies in the world. This terror of incoherence recalls for duBois the imaginary time of bodily dis-integration that precedes, in Lacanian psychoanalytic theory, the child's jubilant self-recognition of wholeness in the mirror phase. Might we forego "a dream of wholeness" and accept partiality, recognizing the possibility for ecstasy in the recollection of disorder? Ultimately what is at stake for duBois is the position of women; she favors a dialectic materialist theory of history that is important for facilitating the questioning of longstanding assumptions about the natural body.

In her reading of Acker's novel, Sciolino also invokes "the imaginary maternal body" as the "site of longing." Maternal absence leads to the desire for what Sciolino calls "full-fill-ment," a desire that decomposes Acker's text of ambiguous genre. For both duBois and Sciolino, fragmentation and de-composition—ancient and postmodern, historical and personal, in textual bodies and human bodies—provokes a culturally-imposed urge to reconstitute the self, circling around the unnameable lack that is the maternal body. But identity, Sciolino reminds us, is a "work in progress." DuBois makes a similar claim when she asks us to acknowledge that "our own relationship to antiquity" (as to our own past) will always be partial and interested, and that postmodern existence is "provisional" and "split," based on a fiction of a coherent ego.

As the culminating essay, Sciolino's reading of Acker's collage echoes the vocabulary of the essays that precede it, surprising us with how the body's treatments in the past are present and transformed in twentieth-century fiction. For example, Sciolino, like Laycock, looks closely at authority and textual bodies while paying particular attention to the economy of plagiarism. Acker's transgressive thefts from, among others, Dickens's novel of the same name and the erotic *Story of O* represent attempts to resist the entrapment of inherited conventions, challenging the distinctions between originality and difference, autobiography and fiction, and canonical and smut as "pornography perversely grants Acker a way of representing woman's psycho-social being."

For Laycock, the plagiarism common in eighteenth-century England, where authors and booksellers shamelessly copied not only the work of others but also stole the names and identities of successful writers, is directly related to changes in the new credit economy. In her richly textured analysis, Laycock shows how the development of public credit and the fashion industry (stimulated by credit) "seemed to contemporaries to threaten the bases of a stable identity or personality, an identity generally conceived to reside in the body of a propertied gentleman." By analyzing how the discourse in the debates about credit overlaps with the discourses about women and fashion, Laycock exposes the misogyny in the current descriptions of a feminized economy that is mutable and without substance, an economy driven by women's criminal desires for a peculiarly eighteenth-century version of Ovidian self-transformation. Value depends not on substance but fashion, which in Baudrillard's words "disqualifies body." In this way the "natural body was thought to disappear" (emblematized in the way a fashionable hoop skirt could easily conceal pregnancy); self-transformation leads to self-alienation, a substitution of fantasy for the real, where reputation (by analogy to credit) is the fashionable version of the self.

Laycock goes on, in another turn, to make the connection between paper money and paper books, the circulation of the insubstantial that justified plagiarism for money and that led to the danger that "people will become paper." She wonderfully shows how the developing economy of the eighteenth century, the critique of Lady Credit, the literature of imitation (particularly false John Gays) and of mock rape (Pope), is rhetorically dependent upon a pre-existing understanding of women's physical insubstantiality, a body thought to be subject to vapors and hysteria. (This medical legacy is the subject of Davis's essay on Aristotelian gynecology and finds further resonance throughout the volume.) Laycock comes full circle by closing with a brief discussion of Lady Mary Wortley Montagu's defense of fashion and a credit economy that apparently resisted her own commodification. When Lady Mary's work as a stockbroker led to her being blackmailed, however, anxieties about the loss of her credit (reputation) affected her physical body, and this sickness brings back to the physical body the consequences of the body's constructions in discourse.

Just as Laycock shows our economy to be built on the foundation of woman's insubstantial body, Davis shows how the contemporary knowing subject of modern philosophy and cultural studies is also based on classical gynecology's "knowledge" of the female body.

Reminding us of the scientific wisdom that the female body is sickly because it is not warm enough, and that woman's blood and semen (yes!) are not pure, as well as of the characterization of the uterus and its behavior in classical medical discourse, Davis supports both Laycock's and Davidson's arguments about how the inherited characterization of women's bodies had material consequences for many centuries to come.

Davis describes how a variety of women's ailments depend upon where the mobile uterus wanders (a woman might drown in menstrual blood, for example, if the uterus wandered between her lungs), to the purpose of proving that the uterus is characterized as willfully perverse, having a perverse intent to go astray. To the point is the second-century Greco-Roman author Arataeus who writes of the womb that it "is like an animal within an animal." Davis shows how the female body, independent and rebellious, takes "a kind of animal pleasure in violating its own order of health." Women cannot control the uterus that becomes a metonym for woman, and the male doctor, who uses remedies such as sweet suppositories, bitter herbs, and massage to trick the errant organ, becomes the master of the female as body and of the female as a body of knowledge.

This triple pun—textual corpus, represented body, and material body—reiterated often in this introduction and in the essays themselves is significant. Davis demonstrates that the Aristotelian concept of the subject of knowledge (passive, a body available for study) is based on a logic of the difference between men and women; the male body becomes the knowing subject (active), "the embodiment of scientific and cultural authority," and the female body is suppressed as the feminized subject of knowledge. This subject (available for study) is defined according to a doctrine of flux that understands the substance of a scientific subject as "the structural pattern of its form always expressed as a contradiction."

Just as duBois brings psychoanalytic theory to ancient attitudes to argue for a particular way of doing history today, Davis brings this slippage in the definition of "the subject" (knower/that which is known) back to contemporary philosophy and cultural studies, asking us to see that these two subjects remain in gendered relationship according to inherited ancient constructions of the sexed body. He shows that Zeus, the cosmic monarch, replicates the function of the human doctor, treating a world that is imagined to be female, orienting it from a fixed position as the male doctor orients the wayward womb. The speaking subject of contemporary critical theory holds this male position in what turns out to be an ancient paradigm.

Bridging Davis on Aristotle and gynecology and Laycock on eighteenth-century shape-shifting is Davidson's essay on cross-dressing in medieval Romance. The Aristotelian tradition persists in medieval thought, categorizing women as more material than spiritual and also, as we have amply seen, as more pliant and subject to the forces of artistic and cultural will. In her engaging reading of several medieval Romances, Davidson shows how women's vulnerability to change makes them particularly responsive to their clothes when they are disguised as men or boys. Davidson's readings illustrate how, in a system consistent with Galenic medical wisdom that females can be literally transformed into males, cross-dressing produced more than superficial gender reversals. When the woman in these romances sports masculine garb, she acquires virility and body powers that once more challenge the boundary between metaphor and literal, between signifier and signified. Davidson provides compelling evidence that straddling the line between active/passive and male/female in the gendered grammar available in Davis's reading of "the subject" is a medieval woman wearing a sword.

The Virgin Mary, exemplary virgin and mother, is the woman on the threshold in Rambuss's contextualization and analysis of Chaucer's *Prioress's Tale*. By contrast with readings of this tale that divorce its devotional character from the gross body, from patterns of abjection, violence, and sexuality, Rambuss convincingly demonstrates that these features of the tale are integral to the genre of Marian devotion precisely because of how the body of Mary was understood in medieval discourses of medical science and theology.

Stories of miracles of the Virgin often feature bodies on the threshold, in particular bodies neither dead nor fully alive, such as that of the "murdered" child who continues to sing the Virgin's praises. Presiding over this threshold is Mary, whose own "perfect virginal/maternal body is made to incorporate a productive liminality between the mysterial and the material, between corporeal abjection and redemption." Rambuss argues that Mary's corporeal status and the processes of pregnancy, lactation, and menstruation illuminate the "choreography between contrary, even impossible modes of existence" in miracle stories such as that recounted by Chaucer's Prioress.

For example, the virgin who conceived without defloration, the paradoxical body, embodies more than a single conundrum: herself conceived without original sin, theologians reasoned that, on the one hand, she surely had to have been spared the defilement and curse of menstruation, a sign of sin, just as she was spared Eve's other curse, pain in childbirth (with a son who would later walk through walls, her hymen remained intact, and she remained "a maid"). On the other hand, medieval medical science taught that menstrual blood was required both for conception and lactation, and the humanity of Jesus therefore depended entirely on the humanity of a mother who, to be fully human herself and more importantly, to endow Christ with humanity, had to have menstruated, had to have been more than a mere vessel.

Rambuss's lively analysis restores medieval constructions of the body to this text and leads to an original and persuasive reading of this tale, reintroducing appropriate complexity to such concepts as youth, purity, and virginity. Figures for bodily orifices and excrement, a "defiling anality" associated here with the Jews and bound up with the tale's anti-semitism, Rambuss shows to be not antithetical to the Virgin and her miracles but rather consistent with the multivalent representations of her miraculous body in the Middle Ages. And in an important final twist, Rambuss exposes an Oedipal drama that positions the innocent child (neither dead nor alive) between two mothers (the Virgin and the biological) and two fathers (the abbot and the Jewish patriarchy), wedding sexuality to violence in Marian devotional literature, in Chaucer's tale, in Mary's body, and, we are left to wonder, perhaps in nature too.

Just as Rambuss's reading, like that of Davis, depends on an appreciation of contemporary medical understandings of the female reproductive body, so too the links of love to violence and Eros to Thanatos find repeated expression in the essays that follow. Sciolino records a confusion of love and violence, and of talking and hurting, in Acker's *Great Expectations,* and Rokem makes a similar connection in his reading of Strindberg's *Miss Julie.* What most strikes me about this repetition is less the association of love and death that Freud popularized than the repetition of the more ingenious grounding of this connection in a longing for the absent maternal body.

Eruditely exposing the multiple metaphorical meanings of the body and its parts in Roman, Arabic, and medieval culture and once more in medical lore, Delany enables us to appreciate the metaphorical associations that give the body, and importantly, particular female body parts, their own valences and connotations. She deepens a background for Rambuss's discussion of decapitation by elaborating on the meaning of the head in medieval culture and literature. The anatomy/architecture metaphor, with body represented as temple, mansion, dwelling, fortress, or tower, is traced through multiple permutations leading to the body of the Virgin Mary as an exemplary Tower in a way that further complements Rambuss's analysis of Mary's body.

Delany also draws our attention to repetitive sadism in medieval hagiography, to "the hyperbolized quality of these zealous adolescents who are flayed, burnt, drowned, maimed, shaved, insulted, raped, disembowelled," etc., who, like the "litel clergeon" in *The Prioress's Tale,* "do not die easily," and persist in defiant devotion. Like Rambuss, Delany describes an endurance that is surreal and often repulsive to modern readers. She then reads Osbern Bokenham's fifteenth-century collection of female saints' lives as a radical moment in the history of the genre, in which the sophisticated author responds "to the great national events of his age" through a literary representation of the suffering but triumphant female body. She shows that Bokenham's array of female saints constitutes a "collective anatomy" with both political and theological implications.

Dividing her essay into body parts just as Bokenham himself fragments and recounts the fragmentation of the female body in his hagiography, Delany sees the body's fragmentation as a metaphor for a series of things from the family (which in a number of these saints' lives proves to be as "fragile and fragmented as the physical body") to the body politic, and ultimately to the body of Christ. Again we see the rhetorical interdependence of literature and medicine, for example in an upward displacement of sex organ to tongue prevalent both in saints' lives and in medical lore.

Delany writes about the separation and fetishization of body parts in the genre of the saint's life, and then makes a rhetorical move that both renders suspect modern revulsion at this practice and foreshadows moments in several of the essays on Victorian and modern literature: She offers us the parallel between the sadist and lover, both of whom practice separation and fetishization of female body parts, exemplified for Delany in a passage from D. H. Lawrence.

Delany's purpose is less to question the lover's discourse than to recognize in Bokenham a rhetorical strategy that rehabilitates "femininity for theological and political purposes." We see the tormented body as central to medieval religious consciousness, and Christ's body is dramatically resituated in a culture in which amputation ceremonies were ritual public events, legal punishments. Bokenham's work demystifies the female body, and Delany's reading of one instance of that demystification in the elaborate medical description of Lucy's mother's dysentery echoes Rambuss's reading of the *Prioress's Tale* with its several examples of the body "open at both ends."

Delany situates the body balanced delicately, for the sake of the soul, between depreciation and appreciation. She sees Bokenham's contribution as a "collective anatomy of inspired women" articulated "from head to foot" and "including face, mouth, tongue, breasts, flesh, guts, womb, and genitals." Like duBois, Delany also tells a story of re-memberment as the author of whom she writes at once reconstitutes woman and reconstitutes the body politic in the re-membering of the body through the parts of his thirteen female saints. This literary re-membering is finally interpreted as a theological statement about death and bodily resurrection; it is a corporeal text about collective membership and ultimate reassembly in the Christian body politic.

The three essays on Victorian literature—Rackin on Carroll, Bailin on Nightingale, and Rajan on Pater—challenge another set of body-defining boundaries. If Davis recognizes the doctor as the knowing subject and the patient as the feminized body of knowledge, Bailin shows how the emergence of the female nurse in Victorian England allows for a lower servant to have a particular kind of authority and a woman to have power over men's bodies. In a wonderfully original analysis, Bailin looks to the life and writing of Nightingale to challenge the opposition of nurse and patient, with the sick body as the mediating term. Nightingale herself went from being a nurse to being a patient, and what Bailin shows is that this move is not ironic; just as nursing "locates ambition in self-sacrifice" so too can illness be used by women "to negate the social body and its cultural ambitions." Bailin reads fictions in which a heroine is transformed from nurse to patient and sees here the ability to "construct a self that can simultaneously command others and submit to them," "authorize self-indulgence and yet exact self-denial, and all within the sphere deemed suitable to women." For Nightingale in particular, "both the interminable work and the terminal illness were expressive of a supervening desire for absolute control over the disposition of her own time and body." At the same time, Nightingale's writings about the body, defilement, and invasiveness theorized a body that, in effect, declared her own "body to be no body." Bailin demonstrates that Nightingale ultimately enacted a different but "familiar narrative of subjection."

Rackin's focus is on the vexed split in the *Alice* books between the cerebral and the erotic and between the author's textualization of body denial and carnal urges. Bowing in the direction of critics who see here narratives ripe for Freudian analyses and submerged autobiography, Rackin reads the "ideal of detached intelligence" that finds one expression in the autobiographical White Knight's question: "What does it matter where my body happens to be? ... My mind goes on working all the same?" as the serious motivating question of these stories. But work for Lewis Carroll (Charles Dodgson) and his characters serves merely as a vain attempt to control the "unholy" inescapable erotic. Positioning us on the boundaries between reality and dream, things and words, and body and mind, Rackin reads the recurrent figures of detachment, mutilation, paralysis, and death through such puns as that on "gravity" (force, seriousness, and pull towards the ultimate grave) and such images of decapitation as the Queen's "off with their heads" and the Cheshire Cat's disembodied grin; the brilliance of the *Alice* books, we discover, comes in large measure from the text's effort and failure to contain an embodied Alice (character, real little girl, and photographic image) in a dream world vexed by Carroll's own conflation of the garden bed, the marriage bed, and the death bed. Moving us between the mind/body problems of the author and those of his characters, Rackin reinterprets the ambivalence of a man at once reluctant and eager to go to bed, a dream lover who worried hard over his mathematical bedtime "problems." Ultimately, Rackin leads us to Alice's triumph over her author in the child's and character's refusals to be a prisoner in someone else's dream.

Rajan also writes about straining limits and challenging body and gender boundaries in Victorian literature, and she sees a "history of misreading" of Walter Pater's text, efforts to "dematerialize" the body of his work in order to make it "safer." Like Sciolino, who makes much of the multiple male and female narrators in Acker's fiction, Rajan attends to Pater's cross-gendered ventriloquism and explains the work of desire in literature. Rajan shows Pater deliberately situating himself on another boundary, the boundary between fiction and history. Just as Pater, as an artist, extended the frame of the canvas, his representation of narrative desire extends beyond the limits that have been imposed on his work.

Rajan's revisionary reading of "A Prince of Court Painters," a portrayal of Antoine Watteau, finds Pater writing a female narrator who attempts to control a desire that her author, Pater, reveals. In so doing, Pater shows how Victorian culture policed the body. Rajan's own analysis layers the effect of policing the body as she suggests that Pater's corpus has been policed by the history of Pater criticism in ways analogous to the policing of women's bodies—a game of desire playing hide and seek—in Victorian England.

Rokem extends to the early twentieth century Davis's and Rajan's analysis of the motives and effects of male authority over and authoring of the female body. Like Rajan, Rokem attends to the work of desire in textual bodies, and like Sciolino, he discusses specular reality in a patriarchal economy. He reads three "scenes," authored by Ibsen, Strindberg, and Freud, in which a woman slaps a man, and he brilliantly develops an analogy between theater and psychoanalysis that, like Rajan, challenges the boundary between fiction and psychic truth.

Theater itself, Rokem explains, is a text translated back to the bodies of actors in which the human "body is a sign," and every production, indeed every performance, "is a concrete bodily realization of the presence of the human body in the dramatic text that draws our attention to the cultural and aesthetic codes of bodily behavior." Structurally and functionally similar, Nora's *(A Doll's House)*, Julie's *(Miss Julie)*, and Dora's (Freud's case history) multiple slaps are female gestures that attack the face, the scopic center and source of the unwelcome male gaze, a gesture that throws a body off balance and both punishes and links (violently) two bodies. Like the sword worn by the Romance heroines analyzed by Davidson, the slap is both female and phallic, a phallic gesture because it thrusts and extends the body of the self onto the body of another.

Rokem shows how in both theater and psychoanalysis one speaks a text that involves the speaker's body, and body signs are overdetermined. Again we are situated on boundaries between sex and violence, history and fiction, and masculinity and femininity as Rokem demonstrates how the slapping women create scenes that are, in each case, related fantastically and convincingly to mother loss, a loss that returns *us,* equally fantastically, to duBois's reading of Sappho and Sciolino's concluding analysis of Acker.

Each essay uses its focus on the body to reinterpret well-known authors and works, but together, and read from first to last, these essays illustrate changing cultural definitions of bodily limits, integrity, transgressions, sexuality, and violation in the history of the Western literary canon. The volume emerges out of the current interest in the body and its history, as well as the related interest in boundaries and transgression. In *The Politics and Poetics of Transgression,* Peter Stallybrass and Allon White attend principally to somatic symbolism and understand transgression as a challenge to a high/low hierarchy mapped, in complex interrelated ways, on the body, social classes, psychic forms, and geographical space. Attention to "boundaries"—physical, geographical, national, disciplinary (as in Stephen Greenblatt's and Giles Gunn's collection *Redrawing the Boundaries: The Transformation of English and American Literary Studies)*—seems to me also connected to research on the human body. One effect of this work is the further problematizing of the concept of identity, whether national, ethnic, racial, or sexual. For example, Sander Gilman's work on stereotypes and his book *The Jew's Body* clarify the association of ideology and image, as he establishes other connections between the history of the body's representation and the themes of identity, boundaries, and the articulation of difference. This collection, *Textual Bodies,* exemplifies how the recent developments in literary theory and history associated with feminism, new historicism, and cultural materialism have been productive of new readings of familiar literary texts; because of these new emphases, we find here a criticism that radically transforms our sense of what is meaningful in the Western canon.

Michel Foucault's work, especially his volumes on the *History of Sexuality,* has taught us to understand that what we have long taken for granted as "natural"—the human body most obviously—has a history. And in recognizing that history, we recognize that the body, real as it seems and experienced at every moment in lived reality, is a construct. Histories of the body have, as a result, proliferated; most recently, Thomas Laqueur's *The Body and Gender from the Greeks to Freud,* and his collection edited with Catherine Gallagher, *The Making of the Modern Body: Sexuality and Society in the Nineteenth Century* contribute to a growing bibliography that includes the three large volumes of *Zone,* entitled *Fragments for a History of the Human Body,* Edward Muir's and Guido Ruggiero's edition, *Sex and Gender in Historical Perspective,* and Elaine Scarry's important book, *The Body in Pain: The Making and Unmaking of the World.* Julia Epstein and Kristina Straub collect essays in *Body Guards: The Cultural Politics of Gender Ambiguity* that discover and discuss gender ambiguity, textual bodies that affirm the idea of body as construct by challenging assumptions about the sexed body *per se,* a challenge posed by much recent work, including Judith Butler's *Gender Trouble: Feminism and the Subversion of Identity* and Marjorie Garber's *Vested Interests: Cross-Dressing and Cultural Anxiety.* The philosophical problem of at once regarding the body as a construct and honoring its material existence in the world is then the subject of Judith Butler's *Bodies that Matter: On the Discursive Limits of "Sex."* The number of these works testifies to our collective fascination with the body and its importance as a site of investigation. At the same time, this confluence of work, like the confluences around the topics of "identity" and "transgression," testifies to a return to thematic criticism, as particular subjects have proven themselves ripe, at this moment, for interesting, sustained conversations.

Theories of the body have material and ethical implications, which is one reason for this subject's continuing attraction to literary critics. The work of French feminists was early to bring theories of the body to practical criticism, Luce Irigaray's voice remaining an important one in that area. This focus on the female body has found a central place too in cultural studies, many with sociological bases; among several, is Emily Martin's *The Woman in the Body: A Cultural Analysis of Reproduction.* Susan Suleiman gathered, in *The Female Body in Western Civilization: Contemporary Perspectives,* essays about the representation of the female body.

Critical theory turned its attention to the body, and we have seen much work in the theory and history of the body. Informed by that work, literary critics have been bringing these theories and histories of the body back to literature. The essays in this collection are among the fruits of that endeavor. The journals and conference section topics in literary studies in recent years show the extent to which the body in literature has engaged people's most serious attention. This book collects some of those efforts, and it distinguishes itself as criticism about the body that is wide-ranging and text specific, practical criticism that is provocative, readable, and exemplary of contemporary critical studies.

Postscript: Scriptures

Hebrew Scriptures, as one important foundation document of the Western tradition, presents us with a useful point of departure for further applying the issues raised by this volume. As in the Greek literature addressed by the first two essays in this collection, Biblical narrative represents the body as a locus of meaning upon which later literature depends for its metaphors and tropes. I want to close these introductory remarks by looking at several biblical body stories, both to represent that text in this volume and to suggest preliminarily what happens when a canonical literature is reviewed through the lens of the body.

In the penultimate chapters of the biblical book of *Judges* (17–21), an anonymous Levite—the last Judge figure—travels through the whole of Israel to recover his woman who has, for reasons not told to us in the story, gone back to her father. The man lingers there day after day, and the reader becomes anxious, suspicious of the apparently excessive hospitality that detains our journey. Finally, he starts home late on the third day with his belongings and his woman. In spite of approaching night, the man and his entourage choose not to stay among strangers, and they travel on to an Israelite tribe, the Benjamites, where they are taken in by the only good man in the town. The townspeople, in a story that echoes the crimes of Sodom and Gomorrah, wish to rape the guest, and they bang on the door so that he might be sodomized. The host is appropriately outraged and offers to send out his virgin daughter instead. But it is the Levite's woman, the one whom he had travelled so far to retrieve, who is thrown out to the men; she is multiply raped, and in the morning, the Levite, the man, finds her lying across the threshold. The Levite says, "get up; let us go," but she cannot; she is dead. The Levite travels home to Ephraim, having now traversed all Israel, all twelve tribes twice, this last part of the journey with the corpse. Once home, he cuts her body into twelve pieces, and parodically repeating the original journey in fragmented form, he mails a piece of the corpse to each tribe in Israel. Each part thereby becomes a mobile and multiple signifier: it signifies brutality (but the text is ambiguous about the agent of the brutality: the Levite? the Benjamites? all Israel?); it is a call for vengeance against the Benjamites, and (for the reader) the parts are metaphors for the fragmented body politic, the land itself.

In this gruesome story, it is possible not to feel much for the murdered woman; we recognize allegory when we are in its presence. This story is about reversals: night and day; family and strangers; hospitality and violation; masculinity and femininity are among the oppositions that are rendered unstable in these unstable times. It is a story about thresholds and transgressions, and they are geographic and political. This Judge has no name because he is everyman, and the unruly body wishes to violate him because it is lawless; the system has failed. As Mieke Bal has shown in *Death and Dissymmetry: The Politics of Coherence in the Book of Judges*, it is possible to read the shaping forces of this story, and of *Judges* itself, as domestic rather than political. To read this story allegorically, as I am suggesting, requires but one transformation: the individual, carnal, sexual body stands for the body politic. But notice that the text forces a substitution; the woman's body replaces the man's body; her body is thrown out to the rapists instead of that of either the anonymous man or the host himself or even the host's virgin daughter, and her corpse is fragmented to symbolize the fragmented polity. The scandal of this story for me is less the threats and transgressions on the surface of the plot—disruption of the family order, violation of hospitality, threats of sodomy, rape, and murder—than the quiet transformation through which the woman's body replaces the man's body as the site of violent representation. The land is intact, but not so the social order; by analogy, the man's body remains whole, while the woman's body is mutilated.

Often, bodies stand in for one another in the Bible: like the body of Jesus sacrificed for the sake of the body politic, in earlier texts, the scapegoat is annually sent into the wilderness bearing the sins of the people; in the book of *Genesis,* Isaac is nearly sacrificed when, at the last moment, he is replaced by a ram; Jacob deceives his blind father Isaac by pretending to be Esau, putting hair on his arms; Leah replaces Rachel at the marriage altar and in Jacob's nuptial bed; later in the story, Leah "buys" Jacob from Rachel for one night for the price of some mandrakes (a phallic medicinal root) which Rachel hopes will make her fertile. The text barely questions the right of one body to claim another's place: the father—whether divine or human—lays claim to the body of the son; we do not know what one sister thinks as she stands at the altar in her sister's place. While it may be a commonplace of our culture that our bodies are our own property, the literature that reflects and informs our culture suggests instead that bodies are iterative, symbolic, and like the discursive subject itself, the body is figured as both independent subject and subject to subjection, a subject to controlling bodies.

A final biblical example: in the book of *Numbers,* God responds with anger to Miriam and Aaron's having slandered their brother Moses, and while Aaron reacts with a cry of remorse, Miriam is instantly stricken with leprosy. As in the case of the anonymous woman in *Judges,* a woman's body is again, is habitually, the site of representation. When Moses pleads on behalf of his injured sister, God replies, "If her father had but spit in her face, should she not hide in shame for seven days?" And like the scapegoat—a punished body that stands for other bodies—Miriam is, at God's command, shut up outside the camp for seven days, by which time she is cured. Miriam's leprosy is here figured as a divine version of paternal spit, an extension of God's own body to the human body: leprosy is the divine spit that punishes Miriam for her moral crime. Among the meanings suggested by this episode is a consequential connection between impiety and bodily illness, a pervasive relationship in Western religious traditions. As Scarry observes in *The Body in Pain*, the Hebrew God's power is often exerted vertically; He is pictured above wielding a weapon, connected to His people by the stick that might beat them, the thunderbolt of Zeus. The power of the gods over the bodies of people is only one of many places where the Greek and the biblical representations of the body are analogous. But the representation and treatment of the body is these two founding traditions are also disanalogous. By focusing on particular texts, the essays that follow allow us to trace moments of continuity and discontinuity in the Western tradition's representation of the body. Looking at familiar texts through the lens of the body changes our perspective; we choose different textual moments, shift the accent, draw other conclusions. Just as developments in critical theory, history, and cultural studies enliven literary criticism by enabling radically new work, such as the essays that follow, this criticism reciprocates by providing new matter for historical and theoretical reflection, as the ever-reshaping corpus develops.

WORKS CITED

Bal, Mieke. *Death and Dissymmetry: The Politics of Coherence in the Book of Judges*. Chicago: University of Chicago Press, 1988.

Butler, Judith. *Bodies that Matter: On the Discursive Limits of "Sex."* New York: Routledge, 1993.

———. *Gender Trouble: Feminism and the Subversion of Identity*. New York: Routledge, 1990.

Epstein, Julia, and Kristina Straub, eds. *Body Guards: The Cultural Politics of Gender Ambiguity*. New York: Routledge, 1991.

Feher, Michel. *Fragments for a History of the Human Body*. Parts 1–3, Zone III–V, 1989; 1990.

Foucault, Michel. *The History of Sexuality: An Introduction*. Vol. I. Trans. Robert Hurley. New York: Vintage Books, 1980.

———. *The History of Sexuality: The Use of Pleasure*. Vol. II. Trans. Robert Hurley. New York: Pantheon, 1985.

Gallagher, Catherine, and Thomas Laqueur, eds. *The Making of the Modern Body: Sexuality and Society in the Nineteenth Century*. Berkeley: Univ. of California Press, 1987.

Garber, Marjorie. *Vested Interest: Cross-Dressing and Cultural Anxiety.* New York: Routledge, 1992.

Gilman, Sander. *The Jew's Body.* New York: Routledge, 1991.

Greenblatt, Stephen, and Giles Gunn. *Redrawing the Boundaries: The Transformation of English and American Literary Studies.* New York: Modern Language Association of America, 1992.

Irigaray, Luce. *Speculum of the Other Woman.* Trans. Gillian C. Gill. Ithaca: Cornell Univ. Press, 1985.

Jaggar, Alison M., and Susan R. Bordo, eds. *Gender/Body/Knowledge: Feminist Reconstructions of Being and Knowing.* New Brunswick: Rutgers Univ. Press, 1986.

Laqueur, Thomas. *The Body and Gender from the Greeks to Freud.* Cambridge: Harvard Univ. Press, 1990.

Lefkovitz, Lori. *The Character of Beauty in the Victorian Novel.* Ann Arbor: UMI Research Press, 1987.

———. "Leah Behind the Veil: The Divided Matriarchy in Bible, Midrash, Dickens, Freud, and Woody Allen," *Hebrew University Studies in Literature and the Arts* XVIII (1990): 177–205.

Martin, Emily. *The Woman in the Body: A Cultural Analysis of Reproduction.* Boston: Beacon Press, 1987.

Muir, Edward, and Guido Ruggiero. *Sex and Gender in Historical Perspective.* Trans. Margaret Gallucci. Baltimore: The Johns Hopkins Univ. Press, 1990.

Scarry, Elaine. *The Body in Pain: The Making and Unmaking of the World.* New York: Oxford University Press, 1985.

Suleiman, Susan Rubin, ed. *The Female Body in Western Culture: Contemporary Perspectives.* Cambridge: Harvard Univ. Press, 1985.

1

Sappho's Body in Pieces

This chapter considers the figure of fragmentation of the body, in relation to the world of the ancient Greeks, and to our own naturalized notions about the body.[1] I am concerned with contemporary feminism's focus on contemporary culture, and with the concomitant loss of a perspective on past and future that might enable other visions of bodies, sexualities, genders. Our lack of relationship to the past, our refusal of its fragmentedness, may depend on a psychological resistance to the fragmented body, a resistance that Jacques Lacan's work can perhaps help us to understand. Our fear of coming to terms with the fragmented historical past leads us to re-member its dismemberment, often to falsify that past. Such misrecognitions have implications not only for how we read the past and its fragments but also for how we read the world and women's place in it. I will argue here that Sappho's poems, their form and the ways in which we receive them, can exemplify an alternative aesthetic. Seeing the possibilities of this alternative—recognizing and accepting our own fragmentation and the inevitably fragmented past—has implications for how we treat bodies of poetry, bodies in poetry, and bodies in the world.

My own perspective on the figure of fragmentation is influenced by Jacques Lacan's model of what he calls the imaginary and the symbolic in psychic life. Lacan argues that in the domain of the symbolic, after the child's acquisition of language, the site of pre-linguistic, pre-Oedipal "imaginary" existence is recalled as a "body-in-pieces," a fragmented disparate collection of body parts. And furthermore, the "I" of the child is produced in the mirror stage as a fiction; Lacan says:

> We have only to understand the mirror stage *as an identification,* in the full sense that analysis gives to the term: namely, the transformation that takes place in the subject when he assumes an image. . . .
>
> This jubilant assumption of his specular image by the child at the *infans* stage, still sunk in his motor incapacity and nursling dependence, would seem to exhibit in an exemplary situation the symbolic matrix in which the *I* is precipitated in a primordial form. . . .
>
> This form would have to be called the Ideal-I. . . . (T)his form situates the agency of the ego, before its social determination, in a fictional direction, which will always remain irreducible for the individual alone. . . .[2]

The "I" is specular, permanent, and always alienated, as in a mirror. It is produced, in a temporal dialectic, by another set of images of what precedes it. If the child celebrates, "jubilates," as Lacan puts it, in the alienated recognition of a whole body in the fictional surface of the mirror, she or he also from the point of view of this fictional integrity recalls or constructs a previous state of disintegration. And the fictional integrity is built upon a concept or experience of disintegration.

> The mirror stage is a drama whose internal thrust is precipitated from insufficiency to anticipation—and which manufactures for the subject, caught up in the lure of spatial identification, the succession of phantasies that extends from a fragmented body-image to a form of its totality that I shall call orthopaedic. . . .
>
> This fragmented body—which term I have also introduced into our system of theoretical references—usually manifests itself in dreams when the movement of the analysis encounters a certain level of aggressive disintegration in the individual. It then appears in the form of disjointed limbs, or of those organs presented in exoscopy, growing wings and taking up arms for intestinal persecutions—the very same that the

visionary Hieronymus Bosch has fixed, for all time, in painting, in their ascent from the fifteenth century to the imaginary zenith of modern man.[3]

The subject, even after it enters into the social network of the symbolic, of collective language, alternates between a fictional I and a memory, a phantasy, of a time before the capture of this I, a time when the body was fragmented, the agent and object of earliest aggressivity.[4] I want to suggest that the dialectic between these two states, the specular ego and the body in pieces, might serve as a model for historicism. Such a historicism would first of all recognize the broken, fragmented quality of the past. And it would also recognize the necessarily fictional yet necessary fiction of the assumption of an "I," a shifter that produces the text that is history, an I that creates a relationship to a past and a possible future.

Such a model of historicism might be especially productive for a perspective on classical antiquity, and our relationship to the Greeks could be conceived in such terms. Our historiographical desire, the need to constitute antiquity as a whole, the "Greeks" as a coherent object, even though all we have of them is heterogeneous fragments, smacks of the need to produce for our own jubilation some mirror image, some wholeness that resembles our own. We need to be conscious of the contradiction here between our desire to register fragmentation, which is certainly a part of our experience of the ancient world, and our more explicit and conscious desire to invent integrity. For example, and I will speak more of this later, what are we to make of the fragments, literal fragments, of ancient poetry? Broken, embedded in foreign texts, in the paragraphs of later, still ancient commentators and critics, unearthed in shreds of papyrus from the sands of Egypt, found scribbled on potsherds, the earliest lyric poems of tradition survive as shattered remnants of a great flowering of culture after centuries of illiteracy and silence that succeeded the collapse of Mycenaean civilization. Who are we, these supposed agents of integrity and coherence, who desire to mend that past? I find especially useful, when considering these texts, Lacan's way of thinking about the alternation between the fictional whole, the "I," and the fragmentary past, as an ongoing dialectic; we are always conscious of the possibility of dismemberment, of the fragility of wholeness, of corporeal and psychic integrity, even as our identity is fashioned against the background of such dismemberment.

Our relationship to ancient Greece is one characterized by fragmentation; I want to use this concept in various ways, to consider not only Lacan's notion of the body in pieces, and my extension of that metaphor to the historicizing, constituting subject of historiography, but also to discuss a particular fragment of ancient literature. Before doing that, however, I would like to suggest some ways in which dismemberment, brokenness, *spolia,* citation—wrenching a text out of context, embedding it in a new context—all of these figure both in our relationship to antiquity and in antiquity's understanding of itself. What follows is a tentative list of ways in which we receive antiquity as fragments, of ways in which the Greeks themselves meditated upon, and used, fragments.

The Greeks themselves were concerned, almost haunted by the image of a former whole, now broken into bits. The figure of the fragment recurs in classical culture. I think of the Dionysiac *sparagmos,* the ritual dismemberment and devouring of animals in Bacchic celebration. Sophocles's heroine Antigone is haunted by the idea of her brother's broken and unburied body. The Athenians buried the broken bodies of the *korai,* the cult statues of Athena, after the Persian invasion at the beginning of the fifth century; they used broken pieces of statuary and masonry to refashion the wall that protected the city. The remnants of the various Greek tribes saw themselves as fragmentary, disseminated bits, broken off into individual cities from original unitary founding ancestors, saw their colonies as similarly dispersed fragments of an original whole. What is the political meaning for Athenians both of tribal dispersion after Ion and of the dissemination of citizens in colonization? What are the discourses on dialects, the attempts to establish leagues, to reconstitute wholeness? The Athenians, in their imaginary integrity and homogeneity, descended from a single ancestor, lived surrounded by refugees, slaves, and metics broken away from their places of origin.

The Greeks themselves saw their existence as haunted by a dialectic between integrity and dissemination. The Athenian citizens who made up the democracy defined their integrity against the background of others, slaves, metics, foreigners. How do we think about democracy—the dispersed, heterogeneous votes, scattered bits of broken shells, ostraka, pebbles—transformed into the single, unified voice of the polis? What is writing—the scattered letters, lots, seeds—which are like the dragon's teeth of Thebes, like the fragmented bodies of Actaeon and Pentheus, the severed head of Orpheus? Can we consider the imaginary opposition between Thebes and Athens in terms of this slippage, this oscillation between fragmentation and integrity? This is one sense in which the historical project must take the fragmentary into account.

What is more, we receive antiquity as fragments. Literary critics for the most part read those archaic Greek poems most whole, most like the textual objects familiar to us from the world of print, poems with beginnings, middles, and ends, poems that at the worst have *cruces,* a few *lacunae,* perhaps a missing line, syllable, phoneme. These are the poems printed in translations, in anthologies, poems with recognizable shape, few ellipses, barely mutilated. Critics have been grateful that the vagaries of transmission have permitted access to a few whole poems, that, for example, Longinus happened to cite most of Sappho 31 as an illustration of sublimity in selection and combination (*On the Sublime* 10, 1–2), even though Longinus's treatise is itself seemingly irretrievably partial and damaged. These poems allow us to construct models of the structure of whole poems, of poetic development and narrative patterning, models that allow the assessment of fragments we possess, that provide a whole against which the part can be measured.

But what are we to make of those poems clearly not whole, lines repeated to illustrate a point, lines retrieved accidentally from a papyrus so damaged that there is no hope of more? Are we simply bound to wait, in expectation that more fragments will be discovered, that the conjectures of textual critics will be confirmed or denied by further findings? Are we to place the truly fragmentary remains of these poets in a limbo of the uncanny, the unreadable, the damaged and partial ruins of antiquity?

These poems seem to lack the charm ruins once held for lovers of antiquity, the mystery of the armless Venus de Milo, the romantic appeal of the constructed ruin in the eighteenth-century garden. There is a resistance to coming to terms aesthetically with these lines of verse as they stand. Sometimes it seems they evoke the same dread as the broken, noseless statuary of antiquity, some primitive shudder at the sight of ruined, mutilated bodies that were first shaped to recall the beauties and perfection of the human form, but that have been reduced to shards, to rubble. The clumsy restorations of plaster in museums resemble prosthetic devices. The ellipses in the published archaic fragments insist on our distance from the past.

Beyond these psychological obstacles, these poems present problems of reading for the critic. Their incompleteness causes unease. How can one speak of poetic development when only one line, one metaphor remains? We have learned to read whole poems, and to see some kind of narrative in whole poems. There is no accessible narrative in some of these fragments; or narrative is of necessity truncated. There is inevitably a sense of something missing, of something yet to be supplied. The critic waits for completion, a completion which may never occur, or she recognizes the sensation of working in the dark, of vulnerability to that text which might appear, which might contradict her reading, or subsume it in a fuller, more adequate reading of a fuller, more adequate poem.

One of the impulses of philology has been to attack the problem of the fragment directly. Classical and biblical scholarship have always been in part efforts at restoration. Philologists have tried to make whole what was broken—to imagine and guess at the missing parts, to repair what was transmitted inaccurately, to change, excise, add, to return to the original and perfect text that we can never know. Their work has been immensely valuable, in reading, deciphering, presenting to us in legible form much that would be inaccessible without the intervention of centuries of erudition. Their efforts at restoration must continue, as labor over textual mysteries, as supplementation of our ignorance. But until the day of glorious resurrection, when all the bodies of ancient poems, of ancient culture, are miraculously restored to their integrity, what are we to do with the fragments of such a poet as Sappho? Are we to leave them aside until they are made whole? Are we to continue to long for restoration, to imagine, for example, what the whole poem that surrounds a two-line fragment must be? Should we not rather accept the fragmentary quality of ancient poetry, of ancient culture, of any cultural artifact, and even as we labor to restore what might be recoverable, should we not read what we have of ancient culture, ancient poems, other cultures, fragments as well as whole poems, recognizing that our relationship to antiquity will always be partial and interested?

Recent literary and psychoanalytic theory has rendered this reading more possible, more pleasurable even, and it has allowed us to see, as I suggested earlier, how our very postmodern existence is fragmentary, provisional, split, and based on a fiction of the ego. Perhaps we can now read otherwise, acknowledging our own fragmentation, our uneasy balancing between a body in pieces and an alienated, mirror image of selfhood. We have come to recognize that our access to the past—our own personal, psychological history as well as the history of humankind—is fragmented, our constructions of that past interested, particular, and historically determined. We are dependent on accidents of transmission—fire, war, loss. Our access to so recent a phenomenon as the early years of television is partial, arbitrary, subject to the peculiarities of archival storage and technological limitation. Our knowledge of daily life in ancient Rome is also limited, perhaps no more fragmentary than our knowledge concerning female literacy in eighteenth-century England, or the history of the Kung. What remains to us of the past, what we know of the present, of the full psychic life of others, or of ourselves, is fragmentary. One way of responding to this recognition is to pursue a dream of wholeness, transparency, perfect access to what we desire to know. Another is to accept the partiality of our experience, even as we yearn for more—more fact, more words and artifacts, more lines of Sappho, more poems of Sappho—to seek to read what we have. And most important of all, to recognize the possibilities of pleasure, of utopian possibility, of libidinality and ecstasy, in the recollection, memory, experience, phantasy of disorder.

Speaking of those ancient writers whose work counted for something for him, in praise of Horace, Nietzsche said:

> This mosaic of words, in which every unit spreads its power to the left and to the right over the whole, by its sound, by its place in the sentence, and by its meaning, this *minimum* in the compass and number of the signs, and the *maximum* of energy in the signs which is thereby achieved—all this is Roman, and, if you will believe me, noble *par excellence.*[5]

Nietzsche's appreciation of Horace does not concern the fragment, nor is it directed to archaic Greek poetry, nor does his praise of Horace as noble suit my purpose. But his remarks on the *minimum* of signs, *maximum* of energy might direct a reading of the fragmentary, one that attempts, not romantically, not lamenting the loss that surrounds the fragment, not to restore its lacks, but to read the minimal signs of the fragment with a maximum of energy. Rather than discarding the historical project, which must always concern the fragmentary, as pointless, as a project concerned with the hopelessly damaged, the frustratingly elusive, let us rather rejoice in the fragment, especially perhaps in Sappho's fragments, almost the only witness we have from ancient Greece concerning women's experiences, their inscription of their own bodies and their pleasures. I want to offer a reading of a necessarily fragmented poem of Sappho, one that recognizes the fragmentary state of my own encounter with the poem, one that recognizes the possibility of pleasure in a celebration of bodily disorder.

This is Sappho's poem 31:[6]

> To me he seems like a god
> as he sits facing you and
> hears you near as you speak
> softly and laugh
>
> in a sweet echo that jolts
> the heart in my ribs. For now
> as I look at you my voice
> is empty and
>
> can say nothing as my tongue
> cracks and slender fire is quick
> under my skin. My eyes are dead
> to light, my ears
>
> pound, and sweat pours over me.
> I convulse, greener than grass,
> and feel my mind slip as I
> go close to death.[7]

The lines break off here, into fragments. This poem was much admired in antiquity; Plato seems to echo it in the *Phaedrus* when

Socrates describes the symptoms of love as beauty enters through the eyes:

> ...first there come upon him a shuddering and a measuring of.... awe.... Next, with the passing of the shudder, a strange sweating and fever seizes him.
>
> *Phaedrus* 251 ab[8]

Catullus translates this poem, retaining the gender markers and thereby transforming it into a heterosexual text. Longinus, in citing the poem in his text, speaks of the skill with which Sappho picks out *(eklexai)* and binds together *(sundesai)* the most striking and intense of the symptoms of love. It is this double action that interests me most here: the selecting out, literally, a plucking out, a gathering from the flow of experience, of the temporal flux, and a yoking, a binding, of the *akra,* the peaks of experience to fashion a poem.

This selection of *akra,* of high moments, is a fragmentation of experience, in that it must perforce break up the flow of lived time. Poetry performs such a splitting up of experience through selection, of course. But piled on top of this sense of fragmentation is another, one peculiar to the thematics of this particular poem, in which the body is represented as falling into fragments, seen as a series of discrete, unconnected, disjunctive responses. As Longinus points out, in remarks that have been found inadequate in the twentieth century, but that suit my purpose admirably: "Is it not wonderful (literally, *ou thaumazdeis?* are you not amazed?) how she summons at the same time soul body hearing tongue sight colour, all as though they had wandered off apart from herself." The editor of the Greek text prints the list of things summoned without commas; Longinus says that the poet effects of all these things a *sunodos,* a meeting, a junction. The poem is a crossroads of emotions, a reassembly of the fragmented, disparate parts of the poetic I that have "wandered off apart from herself." These parts are her heart, which is given a separate existence in her breast, her voice, which escapes her, her broken tongue, her skin, over which fire runs, her blinded eyes, her humming ears. This is Eros the limb-loosener, *lusimeles,* the one that unstrings the assembly of the body and brings the "I" here close to death.

Nancy Vickers has written brilliantly about the ways in which Renaissance lyric, the poems of Petrarch and his imitators perform a sort of dismemberment of the female body, how in their blazons and ekphrases, their descriptions of the physical appearance of the beloved, their lines cut up and cast about the limbs, the parts of women. Such an observation echoes the feminist critiques of contemporary advertising and pornography, which similarly dismember and therefore commodify the parts of women's bodies. What is particularly fascinating about Sappho's poem is that here the woman herself sees the disorder in the body in love, sees herself objectified as a body in pieces, disjointed, a broken set of organs, limbs, bodily functions. This is an occasion on which the supposedly feminine origin of the poem, the fact that this poem was attributed to Sappho, may seem to make a difference in our reading of it, a place where the death of the author has not yet even begun to occur, where the birth of the I has barely begun. In Catullus's version of the poem, his description of the poetic eye and I, and its disintegrated state, the poem resonates in part with its Sapphic origin, so that the complex intertextuality adds to its heterosexual context. But here, in the original poem, I want to say not that we have an example of *écriture feminine,* because I don't believe in such a thing as a transhistorical category, nor that this proves the universal descriptive value of Lacanian psychoanalysis. Rather, this is an important example of a poetics based on a notion of conjunction, of reassembly, of a sort that resonates suggestively with the Lacanian model of historicism I laid out earlier and exposes historical difference, a moment of the constitution of the aristocratic self, perhaps even before the theorization of gender per se. The "I" that speaks and writes, the "I" that is produced in that moment, regards the past, a disordered, fragmented past, from a present in which the poem itself, and the fiction of subjectivity represented in it, are constituted against the backdrop of the fragmentation. The "I" of the poem comes out of that fragmentation, is constructed from it, as Longinus points out so beautifully: "Do you not wonder . . . ?"

The *sunodos,* the junction, must however be read historically, not generalized to describe some absolute and general proposition of feminine composition, not to prove the universality of our postmodern ideas of the split subjectivity. I would argue for a historicist understanding of this poem, relating to Bruno Snell's work on the Homeric body. Although Snell's work has been called into question by Homeric scholars, it seems to be a particularly valuable intervention in the question of the historicity of the body. He argues that the Homeric authors and audience understood the body as such not to exist, but rather to be an assembly of parts, of functions, of disparate organs loosely allied, commanded independently by gods and men. Snell writes:

Of course the Homeric man had a body exactly like the later Greeks, but he did not know it *qua* body, but merely as the sum total of his limbs. This is another way of saying that the Homeric Greeks did not yet have a body in the modern sense of the word; body, *soma*, is a later interpretation of what was originally comprehended as *mele*, or *guia*, limbs.[9]

Snell makes a connection between this conception of the human form and its representation in early Greek art:

Not until the classical art of the fifth century do we find attempts to depict the body as an organic unity whose parts are mutually correlated. In the preceding period the body is a mere construct of independent parts variously put together.[10]

The tribal, collective, pre-political world of the Homeric heroes sees the body, or rather what will become the body, as like its own social organization, as a loose confederation, a tenuous grouping of parts.

Set against the background of this understanding of human beings' physical existence, Sappho's disordered, fragmented body takes on a different resonance than if it were to be understood only as figuring in the Kristevan semiotic. The subject, the I of the archaic lyric is generated in the earliest urban, i.e., literally, "political" setting, in the voice of a dominant aristocracy. According to Snell, these poems record the beginning of the historical evolution of selfhood, of individuality, the aristocratic origin of what will become the male citizen of the ancient polis, the city-state, and Michel Foucault's subject of philosophy in the Platonic tradition. Sappho's view of Eros *lusimeles,* that love that disunites the only-recently constituted body, is that it returns that body to a pre-historic state, to a pile of functions, a loose set of organic capacities; what she represents is regression, a loss of a tenuously held subjectivity, that fresh, new tender sense of the poet as "I," rather than as the conduit of the muses.

What of the pleasure of this text? This particular *sunodos,* the poem which is the intersection, the crossroads, the reassembly of the body of the poetic "I," of her wandering "soul body hearing tongue sight colour" has its beauties and its pleasures. Although I cannot explicate them all here, since to do so would require showing how the stanzas in Greek echo and respond to one another, how the metaphors shock and break the conventions of the lyric, let me mention just one. Sappho says: *glossa eage,* variously translated "my tongue broke, my tongue shivered, my tongue cracked." One editor complains "the hiatus would be irregular, and the meaning, "my tongue is broken, unsatisfactory . . . ;"[11] Campbell nonetheless points out that Lucretius 3.155 seems to echo this passage in *infringi linguam.* The hiatus, however, the two vowels coming together, could be seen to "break" the tongue, to force an awkward, dysphonious phrase, a stumbling into the gap between the two vowels that produces a simulacrum of the poetic I's distress in the reader.

It is crucial to understand here, nonetheless, that the pleasure this poem affords us, in our positions as psychoanalytic subjects of the twentieth century, is not the same as that of the archaic audience of Sappho's day. If Sappho's listeners heard an account of historical regression, of dissolution back into undifferentiated collectivity, we project a psychological state described by Lacan. The richer reading of this poem would acknowledge both dimensions, the historical and the contemporary, and would measure the distance between one pleasure and another. And this poem, in its evocation of distress, even of anguish, of the exaggerated pains of love, is a pleasure for us to read. The "I" of poet and of contemporary reader can take pleasure in Sappho's recollection of suffering because suffering has for us been aestheticized, because the poem has constructed coherence from disorder, reconstituted subjectivity out of a body in pieces. The pleasure of this reconstruction is what allows for readerly transference, to refer back to a psychoanalytic model. If the male lover, who sits across from, *enantios, vis-à-vis*

Sappho's object of desire, is read as caught in a specular, dyadic, imaginary relationship to her, gazing at her, the voice of the poet has, for a modern reader, entered the symbolic, acknowledging the passage of time and the possibility of a linguistic recovery of her fragmented body. The reader's pleasure comes from an appreciation of the disintegration the poet describes, the undeniable pain of Eros, of a disordering desire that shatters the tongue, that brings the "I" to a place near death, but also from the security of that "I" that speaks the poem, the voice that gazes retrospectively at this experience of fragmentation, and from it creates a crossroads, a poem and a self. If, as Shoshana Felman argues, we are both analyst and analysand as we read, if we experience both transference and counter-transference, if we see ourselves as authority and as subject to the authority of the poem, then this poem can offer a model to contemporary feminism that avoids the difficulties of imperial agency, of the colonizing subject and subjectivity of traditional metaphysical discourses. The self constituted from disorder is a self of pleasure and authority that recognizes its construction of itself out of fragmentation, that acknowledges its own fictionality, its own historicity.

One of Walter Benjamin's "Theses on the Philosophy of History" expresses scorn for a certain view of historicism. He wrote: "Historicism gives the 'eternal' image of the past; historical materialism supplies a unique experience with the past. The historical materialist leaves it to others to be drained by the whore called 'Once upon a time' in historicism's bordello. He remains in control of his powers, man enough to blast open the continuum of history."[12] Benjamin here argues, in scandalously sexist terms, against a kind of historicism called by Fredric Jameson "existential historicism," that aesthetic contemplation of an immutable past called "once upon a time," "the experience . . . by which *historicity* as such is manifested, by means of the contact between the historian's mind in the present and a given synchronic cultural complex from the past."[13]

I would argue for a historical materialist historicism, one that is not content merely to contemplate the past from the point of view of an autonomous subject in the present, who comes into contact with the collective past, but that rather engages with the past in order to generate some vision of historical difference. The ancient

Greeks, and Sappho in particular, provide particularly suggestive material for historicist work, in part because we so often name them as our origin, in part because they are in fact so radically different from us, even in such a "natural" domain as life in the body. And if Benjamin, in his vision of the aestheticizing, contemplative version of historicism, uses the image of the whore in historicism's bordello, I want to argue that feminism needs not only to rage against such degrading imagery, but also that we need a dialectical materialist theory of history, need to see difference, to have a richer sense of readings of bodies, to put into question our assumptions about the natural body.

NOTES

1. This essay is a preliminary version of a chapter in a book on Sappho and contemporary theory.

2. Jacques Lacan, "The mirror stage as formative of the function of the I as revealed in psychoanalytic experience," in *Écrits, A Selection*, trans. Alan Sheridan (New York and London, 1977), 2.

3. *Ibid.*, 4–5.

4. See Jacques Lacan, "Aggressivity in psychoanalysis," in *Écrits*, 8–29.

5. Friedrich Nietzsche, *The Twilight of the Idols, or How to Philosophise with the Hammer,* trans. A. M. Ludovici (New York, 1964), 113.

6. *Greek Lyric Poetry,* trans. Willis Barnstone (1972), 67; translation modified.

7. *Greek Lyric Poetry,* ed. David A. Campbell (London, 1967), 44.

8. Plato, *Collected Dialogues,* ed. Edith Hamilton and Huntington Cairns (Princeton, 1961), 497.

9. Bruno Snell, *The Discovery of the Mind: The Greek Origins of European Thought,* trans. T. G. Rosenmeyer (Oxford, 1953), 8.

10. *Ibid.,* 6.

11. Campbell, *op. cit.,* 272.

12. Walter Benjamin, "Theses on the Philosophy of History," XVI, in *Illuminations,* ed. Hannah Arendt, trans. Harry Zohn (New York, 1969), 262.

13. Fredric Jameson, "Marxism and Historicism," in *Syntax of History,* vol. 2 of *The Ideologies of Theory: Essays 1971–1986* (Minneapolis, 1988), 157.

Robert Con Davis

2

Aristotle, Gynecology, and the Body Sick with Desire

> The body sick with desire.
> —Soranus
> *Gyneaecology,* I, 30

> [Aristotle saw that] the relation between men and women is "political."
> —Michel Foucault
> *The History of Sexuality, I*

In this chapter, I want to discuss a concept the ancient Greeks called the *hupokeimenon,* which we call the "subject." I say "subject," and yet the *hupokeimenon* is not precisely parallel to the knowing subject of modern philosophy or cultural studies. Far from it. Through much of this discussion I will be addressing the "subject" in the specifically Aristotelian sense of the focus of science— the classical definition of what can be talked about and examined in scientific terms. I will show that Aristotelian and Western ideas of logic and coherence, seemingly abstract and austere in their formulation, are actually ideas derived from the Greek model of the body. So while Aristotle argues for canons of logical soundness and consistency in various texts on logic, he nonetheless draws his arguments out of the "logic" of the difference between being a woman or a man. Drawing on the differences of gender, he afterwards establishes prerequisites for critical observation and thinking, ultimately canons for logical rigor that become part of the Western project of scientific thinking. In what follows, I will examine the logical relations of Aristotle's *hupokeimenon,* the subject as a model of what critical thinking can know. I will then isolate the assumptions Aristotle makes about logical "form" *(eidos)* and the body, particularly the female body as known through classical gynecology. Finally, I will discuss Aristotle's active suppression of the female body in logic and his silent instituting of the male body as the embodiment of scientific and cultural authority. My ultimate goal will be to define the ideological relationships that link scientific rigor and the classical idea of the body—formulations that still contribute to thinking about the subject in modern science and in contemporary versions of cultural studies.[1]

The *Hupokeimenon*

I am going to start with Aristotle on some philosophical problems that at first will seem quite distant from gender distinctions. In defining the scope of scientific knowledge in the *Metaphysics,* for example, Aristotle tries to resolve two pressing epistemological issues en route to defining how we know anything scientifically. He allows that the world can be projected in two models as unchanging and static or as forever in motion. If unchanging and unyielding of its patterns either to the senses or to reason, the world forecloses the prospect of critical investigation. Nothing can be known of it. If the world is purely in motion, any subject of inquiry will be unreliable and idiosyncratic "knowledge" about an already changed state of affairs. Whether fixed *or* incessantly in motion, the world will vex a critical observer, who then cannot legitimately articulate scientific or critical knowledge about anything.

Within the terms of this dilemma, certainly in the footsteps of Plato, Aristotle creates a dialogue between Parmenides's view of the world as fundamentally "unified" and unchanging and Heraclitus's perspective on a world utterly in flux. Either option will only work to distort the very world and the relation to form *(eidos)* it was supposed to represent or accurately model. The resultant *aporia* concerns the dilemma of the One unified world as opposed to the Many-faceted world-in-flux, the world-as-monolith as opposed to the world-in-continual-motion, and contrasts the knowable *same (tauto)* of understanding to the unknowable other, *an other (heteron)*, of change.

In some of his logical works Aristotle then goes on to theorize the subject as a construction of language and logical relations with no confusion between the subject as *knower* and the subject as *that which is known*. Aristotle does not use *hupokeimenon* to refer to the knowing subject. And yet he takes the "subject" of knowledge as anything but obvious or "given," arguing against the notion of a commonsensical line-of-sight for observation in experience. To approach a "subject" of inquiry in a scientific manner, rather, he specifies a set of operations required for reliable scrutiny, clarifying at every point that his assumptions are open to rational investigation. In contrast to his own position is that of Parmenides and Plato, particularly Parmenides's notion of the world "Being . . . one and . . . nothing else" (*Metaphysics* 1:5,986b9–987a2), that is, knowledge of the world as unified and completely monolithic in makeup. In claiming that unity is manifested directly in the Ideas that structure the intelligible world, Parmenides gives the world a single face in a world model more monist than even Plato suggests. For Plato, the intelligible world is positioned by perfect Ideas regardless of how they are perceived.

Aristotle objects to this approach on the grounds that if we assume the existence of idealized forms directly in relation to their manifestation, as Parmenides does, then we must also assume the continual recreation of new Ideas in order to account for the emergence of new appearances in the world, the ongoing fact of new discoveries and knowledge. Without the generation of new Ideas, which neither Parmenides nor Plato proposes, there would be no explanation for new phenomena in relation to prior knowledge. The ideal forms, in short, cannot account for emergent knowledge, and Aristotle sees this problem as the inevitable result of Plato's and Parmenides's position concerning the world's closed system of forms (*Metaphysics* 1:6,988a).

At the other extreme is Heraclitus's position on the instability of knowledge. In the *Metaphysics,* Aristotle echoes Hercalitus in saying "that the whole sensible world is always in a state of flux" and that from this viewpoint "no scientific knowledge *[episteme]* of [the world]" is possible (1:6,987b). Aristotle even notes that from

Heraclitus's viewpoint not only can one not "enter the same river twice"; it "cannot be done even once." This is so if there is a missing foundation in a world of flux for knowing anything with certainty even a first time (4:5,1010a).

It seems odd at first that Aristotle does not dispute this position and grants indeed "that there is nothing permanent in respect of quantity" in phenomena (4:5,1010a). In the absence of a well-defined subject, "predication *[kategorian]* must [indeed] proceed to infinity" (*Metaphysics* 4:4,1007b). Heraclitus is apparently right in claiming that indeterminacy is a reality of epistemological slippage, the Kosmos's failure to ground directly what Aristotle calls the quantitative and qualitative characteristics of anything. However, when we put a set of substantial relations in place—in effect, define a subject of inquiry, what it is fundamentally we are looking at in order to connect the accidents of experience—the attribution of quantity to a subject under inspection then expresses not the accidents of detail but the patterns of form that actually make up that phenomenon. Aristotle's argument is that scientific knowledge cannot be of details and accidents, because these are infinite in their variety and can be investigated without end. Investigation must be of the natural representation of form itself, for "it is by the *form [eidos]* that we recognize everything" (4:5,1010a). In this qualification to Heraclitus's position, indeterminacy and the subsequent infinite regress of *quantity* in apprehension result from the lack of a definition of what is being investigated (the *hupokeimenon*) and an absence of clear presuppositions for what will be of ongoing interest to scientific investigation.

Aristotle then settles the issue of indeterminacy, still without contradicting Heraclitus, by positing the existence of a scientific viewpoint that scrutinizes a subject of inquiry that will consistently take a particular—I will argue "male"—form. As definitions, both the scientific perspective and the subject of inquiry are at once invariant in their structure, while they remain alterable as concepts in minor ways to be adaptable to the specifics of particular phenomena and texts. Aristotle's notion of a scientific subject of investigation, what John Peter Anton aptly calls the subject as "distributive being" (10), draws from the strengths but not the weaknesses of both the Parmenidean and the Heraclitean positions to imply a subject predictable in form but with the ability to re-

spond to and, in a sense, encompass diversity—unchanging in form
(eidos) but reformulable in terms of the accidents related to form
(quantity and quality). This "subject" can encompass the "substrate"
or "matter" of an argument in the sense of providing a matrix of
assumptions and delimitations that governs the diverse possibilities for representing a particular text or series of propositions. All
of this says that details (quantity) do not ground knowledge with
any certainty, as Heraclitus said, too. In fact, in their ungrounded
state mere details allow an infinite regress of interpretive frames
and conclusions. Aristotle adds, however, that patterns *(eidos)* of
understanding do situate the matrix of a subject as a definition of
something to know. That situating then establishes a stable frame
for critical and scientific inquiry.

So the character, or particular qualities of a scientific subject,
will be conveyed in its form. Within the idea of form, suggested in
the structural relations of *eidos,* is what Aristotle calls the subject's
"substance" *(ousia),* a central set of recognized logical operations
displayed in the pattern of what Aristotle calls "contradiction." The
substance of a scientific subject, in other words, is the structural
pattern of its form always expressed as a contradiction. "Contradiction" formally describes the state of tension wherein two terms
cannot coexist; one must be canceled for the other to be deployed,
as in the contradictions *(antiphasis)* of just versus unjust, generation versus degeneration, good versus bad, etc. That is, the *substance* or general pattern of a subject cannot be both "just" and
"unjust" at the same time. Qualitative distinctions such as light
and heavy, wet and dry, cold and hot, and so on, and quantitative
distinctions about completeness and incompleteness in number (e.g.,
a person with two arms, two legs, etc.) contribute to the relations
of this substance, but they cannot in themselves effect its definition
as something to be known. A "substantial," or structural, change—
what Aristotle calls *metabole*—will always be a change that revises
the largest contradictory opposition (the polarized states) that actually defines a subject's substance, or structure *(Physics* E:1,225a1).

In the *Categories,* Aristotle designates the subject in a further
sense. He also distinguishes between the limited sense of the
hupokeimenon as the grammatical subject in a sentence and the
larger sense of subject as a whole constellation of opposed relations, subject here being what Anton calls "the locus of processes"

(60). Aristotle identifies this "first principle" of oppositional relations as occurring at the moment of instituting a contrary relation (*Metaphysics* 1:5,986b) and, in fact, gives "male" and "female" as primary examples of a contrary opposition (9:8,1058a). The first position of the contrary relationship, ideally considered, actually creates the logical channels for all the developments that will follow in that only once the "contrary" relation has been articulated can the other oppositional relations form the subject in sequence. Aristotle is quite clear on this issue when he says in *The Generation of Animals* that "there is nothing in any argument which does not start from the first principles belonging to the particular subject" (2:8,748a), by which he means the initiation of the subject-in-process (the subject as what is known) in the first, contrary relationship.

This emphasis on the first position of the sequence is consonant with attempts—by St. Thomas Aquinas, for example—to view Aristotle's work on oppositional logic as a theory of language understood discursively as "enunciative speech," scientific understanding as the articulation of an utterance within a particular context of utterances and the critical relations of that utterance as it is so situated. (Aquinas, in his commentary on *On Interpretation,* actually suggests the alternative title of "Enunciative Speech" for this work—see Oesterle 1962.) Aquinas and Cardinal Cajetan (as thirteenth- and fifteenth-century editors of Aristotle) highlight Aristotle's sequence of oppositions as a cross-indexed interpretive grid of the "natural" relations of critical understanding. In this, they follow Aristotle's own suggestions for a discursive heuristic theory given in examples such as the "Man is just" case from *On Interpretation* (10:19b–20a), where Aristotle advances logical procedures as the relations of positions within a scientific discourse.

Aristotle's oppositional thinking here reflects the influence of the Pre-Socratics, particularly Pythagoras, as evidenced in the Pythagorean Table of Opposites. Pythagoras composed a grand scheme of oppositions that were supposed to serve as the scaffolding for the structure of all knowledge in the world. This Table of "all" significant oppositions was advanced by the Pre-Socratic philosophers to represent the "oppositional" form of the Kosmos itself, exactly the oppositional underpinning of reality and intelligibility. Their source could well have been Hesiod, particularly in the

Theogony, where so many genealogies proceed by some variant of opposition. These oppositions—finite/infinite, odd/even, one/many, right/left, male/female, resting/moving, straight/curved, light/darkness, good/bad, and square/rectangular—as G. E. R. Lloyd notes in *Polarity and Analogy,* line up on the Table in large "opposed" groups so that we see "right, male and light on the side of limit and the good, and . . . left, female and darkness on the side of the unlimited and evil" (48). This double alignment points up the structural conditions that would automatically advance the "rightness" and natural priority given to maleness in defining a subject of inquiry and also the privileged scientific perspective, or ultimate cultural authority, in interpretive procedures.[2]

Thus, insofar as the *hupokeimenon* is the "subject" of propositions, it is an abstract pattern of relations, including the entailments of those relations. The *hupokeimenon* specifies that which may be "spoken" and also "heard" from a text in a particular culture. "Allowed" and culturally legitimate, sayable speech and knowledge, the *hupokeimenon* is that which can actually be "voiced" in relation to the boundaries of critical representation in culture. When the *hupokeimenon* as the subject of science speaks, it is speech necessarily *for* the culture it belongs to, and as speech this voicing is the perceptible embodiment, or representation, of cultural authority, the possibility of speech that gives access to sanctioned values and reigning ideological commitments.

In *On Interpretation* and the *Metaphysics,* in sum, Aristotle advanced that an act of understanding, properly conceived, is a complex series of abstract affirmations and negations capable of engaging with and describing the world. The Greek notion of "fate" as the speech of the gods—said or advanced as a decree by Zeus or Moira—catches this dimension of privileged understanding or voicing in the *hupokeimenon.* The linear logic of such reasoning is what Susan Handelman calls the "Greco-Christian ontotheological mode of thinking" (168)—Aristotle's fundamental belief that everything "sayable" is a quality or quantity in the economy of the subject as what can be known in critical terms.

Aristotle's logical texts are also clear in their advancing of the subject as "scientific" arrangement within a hierarchy of values, so that each dimension of oppositional relations is a formalized utterance in speech. Each proposition as a syntactical juncture corresponds to a cultural position of value, meaning that the voicings of the *hupokeimenon* are aligned with assigned values that actually anchor and identify aspects of Greek culture. We can readily interpret Aristotle's oppositional relations as the positions of enunciative speech and the directional relations among those positions, as follows:

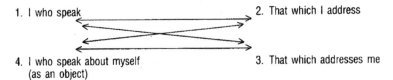

1. I who speak   2. That which I address

4. I who speak about myself   3. That which addresses me
   (as an object)

In this configuration there is the progression of contrary, contradictory, and double-negation relations apparent in other such versions of Aristotle's oppositional square. Here the first position of the speaking subject with "I who speak" is a hierarchically privileged position in that what follows unfolds the entailments of that position. The values assigned to each of the three succeeding positions have the double relation of a movement away from the first position of the speaking subject and *toward* the fulfillment of the subject's logical potential. Placing "male," "female," and other related terms in this grid of relations, we would discover that these positions signify actual cultural and social priorities and values for the agents that occupy those positions—the ideological relation, for example, of males and females. The emphasis here on discourse, the relations of subject and object (though Aristotle does not oppose subject and object as such), and the discourse between the subject and its other *(heteron),* reiterate oppositionally, and "scientifically," what can be known in the situating of cultural values.

Aristotle's formal handling of oppositional relations in his theory of the subject potentially answers the difficulty of reconciling Parmenides with Heraclitus in several ways. In classical epistemology generally, there is the belief that "the object of knowing" and "the intuition of the knowing subject must be stable" for the critical acquisition of knowledge to be possible, which is to say that the act of "knowing may not be affected by movements of the body nor by passionate elements" (Verbeke, 560). Knowledge *(episteme)* must have a stable quality to it precisely because it stands in relation to the "good," and the "good" is not in a state of becoming. If knowledge is to approximate the state of the good, therefore, it must copy the fixity of the good, even if the act of doing so necessarily takes place in a world of apparent motion. God's perspective on substantial relations, if it could only be adopted, would automatically show that there is truth and pleasure to be taken "more in stability than in movement" (Verbeke, 563).

For Aristotle, I am arguing, there is a homology between the idea of a first position or foundation in logic and the ontological foundation of the "good" in the world, the "good" and the *hupokeimenon* being logical representations of ontological and epistemological firstness. This is not to say that Aristotle explicitly advances such a connection. It is the logic of the subject, rather, to be centered as a prime reference in the hierarchies of reasoning and rational interpretation and to be a significant model in epistemology for the centeredness and hierarchical organization of the polis as well as the Kosmos itself. The logic of the subject even suggests a kind of foundation for the institution of cultural law, for without the subject there is no critical discrimination *(diakresis)* about the significance of difference and the subsequent elaborations of culture and truth as they are known to Greek culture. And without the apprehension of difference, there is no hierarchy of values and no cultural law. In these ways, the *hupokeimenon* as a construct catches the sense of cultural order in the most local and also in the broadest cultural terms.

The Logic of Gender

I have been discussing Aristotle's conception of the subject in *On Interpretation* and the *Metaphysics* and several other texts—logical texts that, I will show, draw their principal references from Greek gynecology and theories of the body. Let us look, for example, at *The Generation of Animals,* where Aristotle addresses human physiology and anatomy to establish principles for understanding the medical practices employed by Greek doctors. In his discussion of reproduction and human bodies, he shows the intrinsic importance of gender discourse for Hippocratic medicine but also, more importantly, for his conception of scientific knowledge—that is, his ideas about the authority of science and critical understanding.

Like Hippocrates and the doctors writing under that name, Aristotle posits the order of gender as establishing a fundamental hierarchy of male over female. His general precept is that a woman's body, with weak and ineffective muscles, is a vastly inferior version of a man's with a marked tendency to illness and malfunctions and limited internal structuring or order. The frequent illness among women he attributes largely to a relative lack of body heat, the fact that "male animals are hotter than female ones" (*Generation of Animals* 4:1, 765b). The woman's experience of blood loss during menstruation and the apparent abundance of blood in women at other times could suggest the contrary, that since blood is hot and a woman has a lot of blood, a woman does have an especially warm body. The error here, Aristotle explains, can be explained by the diluted state, or lack of purity, in a woman's bodily fluids. Women actually have too little pure blood and, thus, less body heat (4:1,765b).

He draws on a similar argument about body heat when he says that the human body, male and female, is naturally given "form" *(eidos)* through the presence of semen *(sperma)*. The "concoction" of semen is the result of heat, and the body produces semen only when it is hot enough to do so. And since "the fact that it has been concocted means that it has been set and compacted . . . the more compacted semen is, the more fertile it is" (4:1, 765b). The very warm male body, then, "is that which is able to concoct, to cause to take shape, and to discharge, semen possessing the 'principle' of the 'form'" (4:1,765b). By "principle" he means the *"first motive principle,"* that which "is able to act thus in itself or in something else" (4:1,765b). The "female is that which [only] receives the semen but is unable to cause semen to take shape or to discharge it" (4:1,765b). Males, it turns out, can do precisely these things owing to their active and ample production of semen, and the male as an active agent actually enacts the role of being a *"first motive principle"* of form. The female produces and discharges some semen, too, but with her lower body temperature she produces not the pure product but an adulterated substance not "in a pure condition" (4:1,765b). In *The History of Animals,* Aristotle adds that only the male emits semen "into another individual," whereas the female "will emit semen [only] into itself" (1:3,489a), suggesting the transactional nature of the male in sexual reproduction and the female's self-contained state. The female, in other words, is not characterized particularly as possessing the form embodied in sperm or as being able to produce it.

With her lower body temperature, in fact, and without much semen, a woman really cannot possess the same form, "motive principle," dynamic force, or sense of general "firstness" as a man. Hence a woman's robustness in worldly action and in sex, her ability to orgasm, for example, will be a drastically diminished version of a man's (evidence that contradicts Tireisius's testimony about male compared to female orgasms). Aristotle speculated that even a man severely "deficient of heat" and unable to produce adequate amounts of semen would eventually lose the male "principle" and would at last "of necessity change over into [the] opposite condition" and, in effect, become a woman (*Generation* 4:1,765b). The person of too little semen, whether male or female, is a kind of castrato—as it were, an infertile male. (For a similar distinction, see Plato's *Timaeus* 90E–91E.) The connection here is form *(eidos)* as a natural and intrinsic expression of maleness.

Not always in agreement with Aristotle, Hippocrates (or writers under his name) in *Diseases of Women* elaborates the same doctrine of inherent weakness in the female body owing to her poor physical "form." He differs with Aristotle on the issue of body heat, believing that a woman *does* have an especially warm body. However, this text still provides a context for Aristotle's comments by attempting to offer visible proof, for example, of female deficiency in arguing that a man's body has "more solid [muscle] flesh than a woman" (Lefkowitz and Fant, eds. 1982, 89). Lower amounts of semen cause women to be smaller and weaker overall, but the most vivid example of a woman's lack of solidity and strength, and a cornerstone of Hippocratic gynecology, is the phenomenon of the "displaced uterus"—the "wandering womb." The Hippocratic doctors believed, and from the fourth century B.C. through the second century A.D. the medical notion prevailed, that serious female disorders frequently arose because the uterus was not anchored in place. It could get "displaced" and "wander" through the body's various cavities, especially the chest and lower abdomen, and depending on where the uterus wandered to, a woman could be ill with suffocation, general body limpness, headaches, or liver pains and could even die from this problem.

With the resulting illness, whether minor or fatal, it was the male physician's task to track the errant uterus and discover how to put it back behind the vagina. In several Hippocratic texts there are lengthy explanations about the regions the uterus wanders into and what ailments are then produced. Particularly dangerous, the treatises caution, are movements of the uterus around the lungs. A woman with this trouble might miss up to two menstrual periods because her uterus has lodged between the lungs, and in this condition, the text says flatly, "she cannot survive" because the accumulated menstrual fluid will fill the lungs and drown her (Lefkowitz and Fant, eds. 1982, 90). Less alarming is the situation in which the uterus moves to the upper abdomen and causes non-fatal suffocation, a loss of voice, drowsiness, and chattering teeth (93). On the order of a minor danger is the problem of older women and those sexually inactive women whose dormant uterus gets "empty and light" and then turns until "it hits the liver"; both then might "strike the abdomen...." The uterus hitting the liver "produces sudden [but minor] suffocation as it occupies the breathing passage round the belly" (90–91). This condition, causing only minor suffocation and painful urination, responds well to treatment. The least serious ailment occurs when, because of a woman's "hard work [in her husband's household] or lack of food," the uterus "falls toward the lower back or toward the hips" (91), a problem the Hippocratic text explains reassuringly is minor—temporary and usually self-correcting. Hippocratic doctors came to these conclusions in their writing often based on abstract theory. What little clinical knowledge they had seems to have come from midwives who had considerable experience and information based on their own observation of female anatomy and ailments.[3]

Remedies for these ailments cover a wide range of treatments. If the woman has a marginally displaced uterus, she might be washed with warm water, given several herbal preparations (orally and vaginally), and then directed to "have intercourse with her husband" (94). Severe problems require repeated vaginal insertion of powerfully sweet "pessaries," or suppositories, to draw the uterus close, and fetid or pungent ones inserted in the mouth, to move it away. Along with warm baths, prescribed intercourse, and fragrant oils for the nose, the physician applies the pessaries and massages the woman's body to coerce the uterus back into place before a fatal condition can develop.

The character, and misogyny, of the Hippocratic texts emerges particularly through their attribution of a kind of spiritual and physical animism, a belief in the willfully perverse motivation of the woman's body as it chooses to go astray and be ill instead of remain healthy. Perverse intent is centered in the uterus, as is shown in the following Greco-Latin text by Aretaeus of Cappadocia. A late text of the second century A.D., this passage nonetheless foregrounds the very conceit of female animism and highlights the metaphors fundamental to that tradition since the time of the earliest Hippocratic writers:

> In the middle of the flanks of women lies the womb, a female viscus, closely resembling an animal; for it is moved of itself hither and thither in the flanks, also upwards in a direct line to below the cartilage of the thorax, and also obliquely to the right or to the left, either to the liver or spleen; and it likewise is subject to prolapsus downwards, and, in a word, it is altogether erratic. It delights, also, in fragrant smells, and advances towards them; and it has an aversion to fetid smells, and flees from them; and, on the whole, the womb is like an animal within an animal.
>
> (*The Extant Works of Aretaeus, the Cappadocian,* 285–287)

The passage summarizes many of the precepts of Hippocratic gynecology, highlighting the perverse independence of the female body as it takes a kind of animal pleasure in violating its own order of health. With its own pleasures and aversions, the uterus also has the independent volition of "an animal within an animal," the uterus actually wishing to propel itself away from where it should be according to medical wisdom, all because it has aims not consonant with bodily health as communicated by the male gynecologist. Aretaeus, the Hippocratic doctor, actually condemns the uterus as a primitive and uncooperative organ, errant and rebellious.

The idea of "an animal within an animal," moreover, makes the woman doubly passive. Unable to control her uterus, she is made passive while the uterus follows its own dictates, its inner "animal" urge to go astray. When the woman becomes ill, she becomes passive again as the gynecologist supplies the orientation for the uterus that the woman supposedly lacks in herself. The woman's body, lacking form, is divided into an errant, rebellious part, a kind of dark frontier of incivility and formlessness, and a malleable, colonized part that, while not well-formed in itself, is nonetheless capable of being structured and made healthy by the gynecologist. The woman can be saved and made well, in a sense exorcised of error in the flesh, if the rebellious spirit within her can be kept under control.

In these gynecological texts, not "gynocritical" in the sense of involving women as the producers of knowledge (see Rousselle 1980 and 1983 for a discussion of producing as opposed to appropriating knowledge about women's bodies in Greek gynecology), the woman's body in each case is not properly her own concern. She cannot keep the uterus from getting displaced, does not know where it wanders to, and does not know how to re-position it. She knows only that she needs the doctor's guidance (or conceivably the midwife's help) when the condition develops. The male doctor—and the doctors are male—steps in to position the woman as a female subject. The gynecologist frames the woman's viewpoint with "gynecology," in effect, deploying a male technology to displace female knowledge or self-awareness. From this viewpoint, the woman with no access to a midwife would have no occasion to minister to her own body, for patent in these texts is the assumption of a doctor's mastery of the female-as-a-body and of the female as a body-of-knowledge.

To return to Aristotle, the woman is in this predicament, Aristotle argues, because she is constitutionally inadequate owing to her lack of warmth and firmness. Her condition—in contrast to his repeated assertions of a male's contrary, strong, well-formed state— keeps her weak because her natural state is to be soft and less well "formed" than a man. Further, the doctor's job, *as doctor,* is to provide the structuring or "form" of health that a woman cannot provide for herself—*to make* her healthy. The male's supposed ability as "that which is able to concoct" semen, and the supposed fact that semen possesses "the 'principle' of the 'form'" *(archen tou eidous),* aligns and marks the male "naturally" and irrevocably with form— *eidos (Generation* 4:1,765b). Other "facts" of gender, such as Aristotle's disclosure that a health deficiency in the parents' fluids will "tend to produce females" (4:2,766b), also clarify the significant tie between being male and having the proper *form* of one ontotheologically well suited for life in the Kosmos.

Aristotle argues quite clearly, in other words, that the same form *(eidos)* that is the essence of being male is the form that structures the logical relations of the *hupokeimenon* and scientific inquiry. The male virtually fulfills cultural destiny by aligning his scientific thinking and actions with the dictates of what is taken to be his own body and physiology. The female is alienated from form by her nature as a woman. "Sick with desire" in that the amorphous nature of femaleness renders her dysfunctional, as Soranus describes her, she will be healthier in her dealings with the world to the extent that she receives the impression of male form, what a male doctor or husband must somehow impart temporarily to her. Thomas Laqueur describes an abstract version of this gynecological scenario in classical culture in *Making Sex* (1990), when he says that "conception is for the male to have an idea, an artistic or artisanal conception, in the brain-uterus of the female" (42). This comment implies the same connection I am making between the gendered body and ideas and critical thinking. The woman's body/brain is a poor receptacle, and the natural limits of her constitution and positioning will keep her from imitating form past a certain point. By contrast, the male—who actually *possesses* form—can naturally take the position as a scientific perspective that can make critical observations leading to scientific knowledge. In all of this for Aristotle there is an intrinsic congruence between the *hupokeimenon* as a matrix underlying representation and maleness as embodied in *sperma* as a form-giving substance in the construction of gender. This line of thought shows that the logic of the subject, conceived as scientific rigor, is a logic of the gendered subject conceived principally as male.

In this classical view, women are positioned to reflect a supposedly "open" economy of chance—the certainty of female error that, in turn, functions to define being male as scientific rigor. The figure of the gynecologist evokes and confirms cultural authority in the assumption of an immovable reference of underlying form *(eidos)*— form that stands in relation to an amorphous female, suggesting the male as a stylus writing on the soft, feminine slate of the woman's body. Along this same line, G. E. R. Lloyd writes that the Greek "world-whole" is a Kosmos "subject to orderly and determinate sequences of causes and effects" expressed in "images and analogies from the legal and political domain"—the Kosmos as a large "monarchy" (*Magic, Reason, and Experience,* 247). The cosmic monarch's relationship to the world in fact replicates that of the doctor to the malleable body he treats, and in *The History of Sexuality II* (138–139) Michel Foucault explicitly connects medicine and politics, suggesting that Zeus's mission is to doctor the world. This connection concerning Zeus's doctoring of the world is apparent in book eight of the *Iliad,* when Zeus brings all of the gods to Mount Olympos to warn them about intervention in the Trojan War. Zeus ends his oration as follows:

> Or prove it this way:
> out of the zenith hang a golden line
> and put your weight on it, all gods and goddesses.
> You will not budge me earthward out of heaven,
> cannot budge the all-highest, mighty Zeus,
> no matter how you try.
>
> But let my hand
> once close to pull that cable—up you come,
> and with you earth itself comes, and the sea.
> By one end tied around Olympos' top
> I could let all the world swing in mid-heaven!
> That is how far I overwhelm you all,
> both gods and men. (8:5–27)

Here, Zeus is positioned on Mount Olympos with a fixed orientation for the formless and inherently chaotic world below him. The only one who can stand alone and tend to the structuring and maintenance of the world, he has a fixed vantage point on Mount Olympos from which to regard the world, and if he chooses to break his tie with the world, the world in all its vastness comes unstuck.

The world, in other words, can come unstuck precisely in the way that a woman's uterus comes unstuck in the female body. This similarity exists because the Kosmos itself, as these texts show, was conceived by the Greeks as a female otherness (the *Theogony* makes this point with great force) in relation to Zeus's position as a super-male agency. Zeus and the gynecologist, in other words, have the same approximate relation to the *hupokeimenon* and the discourse that makes the world knowable. The fixed position of the father/doctor, *as doctor,* orients the female body, and Zeus as super father/doctor orients the female world. Also, the technology of gynecology, the pessaries, oils, and various treatments, are the instruments of this orientation, the means of implementation, just as Zeus's "male" technology—his golden cable and various powers of state—implement his rule and give order to the world. The gynecologists, in this way, represent the male's fixed perspective, suggesting the equivalence of the female body and Kosmos in that both are dependent on "male" technology and firstness for form. "Gynecology" as cultural reference and technology of power and the fixity of "mount Olympos," in effect, are the references of Greek critical authority, and in relation to them "womb" and "world" wander without purpose until a male can reposition them. Male technology cures "female problems," that is, female constitutional inadequacy and disorder.

In the passage from the *Iliad,* paternal authority is a position of speech in a discourse that defines "true" speech for the "other" positions relating to it, much as oppositional relations are established in the logical scaffolding of the *hupokeimenon.* Zeus and the gynecologists define "truth" by seeming to arrange the world's otherwise amorphous matter in relation to form *(eidos)* as a sublunary gesture toward the "good." There is also a dialogic relationship in each case between male or paternal authority and that which it shapes and governs. Suppressed in each case is a recognition of the discourse that constitutes the text; each text shows, apart from what it "says," that the "power" of form and maleness is based not in itself but in the social discourse producing the effects of apparently "natural" male form in that text. That dialogic discourse is made evident only when the oppositions that constitute it are identified and exposed.

The discourse of these texts, finally, tends to articulate a central axiom of Western sexuality and gender—what Thomas Aquinas later will assert in the formula of woman as "matter" and man as "form," raw material and mold—in the misogyny of an anonymous Greco-Latin aphorism, *Tota mulier in utero* ("Woman is nothing but a uterus"). The question of the male relation to women necessarily focuses on the issue of form and representation in early Western culture, an issue that—beyond the scope of this discussion—will reappear later with particular significance in the Christian definition and theory of male "firstness" and fatherhood.

Eidos and Ideology

For the Greeks, the position from which one sees the ultimate "good" must be based, in an analytical sense, "outside" of apparent motion, at least "outside" of sublunary imperfection. That scientific position of knowing can then be occupied fully only by those who can see into the natural order of this world—for Homer, the stable viewpoints of Zeus and those in the pantheon, and for Aristotle, the scientific perspective and subject of inquiry. Aristotle's wager is that in any instance of interpretation or knowing there must be a "first mover," and the existence of this perspective addresses the problem of indeterminacy in the world. If there were *more* than one such authoritative perspective, "the series of [subsequent] movers and movables," as G. Berbeke notes, would "be infinite too." And since "an infinite movement cannot be realized [as knowledge] in a limited time" of understanding such as what humans must deal with, the lack of a prime knower would likewise make any knowing impossible (548). Aristotle's scientific undertaking, in this way, demands the postulation of an inherently stable and well-formed scientific subject. The male as a speaking subject is not positioned by Aristotle as such but, rather, is located within the *hupokeimenon* with its suggestion of a privileged and stable view.

The viewpoint of the prime mover, if we could fully occupy it, would allow us to take pleasure, as Verbeke says, "more in stability than in movement" (Verbeke, 563). We in the sublunary world do not have that viewpoint, so we must content ourselves by devising schemes for understanding the world in relation to the postulated stasis of the *episteme* as a gradually perfectible understanding. The critical approach to the *hupokeimenon* then allows us to chart the ratios of imperfection in this world in relation to that which we supposedly can assume is ultimately stable and perfect. It becomes possible to imagine a system of interpretation wherein one can separate mere quantitative and qualitative differences from substantial patterns to find a model of form in human understanding that approximates, or at least is on its way toward an appreciation of, true and reliable knowledge.

In his logical and gender treatises, Aristotle tried to show the potential for constant and reliable interpretation and why logical possibilities necessarily move along certain "oppositional" lines of development and not others. If the interpretation of texts could not be conventionalized at some level, then change, especially important state and political distinctions, would go unnoticed and could be lost in the mundane proliferation of heterogeneity and chance. And "there can be no demonstrative knowledge," as Aristotle says in the *Posterior Analytics*, "of the fortuitous [chance]" (1:30,87b). The logical relationship based on the male body's form as a trope serves the single aim of contextualizing chance within substantial patterns and foregrounding intelligible differences rather than infinite regression.

The move to align the male body with scientific "logic," as if doing so were natural and inevitable, is a strategic move to make a male seem to be the only "natural" speaking subject. The nature of this strategy helps to explain how the strength or weakness of particular manifestations of maleness may do little to change patriarchy. Male "power" lies in the economy of positioning as Aristotle defines that scheme through the *hupokeimenon*, in the institutionalization of the speaking subject's position *as a male position*, and in the Western tradition of this institutionalization. In this way, male authority derives from a fundamentally discursive practice, from privileging males as ideal knowers and the ones who speak of and *for* knowledge—for form as instituted in their own bodies. This privileging has deep ties to Greek science and notions of coherence and reasoning, and Aristotle's texts not only make these connections but, more importantly, cannot help but provide the conceptual frames for critiquing them as well.[4]

NOTES

1. Introductory texts about classical Greek science that discuss Aristotle include Benjamin Farrington's *Greek Science* (Harmondsworth: Penguin Books, 1944) and Morris R. Cohen's and I. E. Drabkin's *A Source Book in Greek Science* (New York: McGraw-Hill Book Co., 1948). Standard texts on this subject by G. E. R. Lloyd include *Early Greek Science: Thales to Aristotle* (New York: W. W. Norton, 1970); *The Revolutions of Wisdom: Studies in the Claims and Practice of Ancient Greek Science* (Berkeley: Univ. of California Press, 1987); and *Magic, Reason, and Experience: Studies in the Origin and Development of Greek Science* (Cambridge: Cambridge

Univ. Press, 1979). More specialized but highly influential, particularly on contemporary French classical studies, is Lloyd's *Polarity and Analogy: Two Types of Argumentation in Early Greek Thought* (Cambridge: Cambridge Univ. Press, 1966).

Other specialized discussions include *Science and Speculation: Studies in Hellenistic Theory and Practice*, ed. Jonathan Barnes, Jacques Brunschwig, Myles Burnyeat, and Malcolm Schofield (Cambridge: Cambridge Univ. Press, 1982); Lloyd's *Science and Morality in Greco-Roman Antiquity* (Cambridge: Cambridge Univ. Press, 1985); and Ludwig Edelstein's *Ancient Medicine: Selected Papers of Ludwig Edelstein* (Baltimore: Johns Hopkins Univ. Press, 1967).

2. For useful and wide-ranging studies in classical gender relations, see Page duBois, *Centaurs and Amazons: Women and the Pre-History of the Great Chain of Being* (Ann Arbor: Univ. of Michigan Press, 1982); Susan C. Jarratt, *Rereading the Sophists: Classical Rhetoric Refigured* (Carbondale and Edwardsville: Southern Illinois Univ. Press, 1991); Eva C. Keuls, *The Reign of the Phallus: Sexual Politics in Ancient Athens* (New York: Harper and Row, 1985); Thomas Laqueur, *Making Sex: Body and Gender from the Greeks to Freud* (Cambridge: Harvard Univ. Press, 1990); Mary R. Lefkowitz, *Heroines and Hysterics* (New York: St. Martin's Press, 1981); Gerda Lerner, *The Creation of Patriarchy* (New York, Oxford: Oxford Univ. Press, 1986); Paola Manuli, "Fisiologia e patologia del femminile negli scritti ippocratici dell'antica ginecologia greca," *Hippocratica*, Colloque de Paris (CNRS, Paris, 1980); S. Pembroke, "Women in Charge: The Function of Alternatives in Early Greek Tradition and the Ancient Idea of Matriarchy," in *Journal of the Warburg and Courtauld Institutes* 30 (1970):1–35; Sarah B. Pomeroy, *Goddesses, Whores, Wives, and Slaves* (New York: Schocken Books, 1975); Aline Rousselle, "Observation feminine et ideologie masculine: le corps de la femme d'après les médecins grecs," *Annales: Économies, Societés, Civilisations* (1980):1089–1115; Aline Rousselle, *Porneia: On Desire and the Body in Antiquity*, trans. Felicia Pheasant (Oxford: Basil Blackwell, 1988; orig. 1983); Ilza Veith, *Hysteria: The History of a Disease* (Chicago: Univ. of Chicago Press, 1965).

3. For a discussion of the relationship of "midwives" and male gynecologists, see Paola Manuli, *Fisiologia e patologia del femminile negli scritti ippocratici dell'antica ginecologia greca*, Colloque de Paris (CNRS, Paris, 1980). See also Aline Rousselle, *Porneia: On Desire and the Body in Antiquity*, trans. Felicia Pheasant (Oxford: Basil Blackwell, 1988; orig. 1983) and "Observation feminine et ideologie masculine: le corps de la femme d'après les médecins grecs," in *Annales: Économies, Societés, Civilisations* (1980):1089–1115. About the "midwives," Rousselle says in

Porneia: "The ancient doctors whose writings have come down to us owe their knowledge about women's ailments to these women, but in the hands of the doctors the knowledge acquired by these midwives lost much of its observational basis" (25). Citing Manuli, Rousselle adds that "the training of [ancient Greek] doctors in medical theory in fact resulted in women knowing less about their bodies than they had in previous eras" (25).

4. This essay is drawn from chapter 3, "Aristotle and the Gendered Subject" in my *The Paternal Romance: Reading God-the-Father in Early Western Culture* (Champaign and London: Univ. of Illinois Press, 1992).

WORKS CITED

Anton, John Peter. *Aristotle's Theory of Contrariety.* London: Routledge and Kegan Paul, 1957.

Aretaeus. *The Extant Works of Aretaeus, the Cappadocian.* Ed. and trans. Francis Adams. London: Sydenham Society, 1856.

Aristotle. *"Categories" and "De Interpretatione."* Trans. and Notes J. L. Ackrill. Oxford: Clarendon Press, 1963.

———. *Generation of Animals.* Trans. and ed. A. L. Peck. Cambridge: Harvard Univ. Press; London: Heinemann Ltd., 1943.

———. *Historia Animalium.* Three Vols. Trans. and ed. A. L. Peck. Cambridge: Harvard Univ. Press; London: Heinemann Ltd., 1965.

———. *Metaphysics.* Two Volumes. Trans. and ed. Hugh Tredennick. London: Heinemann Ltd.; Cambridge: Harvard Univ. Press, 1956.

———. *On Interpretation.* Commentary by St. Thomas Aquinas and Cardinal Cajetan. Milwaukee: Marquette Univ. Press, 1962.

———. *The Organon.* Trans. and ed. Harold P. Cooke and Hugh Tredennick. London: Heinemann Ltd.; Cambridge: Harvard Univ. Press, 1955.

———. *Aristotle's Physics.* Trans. and ed. Hippocrates G. Apostle. Grinnell, Iowa: The Peripatetic Press, 1969.

———. *Aristotle's Physics.* Ed. W. D. Ross. Oxford: Clarendon Press, 1955.

———. *Aristotle's Posterior Analytics.* Trans. and Comm. Hippocrates G. Apostle. Grinnell, Iowa: Peripatetic Press, 1981.

———. *Posterior Analytics.* Trans. and ed. Hugh Tredennick. Cambridge: Harvard Univ. Press; London: Heinemann Ltd., 1960.

duBois, Page. *Centaurs and Amazons: Women and the Pre-History of the Great Chain of Being.* Ann Arbor: Univ. of Michigan Press, 1982.

Foucault, Michel. *The History of Sexuality: An Introduction.* Vol. I. Trans. Robert Hurley. New York: Vintage Books. 1980 (orig. 1976).

──────. *The History of Sexuality: The Use of Pleasure.* Vol. II. Trans. Robert Hurley. New York: Pantheon Books, 1985 (orig. 1984).

Handelman, Susan A. *The Slayers of Moses: The Emergence of Rabbinic Interpretation in Modern Literary Theory.* Albany: State Univ. of New York Press, 1982.

Hesiod. *Hesiod's Theogony.* Trans. and ed. Norman O. Brown. New York: The Liberal Arts Press, 1953.

Homer. *Iliad.* Trans. Robert Fitzgerald. Garden City, N.Y.: Anchor Press/ Doubleday, 1974.

Jarratt, Susan C. *Rereading the Sophists: Classical Rhetoric Refigured.* Carbondale and Edwardsville: Southern Illinois Univ. Press, 1991.

Keuls, Eva C. *The Reign of the Phallus: Sexual Politics in Ancient Athens.* New York: Harper and Row, 1985.

Laqueur, Thomas. *Making Sex: Body and Gender from the Greeks to Freud.* Cambridge: Harvard Univ. Press, 1990.

Lefkowitz, Mary R. *Heroines and Hysterics.* New York: St. Martin's Press, 1981.

Lefkowitz, Mary R., and Maureen B. Fant, eds. *Women's Life in Greece and Rome.* Baltimore, Md.: Johns Hopkins Univ. Press, 1982.

Lerner, Gerda. *The Creation of Patriarchy.* New York, Oxford: Oxford Univ. Press, 1986.

Lloyd, G. E. R. *Polarity and Analogy: Two Types of Argumentation in Early Greek Thought.* Cambridge: Cambridge Univ. Press, 1966.

──────. *Magic, Reason, and Experience: Studies in the Origin and Development of Greek Science.* Cambridge: Cambridge Univ. Press, 1979.

Manuli, Paola. "Fisiologia e patologia del femminile negli scritti ippocratici dell'antica ginecologia greca." *Hippocratica,* Colloque de Paris, CNRS, Paris, 1980.

Pembroke, S. "Women in Charge: The Function of Alternatives in Early Greek Tradition and the Ancient Idea of Matriarchy," in *Journal of the Warburg and Courtauld Institutes* 30 (1970):1–35.

Plato. *Timaeus.* Trans. Francis M. Cornford. Ed. Oskar Piest. New York: Liberal Arts Press, 1959.

Pomeroy, Sarah B. *Goddesses, Whores, Wives, and Slaves.* New York: Schocken Books, 1975.

Rousselle, Aline. "Observation feminine et ideologie masculine: le corps de la femme d'après les médecins grecs." *Annales: Économies, Societés, Civilisations* (1980):1089–1115.

──────. *Porneia: On Desire and the Body in Antiquity.* Trans. Felicia Pheasant. Oxford: Basil Blackwell, 1988 (orig. 1983).

Veith, Ilza. *Hysteria: The History of a Disease.* Chicago: Univ. of Chicago Press, 1965.

Verbeke, G. "The Aristotelian Doctrine of Qualitative Change in *Physics* VII, 3," in John P. Anton and George L. Kustas, eds. *Essays in Ancient Greek Philosophy.* Albany: State University of New York Press, 1971.

Roberta Davidson

3

Cross-Dressing in Medieval Romance

Transformation of females into males is not an idle
story... a girl at Casinum was changed into a boy,
under the observation of the parents, and at the order
of the augurs was conveyed away to a desert
island.... I myself saw in Africa a person who had
turned into a male on the day of marriage to
a husband.[1]

The Berwick tournament of 1347 was enlivened by forty or fifty
mounted women dressed in tunics and armed with knives. Such
women had attended several English tournaments before the one
at Berwick, entertaining the participants and scandalizing the clergy,
for they feared neither the anger of God for their shamelessness,
nor the comments of shocked citizens.[2] Indeed, these masculinely
attired women, like their fictional counterparts, were enjoying the
privilege of license through their sexual disguise.

Cross-dressing in early period literature is never simply about
wearing different clothes. It is always linked to questions about the
established order. When it is perceived positively, it is seen by its
"readers" as manifesting a rebellion against nature or a critique of
literal appearances in the pursuit of a "truer" disguise. In its "dis-
graceful" manifestations, it represents the overthrow of authority,
either playfully or with a more serious anarchic intention. In either
mode, it initially undermines excessive patriarchal authority, but
may also help to reaffirm it:

anthropologists generally agree that . . . rites of sexual inversion, like other rites and ceremonies of reversal, are ultimately sources of order and stability in a hierarchical society. They can clarify the structure by the process of reversing it. They can provide an expression of, and a safety valve for, conflicts within the system. They can correct and relieve the system when it has become authoritarian. But, so it is argued, they do not question the basic order of the society itself.[3]

This is not to deny that cross-dressing could have its practical uses. The Countess Richilde had fought in armor for Hainaut and Flanders in the eleventh century, until she was defeated finally in battle and captured. Despite four years of imprisonment, she retained her rights in Hainaut. It has been suggested that she was the prototype for the warrior maidens found in numerous later French romances,[4] although no model drawn from life was needed by that time. Athena, Camilla in the *Aeneid,* Amazons by the dozen, queens like Semiramis, even the Virgin Mary had donned armor in legends both secular and sacred. (Nor were the only cross-dressers militant ones, or militant women confined to those who wore men's clothes.)

By the mid–fourteenth century, clothing was surprisingly androgenous, even the hoods worn by men echoing women's "decolletage."[5] Nor was it clothing alone which was sometimes androgenous: the ideals of male and female beauty in the high Middle Ages seem at times to have fused.[6] It is possible in early literature as well as in more well-known Renaissance examples for a heroine to be mistaken for or exchange roles with a hero. Yet these factual circumstances and stylistic conventions cannot completely explain the remarkable metamorphoses undergone by the cross-dressing heroines of Medieval Romance—in particular one motif in which the woman *becomes* a man. This is a most telling demonstration, a seeming freedom from the predetermination of the sexual body, yet it is consistent with Galenic medical wisdom and a general conviction about the nature of woman which linked her so strongly to matter and certain forms of behavior that only transformation of her gender could explain her deviation from the norm.

There is not sufficient space in one article to do justice to all the literary examples of cross-dressing in the Middle Ages. What this article explores, therefore, is a sampling of cross-dressing men and women in both fictional and nonfictional texts from late in the period, more with the intention of determining a pattern of perception about gender than a comprehensive analysis of any one work. The actual romances cited—*Tristan de Nanteuil, Estoire de Merlin* (also called the Vulgate *Merlin*), and Sir Thomas Malory's *Morte Darthur*—are not necessarily the most familiar (with the exception of Malory, and in his case the episode I discuss is seldom noted) and are, unfortunately, too extensive to summarize entirely. I will, however, attempt to establish the context of each episode. Other works incorporated in my general argument are even more summarily addressed, but are included to demonstrate the pervasiveness of the belief, documented by Thomas Laqueur in his examination of early medical texts, that "what we would take to be only metaphoric connections . . . were viewed as having causal consequences in the body as being real."[7]

Iphis, in *Metamorphoses* IX, 666–797, was probably the classical model for metamorphosing heroines. Ovid describes Iphis's father as a man of blameless and trustworthy life who desires a male child. Indeed, girl children are so troublesome that he reluctantly decides to put a female baby, should his wife bear one, to death. His wife, Telethusa, begs him to reconsider, but in vain. While not unprecedented historically, this is a good example of excessive paternal control. The father only wishes to reproduce himself through a child of his own gender. Ironically, it will be because he is disobeyed and deceived by his wife and daughter that he will get his wish. The story of Iphis begins as a deliberate, disguised flouting of masculine authority, but it soon becomes clear that the individuals are being manipulated in a reaffirmation of divine order.

While in childbed, Telethusa has a vision in which the goddess Io instructs her to put aside her husband's command and save the child. The little girl, accordingly disguised as a boy, receives the name of her grandfather. When she is thirteen, her father finds her a bride, Ianthe of Crete. The two fall in love with one another, Ianthe innocently, Iphis Ovidianly; the knowledge that her love "cannot" be consumated intensifies her desire. Filled with a sense of her own "unnaturalness," she temporarily comforts herself with the thought that her love is no more strange than the bestiality of Pasiphae (also from Crete—a hopeful sign?), but she despairs that even Daedalus could contrive a sex-change for either herself or Ianthe.

Meanwhile, Telethusa, fearing discovery, finds excuses to postpone the wedding, but finally, all postponements exhausted, she prays to Io.

> The goddess seemed to move, nay, moved her altar, the doors of the temple shook, her moon-shaped horns shot forth gleams of light and the sistrum rattled noisily. Not yet quite free from care and yet rejoicing in the good omen, the mother left the temple; and Iphis walked beside her as she went, but with a longer stride than was her wont. Her face seemed of a darker hue, her strength seemed greater, her very features sharper, her hair, all unadorned, shorter than before. She seemed more vigorous than was her girlish wont. In fact, you who but lately were a girl are now a boy![8]

The secondary sexual characteristics of masculinity are perceived as integral to the change, an assumption shared by Christine de Pizan in the fifteenth century, when she describes the change in fortune that forces her to support her family through writing:

> I felt changed all over.
> My limbs were much stronger than before,
> Which felt strange,
> And the crying had stopped . . .
> And I felt much lighter
> Than I was accustomed to,
> And my appearance was changed and strengthened,
> And my voice became deeper,
> And my body harder and more agile.
> But the ring that Hymen had given me
> Fell from my finger,
> Which troubled me, as indeed it should,
> For I loved it dearly,
> Then I got up easily.
> I no longer indulged in idle crying,
> Which only increased my distress.
> I found myself with a strong and hardy spirit,
> Which astonished me.
> Now I will prove that
> I became a real man.[9]

The loss of the ring seems to be both a reference to the death of her husband and a strong implied reference to the loss of female genitalia. On a material level, she will no longer function as a sexually active woman, and on a psychic one she will think and act as a man. The change is one from the outside in, conflating behavior and identity, as if to say that we are not what we are in any essential way, but, rather, because of what we do. Christine may lament her liberation into the active world at the cost of her identity as a woman—"But it pleased me much more/To be a woman, as I was accustomed to/When I communicated with Hymen"/[10]—but her gender is no longer compatible with the virility she needs as a professional. This attitude would appear to coincide with Laqueur's findings:

> ... it was precisely when talk seemed to be most directly about the biology of the two sexes that it was most embedded in the politics of gender, in culture. To be a man or a woman was to hold a social rank, a place in society, to assume a cultural role, not *be* organically one or the other of two incommensurable sexes.[11]

Iphis's transformation, on the other hand, is more ambiguous. Perhaps it is because she is more suited, in some essential way, to be a husband than a wife. On the other hand, we are left with a strong sense that she is a somewhat arbitrary demonstration of the gods' control, working through a feminine principle of illusion, disobedience, and powerful emotion, showing the futility of human planning and pride, and the paradoxical certainty of the reestablishment of order in human affairs.

A medieval Iphis can be recognized in the plight of Blanchandine in the fourteenth-century *Tristan de Nanteuil*.[12] A. H. Krappe suggests that the Ovidian story reached the West through an Oriental version. K. V. Sinclair largely agrees, although adding "until all Western and Eastern redactions have been surveyed, we must be cautious about how we judge the intercultural transferences."[13] Whatever its transmission, the parallels are striking, and again suggest that the masculine woman is a sexually inactive woman, even if she has a prior history of "womanly" behavior.

In an earlier episode of the story, Blanchandine is the hero's mistress, but later circumstances force her to disguise herself as a knight. She becomes engaged to Clarinde, the daughter of the Sultan of Babilone. At first, Blanchandine refuses to marry a heathen. However, after the Sultan's death, Clarinde becomes ruler and announces she will marry Blanchandine the next day. An initial act of covert disruption—a woman disguised as a man—is therefore compounded by the open overturning of accepted norms of authority by the political power and sexual aggressiveness of the non-Christian Sultan's daughter. Obviously, the possibilities of such wholesale inversion are fictionally entertaining, and the audience, like Blanchandine (but with different motivation), hopes for the period of uncertainty to be prolonged. But it is a dangerous game as well, and if not ultimately resolved by the insertion of a masculine element, likely to lead to the destruction, physical or spiritual, of everyone involved.

The wedding takes place, but the consummation is postponed due to the still-unresolved issue of baptism. The delaying role played by Telethusa in the original is here taken over by the heroine herself. The anxiety about the physical nature of marriage, combined with the suppression of lesbian eroticism as "impossible"—it was also "impossible" for Iphis, for such a conclusion might lead to a permanently rebellious social construction—shows the strong directive of narrative convention underlying the apparent license of the plot. Clarinde, after four days of growing frustration, is told by a messenger that her new husband is a woman. She orders "him" a bath. However, as Blanchandine is being led to it, a wild stag runs into the palace, then out into the woods. Blanchandine seizes the opportunity for escape and follows.

Once in the forest, Blanchandine prays to the Virgin and to God. An angel appears, and allows her to choose between remaining a woman or becoming a man. Moreover, the angel informs her, if she becomes a man, her son will be a great hero. She agrees that transformation is the better option, and is changed. Blanchandin (whose name changes to a masculine form with his gender) then decapitates the kneeling stag and returns to the palace. He strips for the bath, to everyone's visual satisfaction. The disguise is over. Clarinde is baptised with great haste, and the marriage consummated. Power, gender, and faith are again in proper hierarchical alignment.

What in the idea of woman allowed and even seemed to encourage such transformation? Metaphor, in its analogic function, was understood to reveal the proportion between cause and effect.[14] In the relationship between males and females, sexual identity was similarly both given and participatory—a series of behavioral effects as well as biological causes. Under special circumstances, similarity transformed into sameness, or a previously undisclosed sameness, was revealed. Science attempted to understand the nature of women's sexuality through theories that defined her as an inadequately equipped male. Not very far removed from this idea is the perception of woman as a man in disguise.

According to the neo-Aristotelian or Galenic understanding of Woman, her difference from Man was her cold nature which limits her creative (active) abilities. Her own creation and her ability to create were indistinguishable.

> As regards the individual nature, woman is defective and misbegotten, for the active power in the male seed tends to the production of a perfect likeness according to the masculine sex; while the production of woman comes of a defect in the active power, or from some material indisposition, or even from some external influence.[15]

Yet, should this biological prisoner escape into the realm of action, of heat and movement, these careful differentiations might break down. Women were "men turned inside out." Women who spread their legs too far risked having their organs fall out,[16] becoming male genitals, and absence would become presence. Likewise, heat might "ripen" them and cause their dormant maleness to emerge, the woman giving rebirth to herself as a man.

Grammatical law, correspondingly, was perceived as the extension of innate characteristics of being, and grammatical gender the operation of a "law" of sexual differentiation. Masculine gender signified the property of acting, feminine gender the property of being acted upon.[17] Medieval narratives—particularly the most conventional forms such as the lives of saints and the stories of romance—maintained active and passive gender characteristics as "givens."

The woman transformed into a man merges with the disguised woman in the Patristic opinion that "... As long as a woman is for birth and children, she is different from man as body is from soul.

But when she wishes to serve Christ more than the world, then she will cease to be a woman and will be called man"; that ". . . She who does not believe is a woman, and should be designated with the name of her sex, whereas she who believes progresses to perfect manhood, to the measure of the adulthood of Christ. She then dispenses with the name of her sex, the seductiveness of youth, the garrulousness of old age."[18] This can have dramatic consequences, as when Saint Uncumber, who helps to free women from unwanted husbands, was favored with "a long silky moustache and beard."[19] When women are pious and chaste, the man in the woman may throw off his disguise and display, as we have already seen, his secondary sexual characteristics.

Apart from the well-established neo-Platonic tendencies of early Christianity, a secular prejudice may be revealed in some of these stories. John Boswell suggests that the importance of conformity to gender roles defining males as active and females as passive is an early source of prejudice—not against all homosexuals, but against those men willing to take a passive position—as early as Classical times. This same prejudice developed into a partial source of anti-gay feeling in later periods, continuing well into the fourteenth and fifteenth centuries.[20]

There are, of course, no homosexual knights in chivalric romance. There are moments of sexual confusion, but usually, as with Launcelot or Lanval, due to a mistake on the part of another character. The passionate friendships of male characters such as Amis and Amiloun or Galahault and Lancelot in the French Vulgate cycle Prose *Lancelot*[21] are suggestive but are never expressed erotically and, on an emotional level, are left sexually inexplicit. In line with Boswell's finding is an episode in which the Prose Lancelot is so resentful of an attempt to involve him as a passive sexual partner (the knight comes upon Lancelot asleep in his tent and believes that he is his mistress) that he kills the man who kisses him. In Malory's version, this misunderstanding is cleared up with no more than a hasty explanation and a bad wound.[22]

Susan Shapiro has noted that there is little reason to think that before the nineteenth century " '. . . effeminacy' in men and 'mannishness' in women had homosexual connotations either for its practitioners or their critics."[23] Nonetheless, so important was it to the male medieval author that inner masculinity be expressed in concord with outer semblance, that it may have grown to be inconceivable that the two could be separated, perhaps especially when the masculine performer was a woman.

Marina Warner points out that Joan of Arc's transvestism was taken very seriously by those who condemned her for it, and also by herself. It ranked of equal significance for her with the truth of her voices. The visions and the dress were indivisible.[24] In this, as in much of her use of symbol, Joan personalized the sacred and secular traditions of virility, blending them inextricably.

Even in fiction, not all symbolic or literal transformations of females into males were viewed as positive. The active drive incompletely controlling its material host could inspire inferior or deficiently constructed matter to attempt to make anarchy and license a permanent state. Societies of warrior women were monstrous inversions of natural hierarchy; for this reason, perhaps, medieval audiences were fascinated by Amazons. Boccaccio is said to have started a "fashion" for them, and Eustace Deschamps selects five Amazons for his Nine Women Worthies. (It has been suggested that he chose as worthies nine of the fiercest pagan women in response to Boccaccio, who saw women's worth as stemming ". . . not from their good qualities as women, but from their resemblance to men."[25] In the case of his nine secular heroines, Deschamps's criteria appeared to be "courage, their cruel hearts, and their subjugation of their enemies."[26] Boccaccio's treatment of the legend of Pope Joan in *de mulieribus claris* (99)[27] illustrates the awful consequences of female presumption of a male persona. Joan is treated sympathetically at first, her cross-dressing inspired by a desire to be with the young clerk she loves, then continued as she realizes that she also loves learning. She goes too far, however, when she allows herself to be elected Pope. It is not a coincidence that Joan is finally revealed and disgraced through her inability to control her lust. She becomes pregnant and gives birth during a procession.

"Excessive" sexuality is a characteristic Joan shares with Semiramis—who took her son as her lover (one of the more frequently illustrated incidents from her life)—and even the Amazons, whose sexual practices were perceived as unnerving. In the same way, the primary accusation against the women of Berwick was that they were morally loose. It has been suggested that ". . . all deviations from gender-distinct clothing or stereotypes are indicative of sexual license."²⁸ While this is, perhaps, too sweeping a generalization, it is true that the possibility of unconventional heterosexual conduct that cross-dressing seems to invite is a constant anxiety.

The cross-dressing heroine herself may be chaste, but is often associated with a sexually corrupt woman, as if one chaste virgin dressed as a man must be viewed in the company of a sexually experienced, overtly female twin. This is demonstrated by the story of Grisandoles in the thirteenth-century *Estoire de Merlin.*²⁹ This episode is particularly interesting because men as well as women are depicted cross-dressing.

While on a visit to the Emperor of Rome, Merlin discovers two interesting facts.³⁰ The first is that the Emperor's wife has disguised twelve young men as women, and has arranged for them to attend upon her day and night. This is a situation resonant of The Queen of Lydia, Omphale, and Hercules. In Ovid's *Heroides* IX, 54–118, Deianira reminds Hercules that his mistress Omphale commanded him to dress in women's clothes—in particular "bejewelled chains," a woman's turban, Sidonian gown, and "the Maeonian girdle like a wanton girl"—and spin along with the slave girls.³¹ She, in turn, dressed in his lion skins:

> O shame, that the rough skin stripped from the flanks of the shaggy lion has covered a woman's delicate side! You are mistaken, and know it not—that spoil is not from the lion, but from you; A woman has borne the darts blackened with the venom of Lerna, a woman scarce strong enough to carry the spindle heavy with wool; a woman has taken in her hand the club that overcame wild beasts, and in the mirror gazed upon the armour of my husband.³²

Even as the women's clothes Hercules wears bind him physically—around the neck, the head, the waist—the emotional thrall that causes him to accede to Omphale's demands binds him to her as captive. Such emotional excess is, of course, the characteristic of women, as Deianera's own story reveals. Because of Hercules's fear and his passion, the strongest man in the world lies at the feet of a woman and recounts his deeds. To the same extent that he gained glory in the past from the strength of the lion whose skin he wore, when she puts on his clothing she takes his image as the emblem of her strength. So are the twelve lovers of the Empress presumably sexually enthralled, bound by their passions with their clothing, as though they were women. There is, however, a thirteenth man—her husband—who is unwittingly just as much within her power, for, like Telethusa, the submission of the Empress to male marital authority is only apparent.

Merlin's second interesting discovery is that the Emperor himself has a squire (soon a senechal) who, unknown to him, is a woman named Avenable, although she calls herself Grisandoles. The Emperor dreams of a sow wearing a crown—a dream that continually perturbs him. Merlin, in the shape of a stag, gains entrance to the palace. He informs the Emperor that only a wild man can interpret his dream. Merlin also explains to Grisandoles how to find the wild man (who is, of course, Merlin himself). She does so, bringing him back to court. Merlin then exposes the Empress, who is burnt with her twelve lovers.

Finally, it is revealed that Grisandoles is Avenable, the daughter of a Duke, and tells the Emperor to marry her, adding a suggestion that, once they are married, the Emperor not act in any way against Avenable's will. The excessively sexual "bad" woman is therefore replaced by a "good" woman, who will seem to dominate, but ultimately support the needs of her husband and the state.

Like Athena, who sides with men, Avenable's virtue is demonstrated by her successful impersonation of a man. The Emperor, who thought himself in control of his first wife, was, in fact, deceived by multiple disguises. The figure of the magician/wild man is himself a force outside of society, yet even his potentially anarchic voice is used to reorder the patriarchy for its own good. This is a story in which nearly every character, except the representative of secular authority, conceals his or her true identity, but the narrative ensures that all such concealments resolve themselves in revelation and a more insightful understanding of the proper distribution of power.

Male transvestism, even when not employed for adulterous purposes, could be perceived as a serious crime. It was sometimes associated with witchcraft,[33] (as was Joan of Arc's cross-dressing). However, in her discussion of transvestite riots, a seventeenth-century phenomenon, Natalie Zemon Davis suggests that woman's symbolism as an innately disruptive force allowed men in women's dress a license for rebellious behavior: "... the disguise freed men from full responsibility for their deeds and perhaps, too, from fear of outrageous revenge upon their manhood."[34]

In Sir Thomas Malory's fifteenth-century Arthuriad known as *Le Morte Darthur* (although it is unlikely he named it that), Launcelot dresses as a woman in order to deceive Dinadan, whom he has promised not to fight.[35] Dinadan, an anti-courtly knight (in some versions, a cowardly one), is both the source and the butt of much humor in the Tristan section of the book. It is appropriate that the man who is hesitant to ride onto the field for fear of Launcelot, despite a joking pledge, should meet him after all. Dinadan is comforted by the thought that he will recognize Launcelot's shield and be able to watch out for him, but as soon as Dinadan has ridden out, Launcelot dresses in "... a maydyns garmente freysshely attyred."

> Than sir Launcelot made sir Galyhodyn to lede hym thorow the raunge, and all men had wondir what damesell was that. And so as sir Dynadan cam into the raunge, sir Launcelot, that was in the damesels aray, gate sir Galyhodyns speare and ran unto sir Dynadan.
>
> And allwayes he loked up thereas sir Launcelot was, and then he sawe one sytte in the stede of sir Launcelot armed. But what sir Dynadan saw a maner of damesell, he dradde peryllys lest hit shoulde be sir Launcelot disgysed. But sir Launcelot cam on hym so faste that he smote sir Dynadan over his horse croupe. And anone grete coystrons gate sir Dynadan, and into the foreyste there besyde, and there they dispoyled hym unto his sherte and *put uppon hym a womans garmente* and so brought hym into fylde; and so theÄyu blew unto lodgyng, and every knyght wente and unarmed them.
>
> And than was sir Dynadam brought in amonge them all, and whan quene Gwenyver sawe sir Dynadan ibrought in so amonge them all, than she lowghe, that she fell downe; and so dede all that there was.
>
> "Well," seyde sir Dynadan, "sir Launcelot, thou arte so false that I can never beware of the."[36]

The point, of course, is to illustrate Dynadan's "effiminacy" in not wanting to fight a knight he knows is his superior. Male passivity is punished, even at the expense of Launcelot's word, which was, after all, both given and broken in jest and, perhaps, negated anyway by the license of wearing women's clothing. The superficial moral of the story seems to be as uncomplicated (and unamusing, except to the willing participants) as a fraternity prank. This is not a trick that Launcelot plays when fighting a knight whose ability he respects, although the affinity of all the Arthurian knights for fighting disguised, despite the dangers of fratricide, foreswearing and treason, reveals the unbalanced state of that seemingly stable chivalric world. Yet there is a possibility of gender-role ambiguity in Launcelot's own passive interaction with amorous women—particularly Gwenyvere—that sheds an additional light on what is at stake in his behavior.[37] His aggressive nature in battle is highlighted throughout the tales, even as his moral character is as "effeminate" as that of Hercules in the thrall of Omphale. His (compensatory?) physical aggressiveness is so extreme that it must act despite verbal contracts or communal responsibility.

This uncontrolled action is one of the factors that will lead to the discovery of the hero's adultery, the accidental death of Gawain's brothers, and the events that lead to the fall of Arthur's kingdom. The feminine, once again, is found in association with license and anarchy, but in this tale the male principle is unable to restore balance, and the marginal characters—Merlin, Nineve, the ghost of Gawain—are not powerful enough to counteract forces set in motion by the improper use of disguise at the time of Arthur's conception.

In this earlier cross-dressing episode, therefore, as incidental as it may seem, a thematic truth may be found: two men find themselves in maiden's attire, *both* "appropriately."

License, then, is a quality common to both male and female cross-dressers. Some women characters dress as men for the same reason that men characters dress as women—to signify their "dangerous" freedom from inherited or essential structures. It may be a rebellion that reaffirms the roles it rejects, particularly when physical transformation is involved. But cross-dressing can also be an act revealing the dichotomy between the outward and inner selves, and a resolution of that dichotomy. Under such circumstances, it is a denial of the power of matter in the face of will or convention—a denial that is both deeply conservative in its philosophical and spiritual origins and potentially revolutionary in its implications. It is an assertion that the flesh is subject to the sign, the signified to the signifier—not just metaphorically, but actually. Ironically, this insistence upon gender identity may also suggest the infinite possibilities of metaphoric substitution. It is not surprising, therefore, that, as a compensation for this dangerous process, divine devotion or intervention plays such a large role in these narratives, nor that the characters who undergo the ultimate change are most often women.[38]

NOTES

1. Pliny, *Natural History*. 2 vols., trans. H. Rackham. Loeb Classical Library (Cambridge: Harvard Univ. Press, 1942), 2: 7.4.36–38, 531.

2. Stella Mary Newton, *Fashion in the Age of the Black Prince: A Study of the Years 1340–1365* (Woodbridge ÄEng. U: Boydell Press, 1980), 10.

3. Natalie Zemon Davis, *Society and Culture in Early Modern France* (Stanford: Stanford Univ. Press, 1975), 130. Susan Shapiro also notes a "recurrent fear of a degenerate, topsy-turvy world inevitably following from the wholesale adoption of gender-deviant fashions and manners by both sexes." Susan C. Shapiro, "Sex, Gender, and Fashion in Medieval and Early Modern Britain," *The Journal of Popular Culture* 20.4 (1987): 116.

4. Keith V. Sinclair, *Tristan de Nanteuil: Thematic Infrastructure and Literary Creation* (Tubingen: Max Niemeyer Verlag, 1983), 35.

5. Newton, 3.

6. Joan M. Ferrante, *Woman as Image in Medieval Literature From the Twelfth Century to Dante* (New York: Columbia Univ. Press, 1975), 4–5.

7. Thomas Laqueur, *Making Sex: Body and Gender from the Greeks to Freud* (Cambridge: Harvard Univ. Press, 1990), 36.

8. Ovid, *Metamorphoses*, 2nd ed., 2 vols., trans. Frank Justus Miller. Loeb Classical Library (Cambridge: Harvard Univ. Press, 1921), 2: 59–60.

9. Christine de Pizan, *Le livre de la mutacion de fortune*, 1, ed. Suzanne Solente (Paris: SATF, 1959), 51–52, trans. Diane Bornstein; "Self-Consciousness and Self Concepts in the Works of Christine de Pizan,"

Ideals for Women in the Works of Christine de Pizan, ed. Diane Bornstein. Medieval and Renaissance Monograph Series, 1 (1981): 12–13.

10. Bornstein, 13.

11. Laqueur, 8.

12. *Tristan de Nanteuil, chanson de geste inedite,* ed. K. V. Sinclair (Assen: Van Gorcum, 1971).

13. Sinclair, 105. Regarding associations, Sinclair also believes the *Estoire de Merlin* to have been a model for the motif of the Woman Disguised as a Man in the *Tristan de Nanteuil.* Sinclair, 42.

14. Umberto Eco, *Semiotics and the Philosophy of Language* (Bloomington: Indiana University Press, 1984), 105.

15. *The Basic Writings of St. Thomas Aquinas,* 2 vols., ed. Anton C. Pegis (New York: Random House, 1945), 2: 880. Earlier versions of reproduction differed somewhat. See, for example, Joan Cadden's study of Hildegard of Bingen, "It Takes All Kinds: Sexuality and Gender Differences in Hildegard of Bingen's 'Book of Compound Medicine,' " *Traditio* 40 (1984): 149–174, for a theory of reproduction formulated by a twelfth-century woman:

Women are not the same as men of their kind, nor are they a pale imitation: they merit separate consideration and are characterized on their own terms. . . . This full treatment and independent characterization of the sexes is unusual, perhaps unique in the twelfth century. (166)

16. Vern L. Bullough, "Medieval Medical and Scientific Views of Women," *Viator* 4 (1973): 492. This was not, of course, a universally held theory, and is used here rather to illustrate one fairly extreme manifestation of an attitude implicit in much medieval gynecological theory. See also Joan Cadden, "Medieval Scientific and Medical Views of Sexuality: Questions of Propriety," *Medievalia et Humanistica* N.S. 14, ed. Paul Maurice Clogan (Totowa, N.J.: Roman & Littlefield, 1986): 157–171.

17. Jesse M. Gellrich, *The Idea of the Book in the Middle Ages: Language Theory, Mythology, and Fiction* (Ithaca: Cornell Univ. Press, 1985), 107.

18. Marina Werner, *Joan of Arc: The Image of Female Heroism* (New York: Vintage, 1982), 148. Warner cites Saints Jerome and Ambrose.

19. Warner, 154.

20. John Boswell, *Christianity, Social Tolerance, and Homosexuality: Gay People in Western Europe from the Beginning of the Christian Era to the Fourteenth Century* (Chicago: Univ. of Chicago Press, 1980), 137–138.

21. *The Vulgate Version of the Arthurian Romances,* 7 vols., ed. Oskar H. Sommer (Washington, D.C.: The Carnegie Institute of Washington, 1909).

22. Sir Thomas Malory, *The Works of Sir Thomas Malory* 3 vols., ed. Eugene Vinaver (Oxford: Oxford Univ. Press, 1971), 3: 1407–1408; 1: 259–260.

23. Shapiro, 119.

24. Warner, 140.

25. Ann McMillan "Men's Weapons, Women's War: The Nine Female Worthies," *Mediaevalia* 5 (1979): 126.

26. McMillan, 121.

27. Giovanni Boccaccio, *Concerning Famous Women,* trans. Guido A. Guarino (New Brunswick, N.J.: Rutgers Univ. Press, 1963), 231–233.

28. Shapiro, 116.

29. For a survey of "Grisandoles" in literature, see Lucy A. Paton, "The Story of Grisandole: A Study in the Legend of Merlin," *PMLA* 22 (1907): 234–76.

30. *The Vulgate Version of the Arthurian Romances* 2: 281–92.

31. Ovid, *Heroides and Amores,* 6 vols., 2nd ed., trans. Grant Showerman (Cambridge: Harvard Univ. Press, 1986), 1: 113–117.

32. Ovid, *Heroides,* 1: 117.

33. Vern L. Bullough, *Sexual Variance in Society and History* (New York: John Wiley & Sons, 1976), 393.

34. Davis, 130.

35. Malory, 2:668.

36. Malory, 2:669–670.

37. Guenivere, whom he is helpless to resist, even after his penitence and resolutions during the Grail Quest; four lustful fairy queens, including Morgan le Fay, who imprison him in their castle until he is rescued by a maiden; the first Elaine, who drugs and deceives him.

38. Non-cross-dressing metamorphoses are not, of course, unknown to classical literature, as Ovid's story of Tiresias (*Metamorphoses* 3. 324 ff.) illustrates. See also Marie Delcourt, *Hermaphrodite: mythes et rites de la bisexualité dans l'antiquité classique* (Paris: Presses universitaires de France, 1958).

Richard Rambuss

4

Devotion and Defilement:

The Blessed Virgin Mary and the Corporeal Hagiographics of Chaucer's *Prioress's Tale*

Several collections of miracles of the Virgin stories, a popular hagiographical form that flourished in the late Middle Ages, recount the tale of three brothers unfairly dispossessed of their land by a powerful knight. After their eviction, the brothers turned thieves, and lurking in the neighboring woods they plundered everyone who came within their grasp. Eventually, two of them were apprehended by the knight and hanged as bandits. The surviving brother, realizing the same fate awaited him if he too were caught, turned to a certain monk for spiritual guidance. When he was exhorted by this monk to give up stealing, however, the thief indignantly refused, vowing that he would continue his outlaw ways until he had despoiled the treacherous lord and avenged the death of his brothers. "Yet," he added, "I have resolved to keep the feasts of the Blessed Mother Mary so that she will not allow me to die without confession and communion." To this the monk replied, wholly in keeping with sound Christian doctrine: "Your pledge itself is noble, but it will be of little advantage to you if you persist in your intention to sin." Soon afterward, the last of the three brothers was indeed caught by the knight and his squires. In their fury, they hacked his body to pieces. But, the story goes, even when he was thoroughly dismembered, the thief would not die, nor would his severed head stop speaking. "You are wasting your time," he kept calling out. "You cannot kill me until I have first confessed and received communion." The knight and his men then left off their efforts and sent for a priest. After receiving the sacraments, the thief at last died and his soul was ushered into heaven by the Blessed Virgin herself.[1]

This touching and gruesome melodrama of unwavering faith in Mary's saving graces instances only one of any number of bodies that extravagantly refuse to expire, however compromised or mutilated, in the medieval miracles of the Virgin. These stories routinely proffer for devotional effect cases of decapitated heads that go on speaking, of flesh that cannot be melted down in the hottest ovens, of bodies that still draw breath after days of swinging from the gallows, and, of course, of slashed throats that continue to sing. In these miracles stories, the body, not the soul, claims center stage as the fulcrum of heavenly intervention in human affairs. This privileging of the corporeal—of bodies or parts of bodies—as the vector for the most spectacular demonstrations of divine power links the mariales to the medieval cult of relics. Like the relics— fragments of tissue, bone, or bodily excretia that are organically dead but hyper-alive with the powers of bodily healing—these nearly-departed sentimental favorites of the Blessed Virgin call for their own corporeal taxonomies.[2]

The miracles of the Virgin, that is, feature bodies that are neither quite dead nor exactly alive. In the tale with which I began, the body of the thief, even after it has been energetically dismembered, still *operates* as an integral body, inasmuch as it taunts its executioners, makes a confession, receives communion, and so on. The thief and his analogues in other Marian miracles remain for a time in this world, but they no longer quite belong to it nor do they completely abide by its rules. The liminal status of their bodies, moreover, instantiates the marginal condition of their souls, and it is at this point that miracles of the Virgin tend to diverge from hagiography. For generally speaking, the souls in these stories are neither absolutely in a state of grace (many of them, like the thief, are outlaws of some sort, including, interestingly, a good number of sexual transgressors), nor are they utterly depraved (the same story specifies with a certain proletarian bias that the brothers took to thieving only after some noble had first perpetrated a crime against them).[3] Instead, we find these dubious devotional exemplars plotted on the faultlines between excusable human failings and mortal sin, and consequently between the verdicts of heaven and hell. What ultimately wins them heaven is not their piety nor even a deathbed conversion. Rather, it is usually no more than their deeply sentimentalized attachment to the Blessed Virgin. Until she intervenes and personally secures their redemption (her Son, it is to be noted, remains a far more reluctant redeemer in these stories), the thief and others like him are suspended on the margins, their bodies made to perform awkward choreographies across contrary, even impossible, modes of existence.

Over such margins, I want to suggest, the Blessed Virgin Mary herself presides. In what follows, I look to associate the preponderance of threshold sites and states—particularly bodily ones—in the miracles of the Virgin with the liminal corporeal status of Mary herself, whose position, even in heaven, is always *beside* the throne of the one who is her Son, but also her creator, as well as often enough in medieval Mariology her consort. What's more, in terms of her own life in the historical world, Mary's body becomes, as we shall see, thoroughly implicated by medieval devotional and even theological thinking in such manifestly physical processes as pregnancy, lactation, and even menstruation—physical processes that situate her impossibly virginal and maternal body on the thresholds between the ineluctably human (and female) and the transcendent.[4]

In so claiming, I have already begun to trace along the very margins that provide the contours of Chaucer's *Prioress's Tale,* probably the best known miracle of the Virgin story and the text I will be centrally concerned with here.[5] In this *Canterbury Tale,* a "litel clergeon" or schoolboy enrages the local community of Jews with the Marian hymn he sings incessantly while traveling every day to school by way of a street that takes him through the local Jewish ghetto. Eventually the child is kidnapped by the Jews, who, under the incitement of Satan, cut his throat, and discard his corpse, as the Prioress informs us sensationally enough, "in a wardrobe . . . / Where as thise Jewes purgen hire entraille."[6] Having been murdered hardly curtails the boy's devotional performance, however, and he never stops hymning the Virgin from his profoundly abject position in the privy—the Jewish privy. Eventually the body is found, and the culprits are summarily tortured and executed by the Christian provost in retribution for the crime. The child martyr

is then carried to his final burial and then, after a mysterious
"greyn" placed by the Blessed Virgin in his mouth is removed, he
is at last borne away to heaven by her.

As we find in many of the miracles of the Virgin stories, there
is more than one threshold being negotiated here in the Prioress's
Tale. Although the clergeon continues to sing after his martyrdom,
he never really regains what one would think of as consciousness.
The boy is, in other words, more *undead* than either dead or alive.
Furthermore, his suspension between this world and the next results from a wound to his throat, a part of the body figured in the
Tale as itself a gateway by which the hymn of Mary's praise "Twies
a day . . . pass[es] thurgh his throte" (VII.548).[7] Both the street that
leads in and through the Jewish ghetto, as well as the sewer in
which the boy is deposited, can also be seen as marking other
limens. Defilement, Mary Douglas has shown, is typically framed
as a matter of the marginal, as what has passed from the inside to
the outside.[8] Accordingly, the Prioress's surprisingly indecorous
specification of this place "Where as thise Jewes purgen hire
entraille" lines up metonymically with her description of the city's
"Jewerye":

> Ther was in Asye, in a greet citee,
> Amonges Christene folk a Jewerye,
> Sustened by a lord of that contree
> For foule usure and lucre of vileynye,
> Hateful to Crist and to his compaignye;
> And thurgh the strete men myghte ride or wende,
> For it was free and open at eyther ende.
>
> (VII.488–494)

"Open at eyther ende": the Jewish ghetto is thus specified as that
which is for the "passing through"—as an orifice. Situated "Amonges
Christene folk," the whole (and the hole) of the Jewerye, reviled as
it is, shows up here as a necessary part of the Christian civic body
(and, as the stereotypical reference to usury indicates, of its economies as well). Through it the little boy must pass to get to his "litel
scole of Cristen folk" (VII.495), and, in the end, to get his Mother
Mary as well. In this miracle of the Virgin, *"inter urinas et faeces,"*
we are born again.

The "Alma Mater Redemptoris," the hymn the boy sings from out of the privy (metonymically distended, as we have seen, to the entire Jewry), invokes Mary to redeem the devout, her children, by allowing herself to be their passageway to heaven: *"Alma Redemptoris mater, quae pervia caeli / Porta manes"* ("Loving mother of the Redeemer, open door to heaven"). The hymn specifies Mary's body as that open door: *"Tu quae genuisti / Natura mirante, tuum sanctum genitorum / Virgo prius ac posterius"* ("You who, to nature's amazement, became the mother of your holy creator, remaining a virgin before and after"). As Louise Fradenburg puts it, "The hymn thus celebrates not only Mary's own miraculous ability to provide an easy passage to heaven (the inviolate body of the Virgin is an open door) but also her ability to undergo passage from the state of virginity to the state of motherhood without the pain of defloration and labor, indeed without bodily change of any kind."[9] What I would add to this account of Mary's corporeal status, however, is that her power may reside less in what Fradenburg sees as its changelessness and infrangibility, and perhaps more so in its multiple liminalities, in its threshold status between the mysterial and the grossly material.

G. G. Coulton wryly remarked that "If the world knew more about the Virgin Mary, the Middle Ages would have known far less."[10] To supplement what was lacking in the Gospels, an extravagant devotional literature, some of it "official" but much of it popular, accrued around her. The second-century *Protoevangelium of James* provides the details of the Virgin's early life, a good deal of which is modeled on corresponding events in the life of Christ. This "Gospel of Mary" relates the miraculous events of her conception and birth, and even her first steps as a baby. Having taken exactly seven of those unassisted at the age of six months, Mary was swept up by her mother Elizabeth, who said, "As the Lord my God lives, you shall walk no more upon this ground until I take you into the temple of the Lord."[11] And Mary didn't, until she was taken to the holiest part of the temple as a three-year-old. There she remained, waited upon by angels, until she neared puberty. At that point, an anxious council of the priests was called: "Behold, Mary has become twelve years old in the temple of the Lord. What then shall we do with her, that she may not pollute the temple of the Lord?"

The solution was to gather all the widowers of Israel and find her a husband. From this group Joseph was miraculously appointed, though, we are told, he at first refused the divinely appointed match with this unusual girl and only accepted when threatened with the wrath of God.

The Mariology of the *Protoevangelium* remains somewhat nascent (there is, for instance, no mention here of her "Immaculate Conception"), yet this apocryphal account does effectively register the liminality of Mary's position. That is, she seems to be marvelously unconstrained by the usual parameters of the natural world, yet at the same time she remains fully human. For example, the matter of the Virgin being fed by angels, not to mention her taking up residence in the Holy of Holies, prohibited to all women and every man except the High Priest, sets Mary apart from the rest of humankind. But at the age of thirteen and with the crisis of her impending menarche—a graphic sign of a female body's implication in corporeal processes and a matter to which I will want to return—Mary is awkwardly forced out of the Temple and into a marriage neither she nor Joseph appears really to want. Medieval Mariology abounds in similar incongruities, liminally situating the Virgin and her body between the natural and the miraculous. And, I'd further suggest, it is due to her unique threshold status that Mary can be invoked in just the way her often less than immaculate devotees call upon her in the miracles of the Virgin stories— as a mediatrix increasingly preferred before her more aloof Son, a more accessible *via media* between human frailty and perfection, between the processes of the body that tie us to this world and operations of the spirit that lead to the next.

Of her many distinguishing qualities, Mary's "Immaculate Conception" may be the best known. This tenet, popularly maintained long before it actually became dogma in 1854, establishes that Mary was uniquely exempt from the taint of original sin. Her soul's miraculous preservation has important physiological entailments as well. Among them is the widely held notion that she felt no pain in giving birth to Jesus. Despite scriptural teachings that agony in childbirth is the lot of all women since the Fall, in the fourteenth-century *Meditations on the Life of our Lord* Mary's labor is narrated as essentially laborless: "The Virgin rose and stood erect against a column that was there. But Joseph remained seated . . . [and] taking some hay from the manger, placed it at the Lady's feet and turned away. Then the Son of God came out of the womb of the mother, without a murmur or lesion, in a moment."[12] With all the signs of physical birthing apparently effaced (no cry of pain, no blood, no labor, no rupture of the body), there seems to be no reason for Joseph so modestly to have looked away. Christ's birth, at least as it is related in this account, is hardly a biological event at all. The infant seems to be the only agent active in this easy transition: one moment he exists in his mother's womb, and the next he passes through it and out into the world. Mary simply allows her body to be a vehicle for this miraculous passage.

These extraordinary claims about how Mary delivered her child are related to still another miraculous attribute of her body—that, as Chaucer's Prioress puts it, she remained "a mayde alway" (VII.462). Mary's hymen is the corporeal proof of a doctrine that is crucial to Christianity, the tenet that Christ's father was no man but rather God himself. Thus the Virgin's hymen had to remain *intacta* both in conception and in birth:

> Emmanuel has, indeed, opened the gates of nature, because he was a man, but he did not break the seals of virginity, because he was God. . . . [H]e was born as he was conceived: he entered without passion, he went forth without corruption.[13]

Augustine clinched his own case for Mary's postpartum virginity with an analogy to the risen (adult) Christ, who once had entered the lodgings where his frightened disciples hid by passing through a locked door. "Why should he, who, being full-grown, could enter through closed doors, when he was small not also be able to get out without violating the womb?"[14] For the unconvinced, there was also the apocryphal admonitory story about Mary's skeptical neighbor Salome. Informed by her midwife friend that "a virgin has brought forth, a thing *which her nature does not allow*," Salome replied: "As the Lord my God lives, unless I put (forward) my finger and test her condition, I will not believe that a virgin has brought forth."[15] And that is exactly what this female doubting Thomas did, and although her hand shrivelled up as a result, Salome found inside Mary's body the palpable proof she sought.

After Christ's ascension, Mary spent her days teaching the apostles, for from her earliest years she had perfect knowledge, not only of the intricacies of Christian doctrine (her role as confuter of heretics enhanced the perceived antagonism between Mary and the Jews and helps account for the anti-semitism of Chaucer's *Prioress's Tale,* as well as a number of other miracles), but also of rhetoric, mathematics, and the natural sciences. When it came time for her to depart from earth, many believed that Mary did so without dying, avoiding what even her divine Son could not. *"Dedit suum jus natura":* "nature gave up her own law" is the way a Latin carol describes Mary's "Assumption" into heaven and the preservation of her perfect body from the corruption of the grave.[16] Once there, she was crowned its queen by her Son and adored by all the angels. Many of her medieval zealots, in fact, entertained the notion of establishing heaven's queen as an equal consort for its king. Amadeus of Lausanne thus appropriates a biblical prooftext (Colossians 2:9) of Christ's own liminal status as God-Man and recasts it in terms of Marian theology, claiming that "through the mediation of Christ the fullness of the Godhead dwelt in [Mary] corporeally."[17] Peter of Celle, a twelfth-century Bishop of Chartres, even envisions the possibility of Mary's participation in the Deity: "You alone would complete the Quaternity!" he rhapsodizes.[18]

This last remark, in view of the Church's orthodox teachings which have always ranked Mary no higher than the supreme *created* being in the universe, courts the heretical. But such adulation is consistent with a pervasive tendency in the Middle Ages to extol the Blessed Virgin in terms of her approximations of divinity, her borderings on the divine. Interestingly, we also find in the twelfth century a profound devotional concern with the humanity—and specifically the femaleness—of Mary. This striking devotional shift can be read, among other places, in the Marian sermons of Bernard of Clairvaux, who contested the Immaculate Conception and remained cautiously silent on the issue of Mary's bodily Assumption into heaven. Not that Bernard opposed the flourishing cult of the Blessed Virgin; on the contrary, he is perhaps its most esteemed sponsor. Bernard's devotion typifies, however, the displacement of Mary's transcendent status by a new foregrounding of her maternal body, as well as her maternal affects of tenderness, empathy, and merciful, even whimsical, responsiveness to her favorites. Similarly, iconographic representations of the Virgin acquire a new intimacy. As Penny Schine Gold notes, the serenely impassive Regina, who seemed closer to the angels in heaven than to the sinners in this world, was being replaced by the figure of a fully human Madonna nursing her baby, or by the *mater dolorosa,* the supreme embodiment of human suffering.[19] This sentimental rehumanization of the Blessed Virgin is coincident with a larger shift in late medieval piety toward a spirituality of enhanced affectivity. In her study *Jesus as Mother,* Caroline Walker Bynum shows how this transition takes shape from a renewed appreciation of the doctrine that man is created *imago Dei,* as well as from a new insistence on the humanity of Christ—and as a necessary corollary, I would add, an insistence on the humanity of his mother.[20] In charting this shift, Bynum brings forward numerous examples of the feminization of religious language (hence the representation of Jesus as Mother), as well as of the spiritual fetishization of stereotypically feminine roles and attributes: gushing tears, birth pangs, and the nurturing and nursing of children become favored figures for expressing the relations both between God and the individual soul, and between abbots and those in their charge.[21] Though its focus is chiefly Christological, Bynum's argument also helps account for the increased devotion to "Mary as Mother" in the High Middle Ages.[22] It furthermore suggests another context, apart from the usual condemnatory ones I will discuss later, for understanding the exaggerated sentimentality of Chaucer's Prioress. The manifestly affective pitch of her tale—which she terms, resonantly in this context, "my labour" (VII.463)—as well as her deeply emotive investment in the relations between mothers and children, can be plotted in a spiritual tradition authorized by the likes of Bernard of Clairvaux.

For the moment, however, let us set aside pathos for physiology and return to the status of the body of the Blessed Virgin. In doing so, I want now to discuss something of a counter to all those superhuman workings of Mary's maternal body, processes that appear to set her body so completely outside the natural operations of female anatomy. That counter involves an intriguing conundrum over the issue of menstruation. Simply put, the question is whether or not the Blessed Virgin Mary had a period. Menstruation, though not deemed by the Church as sinful *per se,* was nonetheless regarded as a postlapsarian marker of sinfulness, particularly of female sinfulness.[23] The menses were moreover deemed impure inasmuch as they were thought to be linked to female sexual desire. Collecting in the womb,

they augmented feelings of lust, and their emission during intercourse, it was thought, could equal the man's pleasure in ejaculation.
Indeed, as John Benton points out, it was sometimes jealously asserted by male writers on the subject that a woman had twice the
man's pleasure in sex: she both expelled seed and took it in.[24]

In accordance with what we have already discussed about Mary's
unique physiology—namely that she was born without taint of
original sin, that she conceived as a virgin, and that she gave birth
without pain or rupture—it would then seem obvious that her body
could not have been made subject to what was considered such a
defiling physical function. Mary's Immaculate Conception should
have effectively spared her from this part of Eve's curse, just as it
spared her from pain in childbirth. Moreover, as Bynum notes, a
number of medieval female saints saw their amenorrhea as a miraculous somatic manifestation of their piety and devotion.[25]

Yet the impulse similarly to exempt Mary from the natural processes of menstruation opens onto another problem—a theological
one that comes nothing short of the authenticity of Christ's incarnation. In the influential Aristotelian model for procreation employed by many medieval theologians and scientists, the woman's
menses were thought to provide the raw physical matter necessary
for the conception of a child, while semen, the man's contribution,
provided the shaping form and effective cause. In a rival Galenic
or "double seed" theory of generation, mother and father each contributed seed, the woman's being the menstruum.[26] Whatever model
is advocated, for Mary truly to be the mother of Christ, and not
merely a human receptacle for a divine embryo implanted in her
already fully "materialized," her body would have to have produced
the menstrual material out of which Christ's fleshly body was to be
formed. As Julia Kristeva recognizes in "Stabat Mater," her essay
on the cult of Mary, the "Son of Man" is human only through his
mother—"as if Christly or Christian humanism could only be a
materialism."[27] The full humanity of Jesus—in other words, the
core doctrine of the Incarnation—is thus predicated on the full
humanity, as well as the marked femaleness, of Mary's body: even
to the extent, it appears, of her subjection to the natural and culturally defiling processes of menstruation.[28] Thus, Thomas Aquinas,
having noted that in conception the mother "suppl[ies] the matter,
which is the menstrual blood," concedes that Mary necessarily "co-

operated actively in the preparation of the matter so that it should be apt for the conception."[29]

Also at stake in the question of Mary's menstruation is her iconic role as *Maria lactans.* Lactation was well understood in the Middle Ages to be linked to pregnancy, and hence with the menses that made conception possible. In fact, mother's milk was widely thought to be processed menstrual blood, left over from the conception of the child and its nourishment *in utero.* Without her body's production of menstrual fluids, Mary would have been unable to breastfeed the Christ child, as we see her doing in countless, deeply sentimentalized medieval images.

Thus, for all the miraculous powers and exemptions from certain natural processes she was accorded, Mary had to remain fully—and, unlike her dual-natured Son—only human. Though not bound by the historical world, she still belongs to it. In this way, the Virgin comes to represent for her devotees not the abdication of humanity or of the body but the possibility for their ultimate perfection. Her perfection does not so much annul, but rather enables, her glorified (female) humanity. Mary is the second Eve: woman, both mother and bride, as she was meant to be. And it is through her that her devotees route their hopes of being redeemed, born again—to being Mary's children no less than the children of God. It is that hope, to return and take up more fully Chaucer's contribution to the miracles of the Virgin genre, that keeps the "martyred" little boy singing from out of the sewer. It is also the same hope, we shall see, that shapes the Prioress's own childlike invocation of Mother Mary.

Chaucer derives the *Prioress's Tale* from a story repeated in a number of miracles of the Virgin collections. Among other significant alterations of his source, however, Chaucer's retelling reduces the boy's age from ten years, as it appears in most versions, to a mere seven. The significance of this reduction in age is, as Marie Padgett Hamilton noted, the resituation of the tale's protagonist—who is "not merely a little child, but rather the representative of childhood itself"—on the threshold of moral accountability.[30] In the Middle English *Mirror of the Periods of Man's Life,* a child's good angels and bad angels commence their struggle for his soul "Whanne the child was vii yeer olde, / Possying sowking of milke drewis."[31]

That time is chosen, the *Mirror* continues, "because at vii yeer age childhood bigynnes," while at age of fourteen it "blynnes" (ends) and "knowliche of manholde he wynnes." Isidore of Seville offers the same scheme in more prosaic terms: "The first stage of man is infancy, the second boyhood, and the third adolescence.... Now infancy ends at the seventh year, boyhood at the fourteenth."[32]

The diminished age of the clergeon in the Prioress's Tale has regularly been linked to the Prioress's sentimental predilections for what is tiny and childlike as fashioned in the tonally complicated portrait of her that appears in the General Prologue. There the Prioress, "madame Eglentyne," is described as excessively dainty and "al . . . conscience and tendre herte" (11. 121, 150)—though not especially for the world's poor and afflicted, nor even for the nuns in her charge, but rather for her "smale houndes" or any stray mouse caught in a trap (I.144–146).[33] It is no surprise, then, that the Tale she is assigned (itself the most diminutive in length of all the completed *Canterbury Tales*) features a child "so yonge and tendre . . . of age" (VII.524), who attends a "litel scole" (VII.495) where he learns from a "litel book" (VII.516). What's more, the Prioress enacts a similar diminution upon herself. Though described in the General Prologue with a suggestive lack of specificity as "nat undergrowe" (I.156), the Prioress presents herself, at least in the role of storyteller, as a "child of twelf month oold, or lesse" (VII.484).

Is this the meaning of gospel injunction that says we must become as little children to enter the kingdom of heaven? Not according to Alfred David, who finds the Prioress's cathected diminutions less a childlike performance than a childish one—"a fairy story turned into a hagiography," as he disparagingly terms the Tale.[34] For David and many other critics, the Prioress's is a case of arrested, even regressive, development. Yet such readings seem at best only partly right to me in that they unproductively trivialize the Tale by not considering in the Tale's own terms exactly what the "childish" means here. Nor do such readings seriously engage the investment the Prioress has in refashioning herself as an infant storyteller. In order to address these questions, we need to return to the matter of the clergeon's age and his repositioning on the margin between infancy and childhood.

The word *infant*, it is well known, comes from the Latin *fari*—to speak. To be *infans*, then, is to be unable to speak. This incapacity for speech has certain legal and moral consequences. In Roman civil law, Patrick Colquhoun explains, "the expression *fari posse* [to be able to speak] does not imply either a capability of uttering mere articulate sounds, nor does it imply that the child is capable of understanding what it says, but, *between the two,* that it comprehends that it is performing a solemn act."[35] Roman civil law had a powerful shaping influence on medieval canon law regarding moral accountability for actions; canonists, moreover, regularly articulated the capacity for culpability in the same terms as the capacity to take an oath. Neither is ascribed before the age of seven, and seldom until the child is even older than that. Augustine, for one, not only denies full moral responsibility for the "first period of life which passively submits to the rule of the flesh," but also for the second, in which "the will and reason remain weak," even though the ability to speak has been gained and infancy left behind.[36]

Hence the liminal significance of the age of the little boy in the Prioress's Tale. Poised on the threshold of moral accountability, the seven-year-old occupies a privileged position. No longer exactly *infans,* he is able to speak. Yet because of his tender age, his speech passes as pure, unsullied by any (at least attributable) taint. The reduction of the clergeon's age in the Prioress's Tale thus effects his establishment as a model of moral *and linguistic* innocence—a model the Tale's narrator herself attempts to emulate: "o grete God, that parfournest thy laude / By mouth of innocentz, lo, heere thy might!" (VII.607–608), the Prioress exclaims at the climax of her miracle story.

A signal component of the clergeon's innocence, the Tale implies, is his inability to understand the Latin words of the hymn that "pass[es] thurgh his throte." Without comprehension, he instead learns and sings "al by rote" (VII.522). But rather than compromising the worthiness of his sacrifice of praise, the child's lack of understanding opens up an immediacy not otherwise accessible between him and the object of his praise:

> As I have seyd, thurghout the Juerie
> This litel child, as he cam to and fro,
> Ful murily than wolde he synge and crie
> *O Alma redemptoris* everemo.
> The swetnesse his herte perced so
> Of Cristes mooder that, to hire to preye,
> He kan nat stynte of syngyng by the weye.
> (VII.551–557)

Operating under an ultimately deleterious repetition compulsion ("he kan nat stynte of syngyng"), repeating a song learned by rote: the little clergeon hardly qualifies at all as a speaking *subject*. Indeed, one could say that the song he sings uncontrollably is in control of him. The question of agency raised in this stanza more-over recalls the ambiguity of the Prioress's own proclamation, "O grete God, that parfournest thy laude / By mouth of innocentz, lo, heere thy might!" Just who are, or what is, the "innocentz" lauding God here? Who performs this speech act? Is God's praise performed by innocents, who, like the little clergeon, honor him without fully comprehending what they say or do? Or is it some personification of the abstraction "innocence itself" that speaks here? Or is it God himself who performs his own laud through innocent vessels? However we read it, the Prioress's ecstatic grammar effectively elides human agency. Singing "innocentz," the little clergeon be-comes a vessel for embodying the self-performing praise of God. And to this extent he resembles the sinless Blessed Virgin herself: like her, his body has been penetrated by a supernatural force ("The swetnesse his herte perced so") that makes him a kind of human host by which the song that "pass[es] thurgh his throte" gives a virgin birth to itself.

The Tale's investment in the speech of innocents/innocence is crystallized in the Prioress's very first words, which are a recitation from the Introit to the Mass of the Holy Innocents:

> O Lord, oure Lord, they name how merveillous
> Is in this large world ysprad—quod she—
> For nought oonly thy laude precious
> Parfourned is by men of dignitee,
> But by the mouth of children thy bountee
> Parfourned is, for on the brest soukynge
> Somtyme shewen they thyn heriynge.
>
> (VII.453–459)

The Prioress's Tale incorporates several allusions to this liturgy commemorating the victims of Herod's vain attempt to kill the infant Jesus in a mass slaughter of Jewish male babies. In addition to the Bethlehem Innocents, the Tale catalogues several other notable examples of youthful innocence. There is little St. Nicholas

(VII.514–515), who fasted from his mother's milk Wednesdays and Fridays—a remarkable bodily performance of the sacrifice of praise the Prioress claims may be offered even by infants at the breasts of their mothers. There is also the boy martyr "yonge Hugh of Lyncoln," who was, like the clergeon, purportedly slain by "cursed Jewes" (VII.684–685).

What is striking about these child exemplars is the ahistorical immediacy the Prioress claims for them. "Seint Nicholas stant evere in my presence," she declares, and Hugh was killed "but a litel while ago" (VII.514, 686). In reality, Hugh had been dead for more than a hundred years. This elision of history is precisely the effect, according to Peter Brown, hagiographies characteristically reached for:

> In the first place, the *passio* abolished time. The deeds of the martyr . . . had brought the mighty deeds of God in the Old Testament and the gospels into his or her own time. The reading of the saint's deeds breached yet again the paperthin wall between the past and the present. . . . For the hagiographer was recording the moments when the seemingly extinct past and the unimaginably distant future had pressed into the present.[37]

The Prioress's elisions of history are thus part of her Tale's hagiographics. But more than this, the devotional foreshortening of history is also of a piece, I would suggest, with her efforts in the prologue to efface the distance in age between herself and the innocent little boys her tale means to celebrate so innocently.

By now, we should be better able to understand the penchant in the Prioress's Tale for the childlike and the diminutive. What is at stake here is not to be construed simply as a sentimental predilection, nor as a case of arrested development. Rather, the Prioress's efforts to speak about—*and as*—a child proceed from her very serious avocation of what is unsullied by will or even by understanding: the voice of "innocentz." That is what she hears in the song of the little clergeon; that is also what the Prioress herself hopes to ventriloquize in her Tale, which she terms a "song" (VII.487) and sets in hymnic rime royal stanzas.

Furthermore, it is worth underscoring at this point that however "regressive" the Prioress's fantasy of speaking with the voice of infant innocence appears, the setting of that fantasy is wholly apocalyptic:

> O martir, sowded to virginitee,
> Now maystow syngen, folwynge evere in oon
> The white Lamb celestial—quod she—
> Of which the grete evaungelist, Seint John,
> In Pathmos wroot, which seith that they that goon
> Biforn this Lamb, and synge a song al newe,
> That nevere, flesshy, wommen they ne knewe.
>
> (VII.579–585)

The biblical source for this stanza, Revelation 14:1–5, serves as the one of the readings for the Feast of the Holy Innocents. John describes these 144,000 Jewish male virgins as "the first fruits to God and to the Lamb," and they became identified with the Bethlehem Innocents by biblical commentators. Now in heaven as followers of "The white Lamb celestial," the Innocents, who once *"non loquendo, sed moriendo confessi sunt,"*[38] now can sing an everlasting "song al newe." The little martyr of the Prioress's Tale has a place in their company, we are assured, due to his tender age and because he too is a "gemme of chastite" (VII.609). In this apocalyptic troop of boys, the clergeon can continue his song of praise, insulated from all the temptations and dangers of life in the natural world, a world in which he faced the deadly persecution of the "cursed folk of Herod al newe" (VII.574), but also the threat (less remarked in criticism concerned with this Tale) of being "beten thries in an houre" (VII.542) by his own Christian schoolmaster for learning a Marian hymn instead of the assigned lesson. Other versions of this same miracle story conclude with the Blessed Virgin healing her young devotee and returning him to his earthly mother. Obviously such a return would not do as the terminus of Chaucer's apocalyptically scripted rendering of this miracle. Death—that is, being translated to heaven in the care of the Virgin Mary—enables the clergeon to escape a corrupting and dangerous world for one that guarantees the eternal preservation of his voice of innocence. It also enables him to exchange his earthly mother, only a "poure wydwe" (VII.586), for a fabulous heavenly one.

In producing this miracle story and implicating herself in its narrative as another "innocent," the Prioress reveals her own corresponding desire for transcendence. Her prologue and Tale can be seen as an attempt to imitate—in an idiom that is suitably exclamatory and full of childlike wonder—the linguistic innocence of the little clergeon. To state the point in the apocalyptic terms she invokes, the Prioress has styled her own *canticus Agni,* her own song to the "white Lamb celestial." Modelling herself on the clergeon who is too young to comprehend what he is singing, the Prioress maintains that likewise her own "konnyng is so wayk . . . / That I kan unnethes any word expresse" (VII.481, 485). And like the clergeon, she offers her body as a passive vessel through which the anthem of praise may pass: "therfore I yow preye," she appeals to Mary, yet another open vessel, "Gydeth my song that I shal of yow seye" (VII.486–487). Thus the Prioress's "avowal of ineptitude" is not merely a conventional resort to an inexpressibility topos, as Donald T. Fitz determines in his essay on the Tale.[39] Instead, the Prioress stakes her flaunted linguistic and intellectual inabilities as a claim for her inclusion in the company of innocents that follow "evere in oon" the Lamb of God.

Unlike these young innocents, however, the Prioress has not left the profane world behind. She exists in the difficult position—not unlike the abject station of the clergeon churning out the strains of the "Alma Redemptoris" from the privy—of attempting to surmount the natural world and its determinations while still being fully enmeshed in them. Indeed, the central problematic of the Prioress's Tale is that, despite its narrator's various attempts to deny its historicity, to make her song transcendent, the Tale betrays its implicatedness in the historical world at every turn.[40] For all its other-worldly aspirations, the Prioress's miracle story is motored by bodily violence and prurience, and of course by a shaping anti-semitism. Yet the Prioress does not find herself without an advocate. In negotiating these historical and corporeal determinations, she aptly invokes heavenly aid by framing her tale with childlike appeals, not to God or to Jesus, but to "his [human] mooder Marie" (VII.690).

How near, in conclusion, does the Prioress come as a literally rejuvenated storyteller in approximating the speech of "innocentz"?

To address this question, let us briefly return to a stanza we have already considered:

> O martir, sowded to virginitee,
> Now maystow syngen, folwynge evere in oon
> The white Lamb celestial—*quod she*—
> Of which the grete evaungelist, Seint John,
> In Pathmos wroot, which seith that they that goon
> Biforn this Lamb, and synge a song al newe,
> That nevere, flesshy, wommen they ne knewe.
>
> (VII.579–585; *emphasis added*)

Here, in the appropriation of liturgy and apocalyptic song, the Prioress's Tale swells to its devotional and emotional crescendo. The stanza, moreover, is scripted as the Prioress's own most transcendent passage, her voice reiterating the voices of "Seint John" and his heavenly chorus of holy Innocents, whose ranks she would join. Yet this consummate moment of inspired ventriloquism, this moment in which the voice of "innocentz" is supposed to be reproducing itself through a wholly pliant mouthpiece, is arrestingly qualified by the two-word voice-over: "quod she."[41] The interpolation opens up a lacuna in the miraculous performance of this miraculous tale; the marked reassignment of voice back to the Prioress registers the presence of a human speaking and volitional subject here that stands apart from any reified speech of "innocentz." That "quod she," whether it is an authorial oversight or, as some have claimed, a leftover from a pre-*Canterbury Tales* use of the miracle story, breaks the rhythms of her song and sharply recalls the Prioress and the reader back to the historical world, back to a world where songs do not innocently "pass . . . thurgh" singers and where narrators have some measure of agency in terms of the Tales that pass through them.

The devotional recounting of the miraculous is similarly, and perhaps even more jarringly, ruptured by another voice-over in the stanza preceding the one we have been considering. That stanza, however, hardly strikes the other-worldly pitch of the *canticus Agni:*

> *I seye* that in a wardrobe they hym threwe
> Where as thise Jewes purgen hire entraille.

O cursed folk of Herodes al newe,
What may youre yvel entente yow availle?
Mordre wol out, certeyn, it wol nat faille,
And namely ther th'onour of God shal sprede;
The blood out crieth on youre cursed dede.

> (VII.572–578; *my emphasis*)

What shows up in these disturbing lines is the underside of the Prioress's efforts to recover the innocence of youth: a more primitive, elemental aspect of childhood that compromises its innocence, as well as the complex of notions (youth, purity, virginity) the Tale clusters around it. And more than this, the Prioress's emphatic apostrophe ("I seye") on exactly where the Jews discard the boy, as well as what defiling bodily function they use that place for, marks the specification as gratuitous, even prurient. Some readers have commented on how out of sorts this stanza is with the rest of the Tale. Yet, as we have seen, a fascination with the excremental figures in and even structures the Prioress's Tale from its opening description of the Jewish ghetto. Nor, as we have further seen, the attention to bodily processes—even taboo ones—is not wholly out of keeping with the corporealities of medieval discourse on the Virgin herself.

Just as this defiling anality is projected onto the Jews, they are likewise scapegoated in the Tale's violent family romance, which plots the little clergeon between two mothers, but also between two embodiments of paternal authority. Along these axes, the Prioress's narrative of desire and mutilation becomes available for an oedipal reading. The Jews, associated in the Tale with the juridical ("Sustened by a lord of that contree," [VII.490]) and later by Freud, in *Totem and Taboo,* with the religion of the Father, could be seen to be punishing the boy for his devotion to his Heavenly Mother and thereby to prevent his reunification with his earthly one.[42] Their enforcement of the paternal law involves mutilation, a castrative slashing of the boy's throat. But the Tale then turns the law against its enforcers: the Jews, the Prioress relates with satisfaction, are summarily executed "by the lawe" (VII.634). Though this capital penalty is exacted from the Jews, however, it is not they, strictly speaking, who "finish off" the little clergeon. Rather the boy's death is ultimately effected by the action of another father figure, the abbot who plucks the mysterious greyn from the boy's mouth:

> This hooly monk, this abbot, hym meene I,
> His tonge out caughte, and took awey the greyn,
> And he yaf up the goost ful softely.
>
> (VII.670–672)

Though we are told that the clergeon dies "ful softely," the apparent harshness with which the abbot performs this "out catching" and taking away is rendered in terms that link his actions to the mutilation of the throat performed by the Jews as another act of orally-directed, oedipally-sanctioned violence.

Nonetheless, in the "childish" fantasy that is the Prioress's Tale, the abbot's deed ensures rather than forbids the boy's now unbreakable bond with his "mooder Marie." Just so, as an example of the medieval miracle version of the genre, the Prioress's Tale is not undermined by its appropriately sentimentalized contours of violence and desire. Invoking the Blessed Virgin, the Prioress turns to a figure who, we have seen, at the point of her own body incorporates at least some of abject corporealities of the natural world. It is just such Marian corporealities—plotted on the margins between innocence and defilement, between abjection and devotion—which readers stretching back to Wordsworth (though significantly not to the Middle Ages) have found shocking and distasteful about the Prioress's Tale; but it is precisely these liminal corporealities that situate the Tale firmly within its genre. That is to say that within its own devotional terms the Tale's complicated, troubling imbrications of sentimentality and violence, innocence and desire, purity and defilement, and even its hateful anti-semitism, do not compromise but rather bespeak its devotional power as a medieval miracle of the Virgin, bespeak the miraculous powers of Mary's own body. The "sobre" silence (VII.692) of the Canterbury pilgrims, which follows the Prioress's Tale and no other, says as much.

NOTES

1. Johannes Herolt, *Miracles of the Blessed Virgin Mary*, trans. C. C. Swinton Bland (New York: Harcourt, Brace & Co., 1928), 80–81.

2. See Caroline Walker Bynum, "The Female body and Religious Practice in the Latter Middle Ages," in *Fragments for a History of the Human Body,* ed. Michel Feher with Ramona Nadoff and Nadia Tazi, Part 1 (New York: Urzone, Inc., 1991), 160–219. See also Peter Brown's important work, *The Cult of the Saints: Its Rise and Function in Late Christianity* (Chicago: Univ. of Chicago Press, 1981), especially 69–85.

3. In addition to thieves, among the regular recipients of the Virgin's favors are pregnant abbesses, lecherous priests, drunken monks, handsome knights, executioners, adulterers, and, on occasion, Jews.

4. For a related account of Mary's paradoxical corporeal status as a body at once virginal and maternal, at once closed and opened, see Theresa Coletti, "Purity and Danger: The Paradox of Mary's Body and the Engendering of the Infancy Narrative in the English Mystery Cycles," in *Feminist Approaches to the Body in Medieval Literature,* ed. Linda Lomperis and Sarah Stanbury (Philadelphia: Univ. of Pennsylvania Press, 1993), 65–95.

5. After this essay was completed, I became aware of Steven F. Kruger's important essay, "The Bodies of Jews in the Late Middle Ages," in James M. Dean and Christian K. Zacher, *The Idea of Medieval Literature* (Newark: Univ. of Delaware Press, 1992), 301–23. There are a number of points of overlap between my account of the corporeal hagiographics of The Prioress's Tale and Kruger's provocative account of the body's at times both abject and exultant role in medieval spirituality, especially when he turns his attentions to the same Tale: "The miracle of Chaucer's Prioress's Tale is manifestly physical, involving as its central fact the dead-but-not-dead body of the tale's 'litel clergeon'. . . . Bodily injury and intactness are among the tale's central concerns" (301).

6. *The Canterbury Tales,* VII.572–573, in *The Riverside Chaucer,* 3rd ed., gen. ed. Larry D. Benson (Boston: Houghton Mifflin, 1987). All references to Chaucer are according to this edition; further citations will be supplied parenthetically in the text.

7. On this point see Louise O. Fradenburg's important discussion, "Criticism, Anti-Semitism, and the *Prioress's Tale,*" *Exemplaria* 1 (1989): 69–113, at p. 99. This essay also provides a probing discussion of the function of anti-semitism in the Tale, as well as how such anti-semitism has informed a long tradition of critical readings of it.

8. Mary Douglas, *Purity and Danger: An Analysis of Concepts of Pollution and Taboo* (New York: Praeger, 1966).

9. Fradenburg, 89.

10. G. G. Coulton, *Five Centuries of Religion,* 4 vols. (Cambridge: Cambridge Univ. Press, 1929), 1:155.

11. *The Protoevangelium of James,* in *New Testament Apocrypha,* 3 vols., eds. Edgar Hennecke and Wilhelm Schneemelcher (Philadelphia: Westminster Press, 1965), 1:370–388.

12. *Meditations on the Life of our Lord,* trans. Isa Ragusa, eds. Isa Ragusa and Rosalie B. Green (Princeton: Princeton Univ. Press, 1961), 32–33.

13. This is Proculus's seminal fifth-century formulation of Mary's perpetual virginity, as quoted in Hilda Graef's invaluable, if strictly devout, sourcebook, *Mary: A History of Doctrine and Devotion,* 2 vols. (New York: Hawthorne Books, 1963), 1:102–103.

14. As quoted in Graef, 1:96.

15. The story of Salome can be read in, among other places, the *Protoevangelium,* 385. My emphasis here.

16. This anonymous hymn is cited by Marina Warner in *Alone of All Her Sex: The Myth and the Cult of the Virgin Mary* (New York: Knopf, 1975), 96.

17. As quoted in Graef, 1:246.

18. As quoted in Graef, 1:253.

19. For more on medieval iconography of the Virgin Mary, see Penny Schine Gold, *The Lady and the Virgin: Image, Attitude, and Experience in Twelfth-Century France* (Chicago: Univ. of Chicago Press, 1985).

20. Caroline Walker Bynum, *Jesus as Mother: Studies in the Spirituality of the High Middle Ages* (Berkeley: Univ. of Calif. Press, 1982), 130.

21. Bynum, *Jesus as Mother,* 16–18, 110–125.

22. Interestingly, Bynum contends in *Holy Feast and Holy Fast* (Berkeley: Univ. of California Press, 1987) that in the Middle Ages "Mary is not really as important as one might expect in women's spirituality" (269). Instead Bynum calls attention to the number of female mystics who had visions of Christ in the role of nursing mother, baring his breast to them. Other women, Bynum reports, had mystical experiences in which they received the Infant Jesus from the arms of the Virgin and then, in what I read as a scene of a kind of maternal rivalry, refused to give him back to Mary. See *Holy Feast,* 246–249.

Whether or not Bynum's suggestion is indeed historically accurate that medieval female devotees were devotionally disinclined towards Mary (and one wonders why this might be so), we find that many centuries later the female child Dora, of one of Freud's most famous case studies, maintaining a silent vigil before the Sistine Madonna in the Dresden Art Gallery. See Mary Jacobus, "Dora and the Pregnant Madonna," in her *Reading Woman: Essays in Feminist Criticism* (New York: Columbia Univ. Press, 1986). Although she was notoriously well-informed about sexual matters, Dora was, according to Lacan, unable to accept herself as "an object of desire for the man." She forged a way out of this "subjective impasse," Lacan continues, by means of Christianity, in which "woman [becomes] the object of a divine desire, or else a transcendent object of desire." See *Returning to Freud: Clinical Psychoanalysis in the School of Lacan*, ed. Stuart Schneiderman (New Haven: Yale Univ. Press, 1980), 56–58. In other words, Dora (not unlike Chaucer's Prioress) looks to the Blessed Virgin Mary as the liminal figure who can authorize a position between sexual innocence and carnal knowledge.

23. Charles T. Wood, "The Doctor's Dilemma: Sin, Salvation and the Menstrual Cycle in Medieval Thought," *Speculum* 56 (1981): 710–727.

24. John F. Benton, "Clio and Venus: An Historical View of Medieval Love," in *The Meaning of Courtly Love*, ed. F. X. Newman (Albany: SUNY Press, 1969), 32. See also Wood, 716.

25. See Bynum, *Holy Feast and Holy Fast*, 138, 148, 211–214.

26. For more on Aristotelian and Galenic models of human reproduction, see Thomas Laqueur, *Making Sex: Body and Gender from the Greeks to Freud* (Cambridge, Mass.: Harvard Univ. Press, 1990), 29–43. See also Anthony Preus, "Galen's Criticism of Aristotle's Conception Theory," *Journal of the History of Biology* 10 (1977): 65–85.

27. Julia Kristeva, "Stabat Mater," in *The Kristeva Reader*, ed. Toril Moi (New York: Columbia Univ. Press, 1986), 162.

28. In "The Doctor's Dilemma," Wood reports that tourists can visit the Church of the Annunciation in Nazareth and see the tub in which Mary was supposed to have washed away "the ritual defilement periodically caused by her quite normal physiology" (722–723).

29. *Summa Theologica of St. Thomas Aquinas*, 18 vols., trans. Fathers of the English Dominican Province (London: Burns, Oates & Washbourne, 1926), 16:84–85 (3a. qu. 32, art. 4). Aquinas does insist, however, that we understand that the Virgin provided no ordinary menstrual blood, which

would be tainted with corruption and sexual desire. Instead, Christ's body is "formed of the most chaste and purest blood of the Virgin" (p. 68; 3a. qu. 31, art. 5)—a discharge, in other words, that somehow flows between the usual cultural categories of bodily defilement and purity. See also Wood, 720.

30. Marie Padgett Hamilton, "Echoes of Childremas in the Tale of the Prioress," *MLR* 34 (1939): 1. See also Sherman Hawkins, "Chaucer's Prioress and the Sacrifice of Praise," *JEGP* 63 (1964): 599–624.

31. The poem is cited from *Hymns to the Virgin and Christ, The Parliament of Devils, and Other Religious Poems*, ed. F. J. Furnival, EETS, No. 24 (London, 1867), 60–61.

32. Quoted in Hawkins, 607.

33. Interestingly in this context, there is a tradition of Mary's miraculous intervention on behalf of her favorites' favorite pets—a runaway monkey, an injured falcon, and so on. See Benedicta Ward, *Miracles and the Medieval Mind* (Philadelphia: Univ. of Pennsylvania Press, 1987), 149.

34. Alfred David, *The Strumpet Muse* (Bloomington: Indiana Univ. Press, 1976), 209.

35. Patrick Colquhoun, *A Summary of the Roman Civil Law*, 3 vols. (London: V. E. R. Stevens, 1849), 1:350–351, as quoted in Hawkins, 608. The emphasis is mine.

36. Augustine, *The City of God*, trans. G. J. Walsh and D. J. Honan, The Fathers of the Church, VIII (New York: Modern Library, 1954), 376, again as quoted in Hawkins, 608.

37. Brown, 81.

38. The phrase occurs in the Collect for the Mass of the Holy Innocents; see Hawkins, 600–602 and his discussion of the paradox of praise from speechless infants.

39. Donald T. Fitz, "The Prioress's Avowal of Ineptitude," *Chaucer Review* 9 (1974): 166–181.

40. The problematic of how the poetic negotiates between its various enmeshments in the historical world and its impulses to transcend them is not, in my view, a matter confined to the *Prioress's Tale*. Rather I see it is a shaping concern that underwrites a good deal of Chaucer's literary production. For a discussion of these issues in terms of the poem with which Chaucer initiates his poetic career, see my " 'Processe of tyme': History, Consolation, and Apocalypse in the *Book of the Duchess*," *Exemplaria* 2

(1990): 659–683. See also, crucially, Lee Patterson's remarkable study, *Chaucer and the Subject of History* (Madison: Univ. of Wisconsin Press, 1991).

41. H. Marshall Leicester also calls attention, though with a somewhat different emphasis, to this "quod she" and the rupture in the text it enacts. See his *The Disenchanted Self: Representing the Subject in the Canterbury Tales* (Berkeley: Univ. of California Press, 1990), 210–213. "The Prioress's excess," he writes, "has always had an unsettling effect on readers, starting with the poet-narrator, whose extraordinary break in impersonation, the 'quod she' in the above passage, serves notice, among other things, that he wants to dissociate himself from what is being said" (212). I am not so sure, however, that Chaucer is looking to dissociate himself from the Prioress, whose Tale is very much in keeping with its genre as well as with certain strains of Christian devotion.

The issues of impersonation and ventriloquism are, of course, germane to the *Canterbury Tales* as a whole inasmuch as all the Tales are repetitions. Although I do not have space enough to explore that topic here, it should be apparent that the matter of ventriloquism connects the *Prioress's Tale* in a particularly integral way to the project of the *Canterbury Tales* as a whole.

42. Sigmund Freud, *Totem and Taboo*, in *Standard Edition of the Complete Works of Sigmund Freud*, 24 vols., trans. James Strachey (London: The Hogarth Press, 1953–1964), 13:150, 153–155.

5

The Somaticized Text:

Corporeal Semiotic in a Late Medieval Female Hagiography

A collection of lives of female saints seems a perfectly obvious idea to us now, especially for the Middle Ages, when hagiography ranked high among popular genres.[1] Curious, then, that no one seems to have thought of it until the English Augustinian friar Osbern Bokenham, living at the East Anglican prior at Clare, compiled his verse collection of thirteen female lives toward the middle of the fifteenth century.

There were, to be sure, partial models in liturgical, hagiographical, and secular literatures. Catholic liturgy includes ferial lists of male saints followed by lists of female saints, the litanies varying in length with different usages. Outside liturgy, the *liber virginum* was a type of early Latin legendary in which division by sex was a not uncommon mode of classification.[2] Following this taxonomic convention, the Anglo-Saxon scholar Aldhelm divided his treatise *De Virginitate* (c. 680) into accounts of male and female virgins. During the late thirteenth or early fourteenth century, the Franciscan friar Nicholas de Bozon composed, in Anglo-Norman couplets, the lives of nine female saints, though there is no evidence they were intended as a cohesive set.[3] In 1405, Christine de Pizan compiled a group of women saints' lives as a short portion (about one-seventh) of her otherwise secular *consolatio, Le Livre de la Cité des Dames.* Last but not least, there was an English text well known to Bokenham, a verse collection of lives of good women which associated itself with hagiography in appropriating the traditional title for saints' lives as well as its central theme, suffering: I refer to Chaucer's *Legend of Good Women* (1386).[4]

While it might therefore be overstating the case to claim that Bokenham invented the female legendary, nonetheless it is fair to say he reinvented it. He chose the female legendary not as a system of classification, nor to illustrate the virtue of virginity, nor as ancillary to another type of writing, nor in an ironic spirit. In his hands the genre became a carefully crafted poetic artifact, informed by a particular theology and a distinctive vision of contemporary political life.

For Brokenham was no simple cloistered scribbler, no "drivelling monk" (as the eighteenth-century antiquarian Joseph Ritson would label Bokenham's Benedictine contemporary John Lydgate). He led an active social and literary life among East Anglian gentry and nobility on the eve of the so-called Wars of the Roses, produced other works than the one to be discussed here, and travelled in Italy and Spain. He was a Cambridge graduate and master in theology, an administrator in his order, an ardent supporter of Richard Duke of York.[5] The profile, then, is of a sophisticated clerical author, locally partisan but internationally oriented, well prepared to offer a response to the great national events of his age. That he did so through a literary representation of the suffering but triumphant female body is his distinctive contribution to cultural history.

The time was ripe, evidently, for such a project. The previous century had seen the efflorescence of the *devotio moderna* and the development of a new tradition of affective piety both lay and religious, with emphasis on a personal, passionate attachment to Jesus and his saints. In this trend, women played an important role as subjects and objects of devotion, and if by Bokenham's day the new piety had somewhat abated from its fourteenth-century peak, it remained a powerful influence in religious life. This was the case especially in East Anglia where Bokenham lived and where he might well have met, or at least would surely know of, both Margery Kempe and Julian of Norwich, exemplars and products of the new piety. On the continent, women often led small pietistic (or even heretical) groups, or banded together to perform devotion and charitable works in the Beguine movement and other formations.

In England, and especially in East Anglia, women Lollards travelled and taught, sometimes risking their lives to do so. Norwich itself had more anchorites (enclosed solitaries) of both sexes than any city in England, and it is the only English city known to have had communities of devout laywomen resembling the continental *béguinages.*[6] Surviving East Anglian art of the period, particularly the distinctively English form of the rood-screen, reveals intense devotion to several women saints, a phenomenon that led E. F. Jacob to dub this "the age of the women saints."[7]

Bokenham could count on a female component, both lay and ecclesiastical, to his audience. The patrons named in his legendary include women of the East Anglian nobility and gentry, while the endnote to the unique manuscript of the work says that the copy cost thirty shillings and was given "onto this holy place of nunnys."[8] Nuns or other devout women were recipients of numerous pious books, of which two of the best-known also had an Augustinian connection: *Ancrene Wisse* (late twelfth or early thirteenth century) was composed for three anchoresses, probably by an Augustinian canon,[9] and the *Mirror of Our Lady* was written for the Brigitinne convent at Sion, which had a strictly reformed Augustinian rule. The prose life of St. Augustine by John Capgrave, Bokenham's fraternal colleague and fellow Cantabridgian, was composed for a woman patron. The English Austins had two houses of nuns in Suffolk and one in Norfolk, as well as several small establishments of Austin canonesses. In short, the notion of female readership and ownership of books was well established when Bokenham wrote, and is currently being documented by Carol Meale, Julia Boffey, Felicity Riddy, Jocelyn Wogan-Brown, and others.[10]

Bokenham opens his poem with these lines:

> Two thyngys owyth every clerk
> To advertysyn, begynnyng a werk,
> If he procedyn wyl ordeneelly:
> The fyrste is 'what,' the secunde is 'why.'

Considerations of space prevent me from following my author's advice: I am unable in this chapter to address the "why" of his representation of the female body, that is, to discuss at any length its politics or its theology. The interested reader is referred to my other studies of Bokenham mentioned in the notes. What I shall do here is to concentrate on one aspect of the "what": to show that Bokenham's array of female saints is managed so as to constitute a collective anatomy, a structure itself susceptible of both a politics and a theology.

Heads and Feet

The feature of hagiography most puzzling and most repulsive to many modern readers is its repetitive sadism: the hyperbolized quality of these zealous adolescents who are flayed, burnt, drowned, maimed, shaved, insulted, raped, disembowelled, roasted, who have their tongues torn out and breasts torn off, their guts and bones exposed, and are then proposed to, whereupon they answer back spiritedly: No.

They do not die easily, in other words. Their endurance is less superhuman than surreal. They survive ordeals that would kill any of us ten times over. Yet there is a moment of truth that no saint survives, for, as scholars since the sixteenth century have noticed, the commonest *coup de grace* is decapitation.[11] This violation of physical integrity seems more acceptable to God as a cause of death than any other; He could intervene miraculously against it, but (except for St. Winifred—not a martyr) He does not. Dramatically there has to be some gesture to which the saints are terminally vulnerable, something that generic convention understands as finally mortal. Otherwise any legend could continue infinitely, and the concept of martyrdom would lose its meaning. Decapitation is what stands between the saints and Roadrunner, who truly is immortal—and for that reason comic.

But the prevalence of decapitation is more than a dramatic necessity. Ideologically, the role of decapitation as the high road to martyrdom points to all that the head means in classical and Christian thought. Seat of rationality and therefore principle of rule for Plato *(Republic)* and St. Paul (Ephesians 4:15–16, 5:23; Colossians 2:19, 3:18–22), it comes down through Christian tradition as an ontological principle, denial of which is death. The significance of head and headship is carried in medieval political theory, religious literature of all kinds, medical theory—indeed, in the conventional top-down descriptive blazon of medieval lyric and romance. Decapitation is the final ordeal for martyrs for ideological as well as biological reasons. To treat it as only another narreme, another avertible torment, would undercut the hierarchal value system which Catholicism, and civil society generally, had come to exemplify. The rest of the body may be abused in an orgy of sadistic polymorphous perversity, but the head retains its headship.

It isn't however, with heads that Bokenham begins his hagiography, but with feet, and a particular foot at that. This is the foot of St. Margaret, the first body-part to appear in the poem; it is introduced in the prologue. The foot appears there as a subcategory of the fourth (final) cause of the work: authorial intention. Love of St. Margaret was a motive, both the author's own desire to honor the saint, and the devotion of the friend, friar Thomas Burgh of Cambridge, who requested the translation of her life (123–240). The saint's foot, we learn, can be beheld at an old priory of black (Dominican) canons near the author's birthplace. This foot lacks "the greth too only/And the hele" (141–142); these are at a nunnery in Reading. But it is an efficacious foot even without its great toe and heel. The author had experienced its virtue himself only five years earlier in Venice, when a ring previously touched to the relic protected him in an awkward situation in Italy (160–170). If the power of the head is metaphoric, that of the foot is metonymic.[12]

We encounter a single foot again at the end of Bokenham's text. This is the foot of St. Elizabeth, Queen of Hungary, protruding from under the bedclothes as she sleeps with her loving husband. A lady-in-waiting has been instructed to waken Elizabeth gently for nightly prayers, by shaking her foot. Mistakenly the lady grasps the wrong foot, that of the princely husband, who demonstrates his elevated consciousness by pretending that nothing unusual has happened. It seems, then, that Bokenham has framed his work with a pair of feet: a pair of structural pediments on which to construct his architecture of the fragmented female body.

My pun here is not accidental; indeed it is less pun than metaphor, for "pediment" does contain the root that means "foot." Aside from etymology, two traditions perpetuated the analogy of body as building. One of them is medical lore, with its anatomical/architectural analogy in Roman, Arabic, and medieval culture: body as city, castle, or fortress.[13] The other is religious discourse with its gospel,

Pauline, and Augustinian injunctions to think of the body as a temple or altar (*e.g.*, John 2:19–21, I Cor. 6:19, *De Doctrina Christiana* 3.14.22). The body most frequently invoked as architecture—whether temple, palace, dwelling, mansion, or tower—was, during the high Middle Ages, that of the Virgin Mary; this became a topos in the frenzy of naming that constitutes the literature of mariolatry.

These images participate in a cluster of imbricated topoi: body as architecture, text as body (a patristic and commentator's trope), text as architecture (from *City of God* onward, if not even earlier). In connection with this last, a brief return to etymology reminds us that "edifice" and "edify" (as in "an edifying text") share the Latin root *aedifico* meaning to build, establish, or strengthen. Augustine made much of the appearance of this verb in Genesis 2:22, which says, "Et aedificavit Dominus Deus costam quam accepit de Adam in mulierem" (The Lord God built the rib which he had taken from Adam into a woman).[14] Geoffroi of Vinsauf had popularized the idea of text as edifice with his famous opening to *Poetria Nova* (a text which Bokenham refers to in his Prologue, 88). The writer is represented as architect: for both, a vision of the whole work must precede manual effort. In order to construct his own edifying text, Bokenham chose to construct it—loosely but perceptibly—as a body. The body figure allowed him to follow Geoffroi's organicist precept, much as the city-figure (derived from Geoffroi as well as from Augustine) allowed Christine de Pizan to do the same in her *Livre de la Cité des Dames*. Both texts, as collections, require a coherent internal structuration in order to overcome, or at least to balance, the merely agglutinative repetitive tendency of their chosen genre.

I think it scarcely accidental, then, that the image of a single foot appears near the beginning and the end of Bokenham's text. Why would he begin with feet rather than with heads? The descriptive blazon that is so prominent a convention in courtly lyric and romance always begins with the head and works downward, for the reasons elaborated above: what is highest is best and thus comes first. While I doubt Bokenham would want to challenge the hierarchical principle per se, he does, elsewhere in his text, explicitly refuse key elements of courtly eloquence and rhetoric, particularly the courtly-erotic fetishization of the female body and its parts (cf. 407–420, 4996, 5214–5248). To reverse the conventional order of representation is to offer the imagistic paradigm of an alternative system, that of Augustinian doctrine. It lets the work start with a solid foundation, as it were: feet, the lowest part, in touch with the earth (as John of Salisbury had noted in his version of the body politic)—just as the progress through life to a high point of virtue and salvation starts with the solid foundation of humility.

Womb

Feet are not the only bodily motif to frame the legends: childbirth is the other. The central event in Margaret's legend, first in the set, is her encounter with Satan in the shape of a dragon which swallows her entire. Margaret's miraculous escape from the "womb" (ME: belly) of the beast qualifies her to become the patron saint of women in labor (841–844), though she is not mother but infant. It was in infancy that Margaret became a Christian, for her aristocratic parents gave her to a crypto-Christian wet-nurse. Thus, Margaret drew in Christianity literally with her (surrogate) mother's milk. When her biological mother died, Margaret chose to remain with her nurse as a Christian country-girl. She was thus thrice-born: from mother, nurse, and dragon.

The second life too is centrally concerned with childbirth, for it narrates the miraculous late-life conception of Mary by Anne and Joachim. The next ten lives are of virgins, but the last is again a mother, St. Elizabeth, who rejects her natural children, along with all other temporalia which she despises "as dung" (10299). Her children are no dearer to her than others' offspring (10301), and we see that her "real" family is the army of poor and ill people to whom she shows charity over the years. Clearly, then, this framing repetition of childbirth imagery is no celebration of the family. On the contrary, as we will see, family as a social institution is as fragile and fragmented as the physical body. The birth Bokenham wants to validate is the birth into faith.

Face

All young virgin saints are said to be strikingly beautiful, not only in Bokenham's legendary but generally. This is often what brings

them to the attention of an amorous pagan, leading to their martyrdom in defense of virginity and faith. Yet Bokenham's Margaret, first
in his series, is to my knowledge the only saint actually described.
The authorial tactic is interesting if we follow its moves. First comes
one stanza (400–406) of conventional hyperbolic praise of the girl's
beauty. There follow two stanzas of equally conventional refusal to
provide a fuller description, since the author claims he cannot compete in descriptive technique with Boethius, Ovid, Virgil, Geoffroi
Vinsauf, Gower, Chaucer, or Lydgate (407–420). Despite such protest, the description nonetheless comes five stanzas later: Margaret's
face as seen through the eyes of the prefect Olibrius. It is as if
Bokenham is willing, but only if dramatically justified, only in the
right place, and never for sheer rhetorical display.

Margaret's appearance is quite delightful. She possesses several
conventional features—white forehead, grey eyes, straight nose,
ruddy lips, "chyry chekys" (cherry cheeks: 451)—along with two
distinctive ones: a cleft chin and—like young Alison in *The Miller's
Tale*—"bent browes blake" (450). The prefect is smitten.

Thus, Bokenham establishes his priorities from the start. As a
poet he is perfectly capable of description but considers it unneces-
sary to his project (as indeed its usual absence suggests). Margaret's
physical charm can stand for female charm in general. The details
are irrelevant, for there are always beautiful women of one description or another. The reader is not to commit the error of Olibrius,
who "lokyd no ferthere than in hyr face" (456). We are not to be
seduced by the fresh colors of rhetoric—or the fresh colors of a pretty
young face—at the expense of the unsexed spiritual core.

Genitals

St. Anne and her husband Joachim, parents of the Virgin Mary and
subject of Bokenham's second legend, are a Baucis and Philemon
couple, for

> Lyche to lyche ever doth applie,
> As scheep to scheep & man to man,
> Pertryche to pertryche & swan to swan
> So vertu to vertu is agreable.
>
> (1639–1642)

These lines forcefully emphasize what humanity has in common with the rest of *natura naturata,* for reproductive nature as glorification of God is the theological lesson of this legend. The tale starts with a rehearsal of "noble pedegre," a long (1511–1615) multiple genealogy of Mary's parents and of her husband Joseph based on the genealogy that opens the gospel book of Matthew.

Despite their righteousness, Anne and Joachim are a barren couple. Joachim, ashamed at having been publicly rebuked for this failure, leaves home to watch his sheep in the wilderness. There, interrogated by an angel, he poignantly confesses:

> "I want the argumentes of a man;
> & whan men be reknyd I am lefth behynde;
> For no maner isseu may I han"... (1833–1835)

"I lack the evidence of a man": the social evidence of virility is lacking, the family that would create him a patriarch; and so when men are counted he is left out. Anne for her part, lamenting in her garden her husband's absence, glimpses a sparrow feeding its young. She regrets her inability to share the experience of "every creature,/Fyssh, ful and bestis, both more & smal" (1764–1765) to whom God has granted

> "by kyndly engenderrure
> To ioyen in the lykenesse of ther nature,
> And in ther issu, iche aftyr his kynde,
> To worshyp of thy name with-owten ende!"
> (1766–1769)

The two scenes balance each other effectively: Joachim in the wilderness with his sheep, Anne in the garden with her sparrow, both desiring nothing so much as the "fruit" (a constantly reiterated image in this tale) of their "nature" (in Middle English often a synonym for sexuality or the genitals). These are the individuals through whom Christ eventually took on created form, and Leo Steinberg has reminded us how important the genitality of Jesus was to Renaissance painters as an expression of that doctrinal mystery.[15] Here we are asked to see Jesus's parents in their full naturalness, in the animal nature that coexists with their divine mission.[16]

The generative relation explodes in Bokenham's third legend, that of Christine. The heroine is only twelve when the action occurs, and much of her behavior partakes of the insolence and energy, even violence, of that passionate age between childhood and maturity. The story, without a prologue, pulls us directly into a tale of father-daughter conflict. The prefect Urban of Tyre, considering his daughter's adolescent beauty, locks her in a tower, there to perform her (pagan) religious duty. As is the habit of young women kept in towers, Christine does the opposite of what her jailer intends. Unlike the immured heroines of romance, Christine does not take a lover, but she does become a Christian. The outraged father gives a parental lecture-cum-interrogation in the generic form that has survived these many centuries (2237–2250). Their argument centers on the doctrine of the Trinity, for Urban fails to see why, if his daughter can worship three gods, she cannot worship more. Christine will repeat this argument twice more (2835–2842, 2895), for a total of three. Because Christine has three ordeals, threeness is physically inscribed into her body, which thus becomes an emblem of the theology of her tale.

Christine's father is her first persecutor. His professed paternal feelings fail to ensure tolerance, compassion, or even decency. The mother is no more effective, despite a touching scene when she visits Christine in prison, begging her to remember that "I/Ten monethis the bare in my body" (1414–2415). This is the moment of formal renunciation: Christine replies that Christ "is my fadir, he is modir also . . . Wherefor go hense, & labour nomore./Clepe me not doughtyr; here I the forsake" (2426–2436). She is flesh of their flesh, and throws it in their faces—literally, for during her torture, when her body is being torn,

> A gobet ther-of, as she had lyst to jape,
> Sche threu, thus seying, in-to hir fadir face:
> 'O ould shreu of yll dayis that pace,
> Syth thou desyryst flessh for to eet,
> Seke no forthere nere in noon other place.
> Have of thyn own & Faste gyne to frete.'
>   (2467–2474)

Later, when her father dies, Christine—rebel with a cause—kneels down and thanks God.

At the end of the tale, Osbern reminds us of his own efforts to generate this wayward child, his version of Christine. He prays for the saint's mercy

> on-to the translatour
> Wych thi legend compyled, not without labour
> In englyssh tunge . . . (3126–3128)

It is not unlike Christine's mother's appeal for mercy earlier on, and the imagery of birth explicit there is punningly latent here ("labour").[17] Bokenham plainly feels his art deserves proper notice. He cannot afford an *envoi*—this is the wrong genre for it—and his self-conscious little prayer is the closest hagiography can come.

Tongue, Mouth, Language

If an incident is worth telling, it is worth repeating: this often seems to be an aesthetic principle in medieval pious literature. Christine flings a gobbet of her flesh into her persecutor-father's face, taunting his figurative voracity by giving it literal translation: eat this. With her third torturer, the judge Julian, Christine repeats the episode with another part of her body. When Julian has her breasts cut off and her tongue cut out, Christine spits a piece of the severed tongue into the tyrant's face with such force that he is blinded. The lack of a tongue does not prevent her gloating, "Yet have I speche, & thou wurthyly/Off thine oon eye has lost the sycht" (3081–3082).

Three other lives in the collection, the eighth, ninth, and tenth—those of Mary Magdalene, Katherine, and Cecelia—focus on the apparatus and the practise of speech, with a carefully constructed decreasing literality or increasing figurativity. Though the language theme is latent in each of these lives by virtue of plot—Mary becomes a preacher, Katherine debates publicly with pagan scholars, Cecelia is notoriously insolent—nonetheless not every hagiographer chooses to include this material. Bokenham does, and foregrounds it. He inherits a plot, but shapes it new.

The Magdalene's legend is devoted to the incarnation, the real fleshliness of Jesus. Only in this legend is Jesus physically present as a character, and we are forced to be continually aware of that embodiedness through Magdalene's physical attentions: "She mynystyrd hym & hys in there nede" (5505); blessed are those chosen "hym to feden in hys bodily nede" (5526) and so on.

Magdalene is in touch especially with Jesus's feet, which she wipes with her hair, washes with her tears, and often kisses. "The head means the Godhead of Christ," declared St. Cyril of Jerusalem in the third century, and the feet thus represent his humanity. Steinberg offers several statements to this effect:

> The nature of Christ is two-fold; it is like the head of the body in that He is recognized as God, and comparable to the feet in that for our salvation He put on manhood as frail as our own. (Eusebius)
>
> Whoever calls the head of Christ his divinity, and the feet his humanity, he does not stray from the truth. (St. Maximus Confessor)
>
> If it seemed right to St. Paul to describe Christ's head in terms of his divinity, it should not seem unreasonable to us to ascribe the feet to his humanity. (St. Bernard)[18]

Mary's direct oral-pedal contact with Jesus is said to account for her effectiveness as a preacher, for

> no wundyr thow that mowth sothly
> Wych so feyr kyssys & so swete
> So oftyn had bredyd & so devothly
> Up-on cryst oure salvatourys feet,
> Dyvers tymes whan she hym ded mete,
> Past othir swych grace had in favour
> Of goddes wurde to shewe the savour. (5794–5800)

The metaphorical use of "savour" brings the point home. Starting with a mouth, the stanza ends with taste. Between—in the mathematically central line—comes the image of the savior's feet, the physical presence of Jesus as turning-point accomplishing transformation. These feet are the means by which the kissing mouth becomes the preaching mouth. The metaphysical taste of gospel erases any lurking disgust that may accompany the idea of foot-kissing. In its transformative process, Bokenham's stanza formally mimes the working of divine intervention in history.

Katherine is an Alexandrian bluestocking, a highly cultured woman in a city that prided itself on its culture. The emperor Maxence is impressed with her ability to express herself both in philosophical language and in "comown speche" (6490–6499); he praises the saint's "exhortacyoun . . . peroracyoun . . . eloquence . . . prudence" (6257–6260). Well he might, for Katherine is educated in the seven liberal arts "so profoundly, that . . . /Was no clerk founde in that cuntre/ . . . But that she wyth hym coude commune" (6394–6397). This comment immediately establishes Katherine's equality with men. It does more, for in not simply praising her learning but measuring it against that of the other sex, it establishes the culturally threatening quality of her achievement. This implication becomes explicit when Katherine is forced to debate fifty male scholar-rhetoricians, her faith and forensic skills against theirs. Katherine appropriates the ordinarily masculine privilege of oratory and debate—and she surpasses the experts in direct contest. This victory of socially subversive female speech calls into question the pagans' patriarchal notions of order and female subordination.

Katherine's rhetorical tactic is *sermo humilis;*[19] she renounces logic to offer instead a simple profession of faith. Her plain homiletic style is as much an *imitatio Christi* as her death will be, for Christ took on a lower style, as it were, not only to address humanity but to participate in it. The philosophers are reduced to silence; they convert and are martyred on the spot, but not before the outraged tyrant has baited them:

> "O ye lewyd knavys, what eylyth yow?
> Wher is your pompous phylosopye now? . . .
> Why stonde ye thus stylle? be ye tunglees?"
> (6803–6807)

"Are you tongueless?" the emperor jibes. What Katherine has so potently displayed, they have figuratively lost: the organ of phallogocentric supremacy. Only by accepting the faith that animates the saint's speech can the scholars redeem their lack. Until then, they are reduced to silent passivity by a heroic woman who assumes leadership by exercising an organ which is an upwardly displaced version of a sex organ—a displacement well recognized in medieval medical lore.[20]

Cecelia's life, last in this sub-set about the production and use of speech, is the most abstract in its concerns. Its theme is philosophical dualism and the transcendence of dualism in faith. Accordingly, the tale relies on patterns of doubleness. Inner and outer spaces—sartorial, psychological, and architectural—govern the opening movement of the tale: Cecelia's hair shirt beneath her wedding robe, the bride's silent prayer on hearing the wedding music, the enclosed bridal chamber versus the public space of wedding hall and city. Other pairs, not contrasting, repeat the experience of dualism: the marital couple, the two brothers Valerius and Tiburtius, two angelic garlands composed of two kinds of flowers, two conversions, two martyrdoms.

The sense of dualism is interiority and exteriority, or spirituality and worldliness, is also carried in Cecelia's distinctive language practice: the two-levelled wordgames and the stichomythic dialogue which characterize her exchanges with her persecutor. Cecelia herself calls attention to this theme when she reproaches her persecutor for asking questions susceptible of two answers (8108–8109). This style also characterizes Cecelia's two converts, her husband and brother-in-law. After a frustrating interview with the two men, the prefect Almache exclaims, "Where-to we/That cerclyn aboute in batayle verbal?" (7962–7963). He puts his finger on the very spot, for the verbal battle is emblematic of deeper structures.

But of course the conclusion of these pairs, oppositions, and exchanges is that they are ultimately to be resolved in faith. Jesus is the ultimate mediator between the two levels of reality: he participated in both and he exchanged himself for mankind. This is why he can be referred to as the great merchant or celestial negotiator,[21] and why Cecelia is able to use the striking imagery of the marketplace in her important sermon to the Roman soldiers who escort her to her ordeal (8071–8093).

What happens to Cecelia's body is therefore especially significant, for she is the one saint not immediately dispatched by decapitation. Three sword-strokes do not suffice to kill her, but Roman law forbids another blow. The saint survives three days half-living and half-dead—or rather, both living and dead, a liminal-transgressive figure linking and participating in two worlds normally distinct and opposed. She becomes an emblem of the theology of her tale, her living-dead body the visible site of passage between physical and spiritual levels of reality: a bridge, as it were, just as her preaching is a bridge in the linguistic realm. Her half-dead body both is and represents the resolution of opposites or paradoxes, a vision of the kind revealed to her husband Valerian in his conversion, of "o lord & oon feyth ther-to,/O baptem ... & o god also" (7625–7626).

Breast, Gut and All

Bokenham's last three legends form a coda to the collection, concentrating more densely some of the themes of the body present in the other lives. In an appropriate stylistic adjustment, the eleventh and twelfth lives—those of Agatha and Lucy—display a sustained grotesque creatural naturalism not present elsewhere.

St. Agatha's iconographic attribute is the breast. She is often represented holding a breast in a pair of pincers, or with a sword driven through her breasts, or with the flesh-hook that was used to rip her breasts. Though the removal of breasts is not unique to Agatha, it is distinctively the central feature of her ordeal and of her sanctity, and only Agatha has the breasts restored to her body. Bokenham makes every effort to amplify references to this part of the saint's body. The consul Quincian does not merely order her torture, he specifies attention to "pappys ... And let hyre knowyn whayt ys peyn" (8584–8589). We learn of the "tendyr brestys" being pulled with pincers, burnt with fire-brands, torn with forks, and finally cut off and thrown away, both flesh and skin (8590–8603). Agatha denounces the tyrant for disfiguring a woman and for cutting away that which he sucked as an infant (8605–8615). She claims to possess spiritual breasts that can never be lost, and with which she nourishes herself (8619–8623). Afterward, an old man appears to the saint in prison, offering to heal her and restore her breasts. She refuses: not out of modesty, as the old man thinks, but because her only confidence is in Jesus. When the old man reveals that he comes from Jesus—he is St. Peter—the cure is effected and the breasts are restored.

Now, it is the case that the female breast was at the time particularly hard to ignore. Naked breasts were in vogue among noble-women from 1429 on, and though it is unlikely they were to be seen at festivities at Clare Castle—next door to Bokenham's priory and the residence of his patron Isabel Bourchier, Countess of Eu and sister to Richard of York—still anyone with Bokenham's connections would have been aware of this courtly fad. The Oxford chancellor and cleric Thomas Gascoigne deplored it as conducive to sins of word and touch.[22] King Henry VI was known for his innocence and even prudery, but his courtiers were not; they "introduced a bevy of unclad dancers into a Christmas ball," which Henry fled, crying "Fy, fy, for shame!"[23] In France, even more scandalous events took place at court from 1444 on. Fashionable women strove to imitate the king's mistress, Agnès Sorel, in her innovative display of naked breasts, a style for which she was notorious among French and English alike.[24] But if Bokenham's treatment of the breast comments on courtly fashion, that is incidental to its aesthetic and ethical purpose.

Certainly Bokenham's treatment of Agatha succeeds in demystifying the female breast as a focus of sexual attraction. It reifies the breast as a functional, even removable, object whose primary use is nursing, as Agatha stresses in her reproach to Quincian. Paradoxically, the separation and fetishization of body parts is a practice shared by sadist and lover, for the rhetorical device of the descriptive catalogue, or blazon of female charms, also reduces and fragments its object. A wholly sexualized view of the body, like a sadistic one, singles out one or another biological feature for scrutiny while ignoring the individual's integrity as a physical and moral being. (One is reminded of a modern instance: in D. H. Lawrence's *The Rainbow*, Chapter 8, Will Brangwen worships his wife Anna's ankle and other parts *seriatim*.)

In other registers too the Middle Ages were intensely conscious of bodily fragmentation. Chaucer's Pardoner denounces oath-swearers for blasphemy, for in swearing by the various parts of Christ's body, they have "Cristes blessed body al torent" (VI, 709). This injunction against swearing participates in a widespread topos in late-medieval pious art, literary and visual, which represents the swearer as archetypal persecutor of the archetypal martyr.[25] This is the tormented body at the center of medieval religious consciousness, *the* hegemonic image of the period, displayed in every crucifix and pietà and, according to the moralists, duplicated in every casual conversational oath (by God's body/blood/bones, etc.). But the visualization of detached body parts was not linked with religious doctrine only, not in a culture where the amputation of head, hand, tongue, eye, or genital was a possible penalty for various treasonous or "immoral" acts; where the ceremony of amputation was a ritualized public event; where a severed head or hand or extruded guts might be placed on display for weeks as a political or moralistic warning.

If oath-swearers can be accused of verbal sadism, how vulnerable to the charge are lover-poets who rip apart the female body in their verse! For the critic of such verbal tactics, what more effective way to deflate the lyric-erotic overvaluation of a lump of fat than by asserting its biological use, showing the worst physical instances of fragmentation, and re-presenting the body part completely estranged? That, I believe, is Bokenham's rhetorical tactic in an overall strategy aiming to rehabilitate femininity for theological and political purposes.

The legend of Lucy continues to demystify the body, though from another angle. We are assaulted with a description of the saint's mother's dysentery. This is a traditional detail, and necessary to the plot, for the mother will be cured by her daughter's devotion to Agatha. But the rhetorical amplification of this minor point is unique to Bokenham, who offers a lengthy (some thirty lines) medical digression on the red or bloody flux, the balance of humors, excoriation of guts, and other theoretical and empirical details of the disease. After the cure, which reveals Lucy's powers, the saint's ordeals commence. She is condemned to a brothel, there to serve the lust of every comer "Of nature aftyr the condicyon" (9251). Again, Bokenham amplifies enormously. We are told that the girl will be "with corupcyon/Defouled" (9252–9253): the triple corruption of sexuality itself, of semen, and of venereal disease. We are spared no detail about prostitution and pimping. The consul's proclamation calls upon all and sundry to fulfill their lust on the fair young virgin until she is dead from multiple rape.

In this way, both sections of the Lucy story reduce the body to sheerest functionalism: a foul bag open at either end, site of diseases, a vessel for humors and semen, a thing. Yet such reductivity is only half the story. Needless to say, the requisite miracles are performed so that Lucy remains untouched. She never enters the brothel because she is miraculously rooted to the spot where she stands and cannot be moved: a physical manifestation of her immovable will. Her body cannot be defiled, for Lucy understands, echoing Scripture, that

> Of the holy gost I hys dwellyng-place
> And his temple am made, by a special grace.
> (9375–9376)

That potential, present in every Christian, is the still center—the soul, as it were—of this tale whose literary body is an intense and revolting naturalism. The stories of Agatha and Lucy alienate the body, defetishize it by stripping it of its association with beauty and desire. Simultaneously, they re-fetishize the body toward functionalism and, consequently, the necessary subordination of all nature to the Christian imperative. It is a delicate position, for the body has to be depreciated, but not so far as to damage a creation of God, and it has to be appreciated, but not beyond the claims of spirituality. The point is proper balance—an attitude of moderation for which the Augustinians were traditionally known and distinguished from harsher rules.

Elizabeth's life seems to contradict the ethos of the body just sketched, for although Elizabeth is not tortured, her self-imposed privations and those imposed by her harsh confessor, Master Conrad, constitute a lifelong ordeal. No other saint in the collection displays such consistent asceticism. Yet at no time does the poet recommend it as a model; rather he displays it as a possible, not a typical or necessarily desirable, mode of worship. What Bokenham does explicitly recommend as a model for men and women alike is not Elizabeth's self-deprivation but rather her patience, humility, and obedience (9834–9845), virtues available to all. As princess, queen, wife, and mother, Elizabeth has every opportunity for self-indulgence. Yet she dedicates her life to prayer and service, maintaining the proper spirit in prosperity and adversity. In this sense her life is exemplary: no melodramatic exotica set in the distant Roman or Egyptian past, but as contemporary as someone like Margery Kempe of King's Lynn, whose married status and fits of crying might be recognized in the life of the late-medieval Hungarian saint.

From head to foot, then, and including face, mouth, tongue, breasts, flesh, guts, womb, and genitals, Bokenham has given us a collective anatomy of inspired women whose strength and assertiveness assure their death and, in the spiritual and literary senses, their life. I began by writing that this representational strategy is susceptible of both a politics and a theology. Though I can't expand on the politics here, I have proposed, in my other work on Bokenham, that it is to do with the body politic, that is, with the politics of reproduction and particularly with rival claims to the English throne. The strongest genealogical claim of Bokenham's landlord and patron, Richard Duke of York, came through female descent, while the Lancastrian pedigree was exclusively male (though weakened in other ways). The question of women's ability to transmit rule had been a significant one to English and French theorists and propagandists for over a century, since the start of the Hundred Years War to which it was a contributing issue. To vindicate the nature and capacities of women as powerfully as Bokenham does in his legendary constituted a useful, if minor, propaganda service to Yorkist aspirations.

As for the theology, I want to take a long running jump at this by looking at several ways in which we might interpret the entire array of stories considered here. To begin, there are thirteen lives—a curious number, not usually associated with the Pythagorean numerical symbolism often found in medieval and Renaissance works. On the simplest physical or biological level, thirteen is the number of months in a year measured in months of twenty-eight days, the length of a menstrual cycle. This is the calendrical calculation Bokenham uses in his life of Christine, whose mother poignantly reminds her daughter of the ten months she bore her in her body (2414–2415), a period correct only when a month is reckoned as four weeks long, or twenty-eight days. We need to recall here how much attention was paid by scholastic philosophers to matters of natural science, including embryology, which posed the crucial question of matter and form. Augustine, Avicenna, Aquinas, and many others had addressed the topic, as had Giles of Rome— the thirteenth-century Augustinian scholar whose works every Austin was required to read and defend—in his treatise *De formatione corporis humani in utero*.[26]

Another important set of thirteen with special relevance to hagiography is the number of primary apostles, including St. Paul. All were missionaries and martyrs, hence the first imitators of the teacher and protomartyr Jesus. The significance of their number was commemorated in the number of members admitted in 1415 to the newly founded monastery at Sion near London, the only religious house in England professing the reformed order of St. Augustine. It accepted eighty-five, representing the thirteen apostles and seventy-two disciples.[27] If Mary can be referred to as "apostoless" (5068), then the complete array can be seen as a female apostolate, teaching by word and by example.

The coexistence of physical and symbolic (or historico-literal and spiritual) interpretations of a given text or event is a key principle in Augustinian hermeneutics. If biology provides the physical or literal level of meaning for the number of Bokenham's saints, and the apostles its ethical or moral level, then what about the third and fourth levels of medieval allegorical interpretation, the allegorical and tropological (often collapsed into a single doctrinal statement)? What would be the ultimate theological meaning of Bokenham's literary re-memberment of the female body? It is to be found, I believe, in the central problems of eschatological theory: death and resurrection.

Resurrection theory was controversial virtually from the start of the Christian era.[28] Despite many varied contributions—Jewish, Christian, and Gnostic—what eventually came to be mainstream orthodoxy taught that the resurrected body will be the same body as during life, complete in all its parts, lacking only concupiscence and corruption. As might be expected, Augustine devoted a great deal of attention to this topic, nowhere more effectively than in the last book of *The City of God*. What about aborted fetuses, dead infants, cannibalism, obesity, or other deformity whether excess or deficiency (chaps. 12–20)? The solution—a paean to the theology of rassemblage—is that the risen body

> will be transformed from its former condition as a natural
> body into the new condition of a spiritual body. . . . And, even
> though by some accident of life or by the savagery of enemies
> the whole body has been reduced to dust and thrown to the
> winds or scattered on the waters so that not a trace of it

seems to be left, nothing in fact will escape the omnipotence of the creator, and not a hair of its head will perish. (22.21)

"If corruption or fragmentation," writes Caroline Bynum, "or division of body . . . is the central threat [to survival], resurrection (the reassemblage of parts into whole) is the central victory."[29] And so it is for the impolitic bodies represented by the fifteenth-century Austin friar: those supremely tactless, rebellious adolescents, those nonconforming citizens, those militant virgins and controlling wives who constitute his array of female saints. The resurrection of the body is, for the Augustinian poet, humanity's final hope, as it was the martyrs', to live again and to live in triumph. Yet besides being individuals, his saints are, theologically, the limbs—the members— of a single body. This is institutionally true for every Christian, but even more intimately so of saints, who are "of the body of Christ, whose members are in common."[30] In the collective anatomy that is his text, Bokenham re-enacts this membership, figuring in its reassemblage the universal one at the end of days.

NOTES

1. Charles Jones characterized saints' lives as "the popular form of creative literature from the sixth to the tenth centuries," and demonstrated numerous points of contact with romance: *Saints' Lives and Chronicles in Early England* (Ithaca: Cornell Univ. Press, 1947), chapter 4.

2. Guy Philippart, *Les legendiers latins et autres manuscrits hagiographiques* (Turnhout: Brèpols, 1977). Philippart lists forty manuscript collections, all Latin, divided *sancti/sanctae,* from the eighth through fifteenth centuries. Of these, only one—from the fifteenth century—is in England (at St. John's College, Oxford).

3. That is, no one has yet, to my knowledge, made that argument, although my examination of one ms.—British Library Cotton Domitian A XI—suggests the possibility. Bozon's lives have been edited piecemeal by Sister M. Amelia Klenke: Margaret, Mary Magdalene and Martha in *Three Saints' Lives by Nicholas Bozon* (St. Bonaventura, N.Y.: Franciscan Institute, 1947), the others in *Seven More Poems by Nicholas Bozon* (St. Bonaventure: The Franciscan Institute and Louvain: E. Nauwelaerts, 1951). See also

Mary R. Learned, "Saints Lives Attributed to Nicholas Bozon," *Franciscan Studies* 25 (1944), 79–88.

4. For Bokenham's knowledge and use of Chaucer's work, particularly the *Legend of Good Women,* see the Introduction to my translation of Bokenham's *Legends of Holy Women* (Notre Dame: Univ. of Notre Dame Press, 1992) or my study of Bokenham, *Patronage, Politics and Augustinian Poetics in Fifteenth Century England* (forthcoming).

5. On Bokenham's biography and other works, see the above; also documents in Francis Roth, *The English Austin Friars, 1249–1538,* 2 vols. (New York: Augustinian Historical Institute, 1961).

6. Norman P. Tanner, *The Church in Late Medieval Norwich, 1370–1532* (Toronto: PIMS, 1984), 58, 64. For context, see Gail McMurray Gibson, *The Theatre of Devotion. East Anglian Drama and Society in the Late Middle Ages* (Chicago: Univ. of Chicago Press, 1989); Ralph A. Griffiths, *The Reign of King Henry VI* (London: Benn, 1981); Samuel Moore, "Patrons of Letters in Norfolk and Suffolk, c. 1450," *PMLA* 27 (1912): 188–207; and 28 (1913): 79–106.

7. E. F. Jacob, "Cusanus the Theologian" in *Essays in the Conciliar Epoch* (Notre Dame: Univ. of Notre Dame Press, rev. ed. 1963), 155; Peter Lasko and N. J. Morgan, *Medieval Art in East Anglia, 1300–1520* (London: Thames and Hudson, 1974); W. G. Constable, "Some East Anglian Roodscreen Painting," *The Connoisseur* 84 (1929): 141–147, 211–220, 290–293, 358–363.

8. The most recent edition, and the one I have used, is by Mary S. Serjeantson for EETS, o.s. 206 (1938 for 1936; repr. 1988).

9. E. J. Dobson, *The Origins of Ancrene Wisse* (Oxford: Clarendon, 1976).

10. See essays in *Book Production and Publishing in Britain, 1375–1475,* ed. Jeremy Griffiths and Derek Pearsall (Cambridge: Cambridge Univ. Press, 1989) and *Women and Literature in Britain, 1150–1500,* ed. Carol Meale (Cambridge, Cambridge Univ. Press, 1993); also Janet Coleman, *English Literature in History, 1350–1400: Medieval Readers and Writers* (London: Hutchison, 1981); Michael G. Sargent, ed. *De Cella in Seculum. Religious and Secular Life and Devotion in Late Medieval England* (Cambridge: Brewer, 1989); Jocelyn Wogan-Brown and Bella Millett, *Medieval English Prose for Women* (Oxford: Clarendon, 1990).

11. Half of Bokenham's ten martyrs die of decapitation, and the same proportion holds for the *South English Legendary.* For a survey of

theories, see Baudouin de Gaiffier, "La mort par le glaive dans les passions des martyrs," *Subsidia hagiographica* 52 (1971): 70–76; a more general discussion is that of Paul-Henri Stahl, *Histoire de la Décapitation* (Paris: Presses Universitaires de France, 1986).

12. On the history of reliquary devotion and law, see Nicole Hermann-Mascard, *Les Reliques des Saints* (Paris: Klincksieck, 1975); André Vauchez, *La Sainteté en Occident aux Derniers Siècles du Moyen Age* (Rome, 1981); Peter Brown, *The Cult of the Saints* (Chicago: Univ. of Chicago Press, 1981) and *Relics and Social Status in the Age of Gregory of Tours* (Reading: Univ. of Reading, 1977); Patrick J. Geary, *Furta Sacra. Thefts of Relics in the Central Middle Ages* (Princeton: Princeton Univ. Press, 1978).

13. Marie-Christine Pouchelle, *Corps et chirurgie à l'apogée du moyen age* (Paris: Flammarion, 1983), Part 2, chapter 3; Roberta Cornelius, *The Figurative Castle* (Bryn Mawr, 1930) on "the castle of the body [as] a species in the genus of the bodily edifice" (73).

14. Augustine, *The Literal Meaning of Genesis,* trans. John Hammond Taylor, 2 vols. (New York: Newman Press, 1982), Book 9, chap. 13, 86.

15. Leo Steinberg, *The Sexuality of Christ in Renaissance Art and in Modern Oblivion* (New York: Pantheon, 1983).

16. A key theological point arising from Bokenham's treatment of Anne and Joachim is the immaculate conception of Mary; for a full discussion see *Patronage, Politics . . . ,* where I argue that Bokenham implies the maculist position common to his order and to many late medieval ecclesiastical writers, including Aquinas. The question was highly controversial during the late Middle Ages; the immaculate conception of Mary was declared official doctrine only in 1439 at the Council of Basel— a few years before Bokenham compiled his legendary—but was by no means universally accepted. See *The Dogma of the Immaculate Conception. History and Significance,* ed. Edward D. O'Connor (Notre Dame: Notre Dame University Press, 1958).

17. See *MED* s.v. "labour." Meaning 1.(e) is "the fruits of labour, product; a book," and 4.(b) includes several medical and other instances of "labour of birth," among them citations from *The Book of Margery Kempe* and a translation of Boccaccio's *De Claris Mulieribus. OED* includes an instance from the Paston letters (1.244). These examples are by and large clustered in the first half of the fifteenth century, so it seems that Bokenham took advantage of a fairly recent linguistic development. OED does not mention the Claudian translation done at Clare in 1445, probably by Bokenham, which mentions "labours of . . . childyng"; line 377 in Ewald

Flügel, "Eine Mittelenglische Claudian-setzung (1445)," *Anglia. Zeitschrift für Englische Philologie* 28 (1905): 255–299 and 421–438.

18. Steinberg, Excursus XVIII (143), "The body as hierarchy."

19. Erich Auerbach, *Literary Language and Its Public in Late Latin Antiquity and in the Middle Ages* (New York: Pantheon, 1965), Chapter 1 for *sermo humilis*.

20. In some texts, head and penis-tip *(caput virgae)* are analogous, as are mouth and vagina, tongue and clitoris. See Danielle Jacquart and Claude Thomasset, *Sexuality and Medicine in the Middle Ages* (Paris: Presses Universitaires Françaises, 1985; trans. Cambridge: Polity Press, 1988).

21. R. A. Shoaf, *The Poem as Green Girdle. Commercium in Sir Gawain and the Green Knight* (Gainesville: Univ. of Florida Press, 1984), 9.

22. *Loci e Libro Veritatum*, ed. James E. Thorold Rogers (Oxford: Clarendon, 1881), 144–145, s.v. *Ornatus*.

23. *Henry the Sixth. A Reprint of John Blacman's Memoir,* ed. M. R. James (Cambridge, 1919); also B. P. Wolfe, "The personal rule of Henry VI" in *Fifteenth-Century England,* ed. S. B. Chrimes et al. (Manchester, 1972), 37; Paul Murray Kendall, *The Yorkist Age* (New York, 1962), 162. Wolfe adds: "The sight of naked men in public baths similarly incurred [the king's] rebuke. He spied on his entourage from a secret window in his chamber, lest they should be corrupted by bad company" (37). Further on the king's piety, see Ralph A. Griffiths, *The Reign of King Henry VI* (London: Benn, 1981), 235.

24. Margaret Scott, *The History of Dress Series. Late Gothic Europe, 1400–1500* (London: Mills and Boon; Atlantic Highlands, N.J.: Humanities Press, 1980), 26; M. G. A. Vale, *Charles VII* (London: Eyre Methuen, 1974), 94.

25. The tradition has been documented by G. R. Owst, *Literature and Pulpit in Medieval England* (Oxford: Blackwell, 1933; repr. 1966), 414–425. A remarkable fifteenth-century wall-painting illustrating the theme, from Broughton (Bucks.), is shown in Christopher Woodforde, *The Norwich School of Glass-Painting in the Fifteenth Century* (London: Oxford University, 1950), 185.

26. M. Anthony Hewson, *Giles of Rome and the Medieval Theory of Conception* (London: Athlone Press, 1975).

27. George James Aungier, *The History and Antiquities of Syon Monastery* (London: J. B. Nichols, 1840), 21.

28. Two useful surveys are by Joanne Dewart, *Death and Resurrection* (Wilmington: Michael Glazier, 1986) and *The Resurrection of the Body,* ed. H. Cornélis et al. (Notre Dame: Fides Oublishers, 1964). A sampling of scholastic treatises on the topic can be found in Richard Heinzmann, *Die unsterblichkeit der Seele und die Auferstehung des Liebes* (Münster: Aschendorffsche Verlagsbuchhandlung, 1965).

29. Caroline Bynum, "Bodily Miracles and the Resurrection of the Body in the High Middle Ages," in *Belief in History. Innovative Approaches to European and American Religion,* ed. Thomas Kseiman (Notre Dame: Notre Dame University Press, 1991), 68–106; citation to 77.

30. From a ninth-century life of St. Gregory by a monk at Whitby, translated in Charles Jones, *Saints' Lives and Chronicles in Early England* (Ithaca: Cornell University Press, 1947), 118.

Deborah Laycock

6

Shape-Shifting:

Fashion, Gender, and Metamorphosis in Eighteenth-Century England

In 1747, Richard Campbell, author of *The London Tradesman,* in an otherwise unprepossessing account of the trades of London ("calculated for the instruction of youth in their choice of business"), attempted to account for the tailor's symbolic and commercial investment in fabricating and accommodating an economy of desire, an economy that could only be represented as "fashion" and figured through metamorphosis. The tailor, according to Campbell, was a "shape merchant," a "perfect Proteus," "chang[ing] Shapes as often as the Moon":

> No Man is ignorant that a Taylor is the Person that makes our Cloaths; to some he not only makes their Dress, but, in some measure, may be said to make themselves. There are Numbers of Beings in and about this Metropolis who have no other identical Existence than what the Taylor, Milliner, and Perriwig-Maker bestow upon them, Strip them of these Distinctions, and they are quite a different Species of Beings; have no more Relation to their dressed selves, than they have to the Great *Mogul,* and are as insignificant in Society as Punch, depriv'd of his moving Wires, and hung up upon a Peg.
>
> This makes some fanciful Persons imagine, that the *Prometheus,* so much mention'd in *Heathen* Theology, was really no more than a Taylor, who, by his art, metamorphosed Mankind so, that they appear'd a new Species of Beings.[1]

In this passage, Campbell's anxiety about how not only clothes but bodies and identities are the products of fashion leads him to situate himself at an ironic distance from the trade that he is teaching youth to profit from. The ambivalence expressed in this directive to tradesmen, which skeptically articulates the commercial fabrication of identity at the same time that it attempts to encourage those who might capitalize on it, was earlier expressed by Bernard Mandeville, the author of *The Fable of the Bees* (1714), but less as fascinated horror than as realist paradox. Mandeville depicted a world in which a fashion system predominated in all aspects of eighteenth-century culture. "Laws and Clothes," he observed, "were equally/Objects of Mutability."[2] The politics of state were intimately connected to the transformative economy of the body, and both were acted upon by the forces of fashion. And in such a society, as Richard Campbell noted, the tailor played a powerful and profitable role as artificer.

In this chapter, I will examine how new economic forces in seventeenth- and eighteenth-century England, particularly the development of public credit and the associated fashion industry stimulated by credit, seemed to contemporaries to threaten the bases of a stable identity or personality, an identity generally conceived to reside in the body of a propertied gentleman. To opponents of luxury, the new economy appeared to be driven by the fashionable desires of women. But defenders of the credit economy appropriated the figure, if not the body, of the fashionable woman in order to represent and contain the danger of instability embodied in public credit. The Promethean metamorphoses of mankind to which Richard Campbell compared the art of the tailor were brought more under male control in the form of Ovidian metamorphoses of mankind. Further, the topic of women's fashionable consumption seems inevitably to elicit from early eighteenth-century authors, both major and minor, male and female, Ovidian tales of transformation.

I

The continuous permutations allowed to fashion by an economy of desire, especially an economy that was stimulated by paper money and credit (Anthony Ascham in 1649 referred to paper money as "an invention for the more expedite permutation of things"[3]), contributed, according to such promoters of credit ideology as Mandeville, to the wealth of the nation:

> To this Emulation and continual striving to out-do one another it is owing, that after so many various Shiftings and Changings of Modes, in trumping up new ones and renewing of old ones, there is still a *plus ultra* left for the ingenious; it is this, or at least the consequence of it, that sets the Poor to Work, adds Spurs to Industry, and encourages the skilful Artificer to search after further Improvements.[4]

Women's fashions, Mandeville argued, even the hooped petticoat, have enriched the nation, for "the variety of Work that is perform'd, and the number of Hands employ'd to gratify the Fickleness and Luxury of Women is prodigious."[5] Female luxury becomes a central piece of evidence for Mandeville's famous contention that private vices have public benefits.

Mandeville and Campbell were certainly not the first writers to comment on the impact that fashion and the desire for luxury had made upon the economy and the social structure of England. For a considerable period of time in England (but a shorter period than on the Continent), laws were enacted to regulate and control the potentially disruptive expressions of social mobility that might be occasioned by shape-shifting through dress. Between 1337 and 1604, sumptuary laws legislated which apparel was deemed most suitable for the preservation of a rigid social hierarchy, for the effective distinguishing between the sexes, and for the mercantilist protection of native textile industries.[6] Even when, however, such legislation, excepting the protection of domestic textile production, failed to find the support of the House of Commons (when in 1604 the Commons more effectively began to thwart the exercise of the royal prerogative in control of dress), there was still a great deal of support for the maintenance of sumptuary laws. Through the seventeenth century, numerous attempts were made in the House of Commons to reintroduce such legislation, and there were frequent discourses on the subject of regulation of dress throughout the seventeenth and eighteenth centuries.

John Evelyn, in an appeal for the resumption of sumptuary laws entitled *Tyrannus or The Mode* (1661), chastised the English for allowing the French tailor to exercise a Circean transformative power over the nation, erasing distinctions between the classes and the sexes. He clearly was less sanguine than Campbell about the tailor's promethean power of transformation: "Methinks a *French Taylor* with his Ell [measuring stick, about forty-five inches in length] in his hand, looks like the Enchantress Circe over the Companions of *Ulysses,* and changes them into as many formes. . . ."[7] At least the "new species of Beings" created by Campbell's tailor had a human form; they were not the grovelling beasts of Circe's island. Mandeville, however, was one of the first to express an enthusiastic interest in capitalizing on an economy that was not only driven by fashion but for which "fashion" was a metaphor— clothes and laws equally were "objects of mutability." Eighteenth-century culture, being a "culture of travesty," as Terry Castle has recently argued, was itself "the ultimate product of fashion."[8] *All* was transformation, and clothes were the visible sign of it.

Luxury stimulated an endless cycle of transformations prompted by desire. More particularly, a new economic system of speculation and credit stimulated this desire. As P. G. M. Dickson has shown, such an economy was made possible by what he calls "the financial revolution" of the 1690s—characterized by the incorporation of the Bank of England in 1694, the establishment of the National Debt for the funding of wars generated by competition for new markets, and the large numbers of joint-stock companies associated with projects and schemes financed by new systems of credit.[9] Trade itself seemed to be falling into the hands of joint-stock companies allied with the bank and the credit structure. And in an exchange economy, sumptuary laws were counterproductive, impeding the necessary "Shiftings and Changings of Modes" that fuelled an economy of desire. Such laws, Mandeville argued, "may be of use in an indigent Country, after great Calamities of War, Pestilence, or Famine, when Work has stood still, and the Labour of the Poor been interrupted; but to introduce them into an opulent Kingdom is the wrong way to consult the Interest of it."[10] J. G. A. Pocock in his important study of the recurrence of the "Machiavellian moment" in history, convincingly demonstrates that, following the financial revolution, "money and credit dissolved the social frame into a shifting mobility of objects that were desired and fictions that were fantasized about."[11] Increasingly, little remained that was not subject to an economy of desire and transformation.

Increasingly in seventeenth-century England, with the progressive disappearance of sumptuary laws, the impact of the financial revolution, the disproportionate growth of metropolitan London, and the general burgeoning of wealth and consumption, it became apparent that women were being held accountable for the forces of transformation unleashed by luxury. Sumptuary laws of the fifteenth and sixteenth centuries, as well as general writings on fashion and other threats to the social order, focused less on women than on men. Men were seen more as creatures of display, and, as N. B. Harte has suggested, "women, like children, were dealt with only incidentally, and they took their status and their dress eligibility from their husbands or fathers."[12] Even in 1661, John Evelyn focused in his *Tyrannus or The Mode* on the apparel of men, expressing his anxieties about the desire of English men to emulate and rival the French.

More insistently, however, it was the fashion industry associated with women that was deemed responsible for disrupting the order maintained by sumptuary laws. When sumptuary laws began to lapse in the seventeenth century, especially in the latter half of the century when the credit economy opened up new markets and new mechanisms for the importation of luxury items, countless writers attacked or promoted what they claimed to be the prodigious desires of women as the cause for new and disturbing social transformations. For Mandeville, an ardent supporter of the new credit economy, women were pathologically but gloriously accountable for these transformations: the economy was dependent on their criminal desires. Ideological opposition to the economy of credit also focused on women, but without allowing for the paradoxical redemption of their supposed vices.

One way to account for this intensification of misogynistic discourse from the late seventeenth century and through the eighteenth is to examine the economic changes occurring at this time effected by credit, changes that were represented in gendered terms. If fashionable women were increasingly represented as demanding and stimulating an economy associated with luxury, such a representation was tied to the way in which the credit economy was emblematized—surprisingly, by the proponents of credit. Credit, associated with speculation, exchange, fantasy, the passions of hope and fear, hysterical fluctuations, the illusion of substance—was represented as female, particularly as a woman of fashion. The economy of desire as facilitated by credit is depicted as a feminine economy; mutability is inscribed onto the very character of credit, the symbol of the new economics. For example, in his periodical *The Review*, Defoe refers to "the Lady Credit"—his "beautiful countess."[13] Significantly, a healthy economy for Defoe is best represented by Lady Credit's being fashionably attired and available to be circulated among the greatest number of men: In King William's time, he observes, she was but in Rags, but now "my Lord T[reasure]r has bought her new Cloaths, dress'd her up like a Princess—And now she is as Gay and as Bright as ever she was, and is become the whole Nation's Mistress" (Aug. 8, 1710).[14]

Defoe brings to this characterization of credit an assumption that he shares with Mandeville: women's vices are necessary to an economy that, for better or worse, is based on luxury. "In the open, Large, and Plentiful Living," Defoe argues, "is that Luxury Maintain'd, which I say however it may be a Vice in Morals, may at the same time be a Vertue in Trade, and of this, I confess I cannot be forward to say, I would have it Suppress'd, a great share of our Trade, and for ought I know, two Millions of our People live by it, and depend wholly upon it" (Feb. 7, 1706).[15] Although Defoe expresses considerable trepidation about an economy that is dependent upon luxury, an "investment" economy emblematized as a woman who, if not decoratively attired, is subject to the vapours and hysteria, some of his fears have been allayed as he depicts women being dressed *by* men and circulated among them.[16] Defoe's fears could be partly allayed, because women's bodies were deprived of substantiality in the market of male texts.

As Luce Irigaray has argued in her essay "Women on the Market," "when women are exchanged, woman's body must be treated as an *abstraction*."[17] When women are exchanged between men, she explains, they assume two bodies: *A commodity—a woman—is divided into two irreconcilable "bodies":* her "natural" body and her socially valued, exchangeable body. . . ."

> At the most, the commodities—or rather the relationships among them—are the material alibi for the desire for relations among men. To this end, the commodity is divested of its body and reclothed in a form that makes it suitable for exchange among men.[18]

One consequence of the new exchange economy, as Nicholas Barbon observed in 1696, was that "things" or commodities had been deprived of their bodies or "substance" previously guaranteed by the stable values of land: "For *Things have no value in themselves,* it is *opinion* and *fashion* brings them into use and gives them a value."[19] The credit economy demanded that things be reclothed, be invested with value, just as Defoe symbolically represents in his reclothing of "Lady Credit." As this economy is emblematized as female, so too are *women* assumed to have no other substance than that which they externally acquire from fashion. In an economy of "investiture," dominated by fashion and represented as female—a potentially hysterical "Lady Credit" being dressed and constrained by men—women are the visible objects for adornment and are depicted as the inert site of the tailor's art. Like Prometheus, according to Campbell, the tailor (in this case, Defoe) animates the human—the female—"form," but does so merely by dressing it. Although Campbell does not substitute "female" for "human" in his work, the implication nevertheless is that those who "dress," those who have given themselves up to the forces of a commodity culture, are symbolically female. Displaying their identity through outward forms, they surrender the material body culturally associated with the male.[20] Insofar as men became the objects of fashionable display, they were perceived to have been feminized—symbolically accorded the exchangeable bodies of women. If men were referred to in relation to fashion, it was as men who were effeminized by fashion—beaus, fops, gallants.

In this economy, women are presented (both by advocates and detractors[21] of the credit economy) as having no substance; they merely have desires, which may not be their own. Feminine desires for investiture merely promoted capital investment by men. In describing credit (and, by implication, the women in a credit economy whose activities and characteristics imitate Lady Credit's), Defoe describes its essential nothingness. It is a nothingness so profound that it confounds all attempts to read beneath the surface. According to Defoe,

> Like the soul in the body [public credit] acts as all substance, yet it itself is immaterial; it gives motion, yet it cannot be said to exist; it creates forms, yet it has no self to form; it is neither quantity nor quality, it has not *whereness,* or whenness,

site or habit. If I should say it is the essential shadow of something that is not, should I not puzzle the thing rather than explain it, and leave you and myself more in the dark than we were before?[22]

Credit, and hence woman, is depicted as an insubstantial creature of fashion who can only be known through her effects in the marketplace. And "Nothing" (as we know from Pope's depiction of a culture of metamorphosis ruled by a feminine "Dulness" or animate nothing in *The Dunciad*) is the absent center of Fashion. The substantiality and corporeality of the body is replaced by the materiality of the sign.[23]

Jean Baudrillard, in his *Critique of the Political Economy of the Sign,* argues that fashion constitutes "the final disqualification of the body, its subjection to . . . the total circulation of signs."[24] Fashion contributes to the disappearance of the body. Women, thus, are not shown by the proponents of the credit economy actively participating in the economy; at least, they do not *consciously* control it. Within this system, men are thus burdened with the privilege of capitalizing upon the amoral and largely unconscious desires of women and translating them into what they conceive to be the common good. The contempt for women and for the vices Mandeville attributed to them in his *Fable of the Bees* is contained by his admiration for an economy of credit, the symbolic representation of which was woman—"Lady Credit." The credit economy controlled by men could exploit and capitalize upon these vices. Mandeville could simultaneously express his antipathy toward the real body of woman and venerate her symbolic, "reclothed," body in the context of the new credit economy—an economy of fashion and metamorphosis. The real body of woman is subsumed by her exchange value.

The debate about luxury and the new economy that sustained it was carried out in terms of fashion and with reference both to the symbolic (or exchangeable) and the natural bodies of women. Few agreed with Mandeville on the beneficial economic effects of women's "prodigious" desires cultivated by, and even represented through, credit. Many feared the associated realm of transformation being opened up by an economy driven by the demand for luxury, the desire for which was increasingly attributed to women. The symbolic body of woman figured forth as Lady Credit was rejected by many who argued against this economy by cleaving to nature. The anonymous author of the pamphlet "Whipping Tom, or a Rod for a Proud Lady" (1730) derides women for "look[ing] more like Poppets, or Anticks in some Carnival, than the production of human nature."[25] And they have become, Whipping Tom insists, nothing more than they appear to be. They were accused of having no more substance than the wooden fashion dolls sent from France to England during the eighteenth century.[26] Behind the drapery, which itself was subject to continuous transformation, there was no essential substance. The impression that women made was created neither by weight nor substance, but through display. Not only were their transformations dictated by fashion but they themselves, in having no bodies but their fashionable ones, were emblems of fashion and the credit economy that made the metamorphic world of fashion possible. They were constituted by their ever-mutable and interchangeable appearances. The demand for luxury, many argued, replaced the substance of culture by "outward Forms." "All Ages, and all Countries," according to Andrew Fletcher, a Commonwealthman writing in the late seventeenth century, "concurred to sink Europe into an Abyss of Pleasures; which were rendered the more expensive by a perpetual Change of the Fashions in Clothes, Equipage, and Furniture of Houses."[27]

With sumptuary laws, dress had once been the sign of a fixed and unvarying social structure. Clothes had once provided, at least in theory (the laws were actually quite difficult to enforce), a symbolic register of social hierarchy and of identity. John Evelyn, while acknowledging that "Garments be Superficials, and extrinsecal to us," maintained that a person's character can be deduced from them: "if (as *Solomon*) a Wise Man may be known by his gate; a Fantastick may be no less by his Apparel."[28] There existed for Evelyn a necessary conjunction between appearance and identity, as well as between clothes and the body. Clothing rendered the body—the body deemed by Evelyn to be "natural" and derived from God, but which to us appears more a register of a cultural identity (one's class position, gender)—visible. Evelyn argued that clothes must reveal substance—of the body, and of character. How was it possible, Evelyn queried, to be true to the commandments of God and to nature when, through fashion, men and women neglect to preserve the "Lineaments of their Bodies?" Plato, according to Evelyn, allowed it "only to *Curtesans* and *Comedians* to vary Dresses: since 'twas but a kind of Hippocrisie to be every day in a new Shape, and *Masquerad*."[29]

When fashion and women began to be associated with capital investment, however, the destabilizing forces of transformation (the same generated by the institution of the masquerade)[30] were put into play. The natural body was thought to disappear, and with it, the means by which identity could be read. Indeed, identity itself was pronounced to be so mercurial, so subject to fashion, that clothes seemed an emblem of it (as we see represented in Swift's *Tale of a Tub*). With the rise of the credit economy, the self too was thought to have mere *contingent* value when the reality of the body and even of land (and therefore property in oneself) were brought into question. As Pocock has observed:

> Once property was seen to have a symbolic value, expressed in coin or credit, the foundations of personality themselves appeared imaginary or at best consensual: the individual could exist, even in his own sight only at the fluctuating value imposed upon him by his fellows. . . .[31]

That one's value (in this system) existed only in one's name or reputation, and that this was a property held by others, had enormous consequence for writers.

It is not surprising in an age dominated by credit and fashion, both of which were depicted in terms of metamorphosis, that writing concerned with fashion itself, or with articles of fashion, should reformulate Ovid's *Metamorphoses* for a new world of transformation. Many writers on the subject of fashion felt inspired to emulate Ovid, to see themselves as neo-Ovids and imagine that if Ovid were to appear in the eighteenth century, he would write not about transformations of women's bodies, but of women's fashions. An anonymous poem on the subject of the "hoop petticoat,"[32] entitled "The Farthingale Revived, or more Work for the Cooper" (1711), suggests that

> Ovid's mistress in her loose attire,
> Would cease to charm his eyes, or raise Desire.
> Were he at *Bath,* and had these Coats in View,
> He'd write his *Metamorphoses* a new.[33]

To explore the relationship between credit and fashion, I will examine in the remainder of this chapter some eighteenth-century writings on fashion, to reveal their assumptions about the new credit economy. I will deal not so much with fashion itself (the details of various garments and styles) as with *writing on fashion* and its participation in an Ovidian metamorphic world created by public credit. I am particularly interested in observing the ways in which the transformations were depicted in Ovidian narratives, not only because Ovid was the writer of metamorphoses, but because there was also a fashionable industry in translations of Ovid. Such an interest in Ovid at this time is connected with a larger cultural interest in the shape-shifting brought about by the financial revolution. One way in which to read the credit economy and the responses to a society of transformation created by credit is to examine how Ovidian myths of metamorphosis are rewritten in discussions regarding fashion.

II

Ovidian narratives of metamorphosis, as Richard Campbell observed, provided both a way of reading this protean economy of desire and also a way of capitalizing on it. Not only was Ovid's text a fashionable site for the emblematic representation of the mutability of fashion, but it was incorporated into the vestimentary signifier itself: Ovidian tales were depicted both on buttons (the size of large coins) or embroidered onto the fabric of coats and dresses.[34] Fashion's "fabrications" were always narratives of metamorphosis. Ovid was investment capital in a culture that both feared and embraced transformation, transformation both sublime and monstrous.

Ovid was everywhere translated and adapted in eighteenth-century England, especially his *Metamorphoses*. As Margaret Doody has observed, "Augustan poets in their use of classical authors were constantly engaged in transforming the transformers."[35] One of the most significant translations was Samuel Garth's 1717 edition of Ovid's *Metamorphoses* in fifteen books, published by Jacob Tonson and translated by several "eminent hands"—Joseph Addison, Matthew Prior, Alexander Pope, John Gay, and incorporating Dryden's translation of Book XII. A rival edition appeared in the same year, published by the notorious hack bookseller Edmund Curll, and compiled (and partially translated) by an extremely reluctant and self-deprecating author working for Curll, George Sewell.[36] That there should be a competitive struggle for translations of Ovid at this historical moment indicates a broad interest in *The Metamorphoses* that was hardly accidental. This revival of interest in Ovid, this culturally significant demand for tales of transformation, arose in a society that was itself one of fashion and metamorphosis, brought about by an economy of credit and speculation. Garth, in the preface to his edition, laments that in his own time, in contrast to Ovid's, not only has commerce dictated what is to be produced and read but authors themselves have banded together in rival corporations. Further, to produce any work of literature, one has to compete with the only game in town—the stock market: "The only Talents in Esteem at present are those of *Exchange Ally;* one Tally is worth a Grove of Bays; and 'tis of much more Consequence to be well read in the Tables of Interest, and the Rise and Fall of Stocks, than in the Revolution of Empires."[37] Participating in this rivalry, Garth is, of course, implicated in this fashionable literary economy, however much he would like to distinguish himself and his miscellany translators of Ovid from the Grub Street hack writers imitating his imitations of Ovid.

Immediately prior to the publication of Garth's compilation of imitations, Pope reflected on the metamorphosing of Ovid in the publishing industry. In his poem "Sandys's Ghost: Or a Proper New Ballad on the New Ovid's Metamorphosis" (1717),[38] he describes all of the authors of disparate interests and political ideologies that Tonson has pressed into service and doubts that anything significant can come of his project:

> Now, *Tonson,* list thy Forces all,
>   Review them, and tell Noses;
> For to poor *Ovid* shall befal
>   A strange *Metamorphosis.*
>
> A *Metamorphosis* more strange
>   Than all his Books can vapour;
> 'To what . . . shall *Ovid* change?'
>   Quoth *Sandys: To Waste-Paper.*[39]

Even the Garth edition of Ovid's *Metamorphoses* to which Pope contributed, Pope fears, might undergo a frightening transformation into "Waste-Paper" ("Sandys's Ghost"), especially as this edition was in competition for readers with Curll's rival edition. As we shall presently see, Pope's reference to waste paper is connected to a fear of paper money or paper credit. The new economy of credit penetrated all aspects of culture. The literary work itself yielded to its transformative powers, yielded to fashion. Many authors in fact joyfully succumbed to the literary marketplace presided over by fashion. The anonymous author of the play *The Humours of the Court; or, Modern Gallantry* (1732), a ballad opera inspired by Gay's *Beggar's Opera,* discusses the literary modes in relation to the metamorphic world of fashion. His compliance with fashion is appropriately figured as fashion, with the preface to his play appearing to be the necessary fashion accoutrement to adorn his book:

A Preface is become so much the Fashion now-a-Days, that a Book looks as much in a *Dishabille* without it, as a Lady without Stays. . . . However, as one had as good be out of the world as out of Fashion, partly to comply with that, and partly with the Importunity of my Bookseller, who would not buy the Opera without it, I have condescended to say a few Words in Behalf thereof.[40]

Even works of literature, succumbing to fashion, resemble women's bodies that must be fashionably decorated and adorned to be circulated and exchanged. On the one hand, fashion dictates that all works and bodies appear in a prescribed form, the modish dress. On the other hand, fashion requires continual novelty.

In this regard, the survival of an older literary form—the imitation—is curious. But the imitation appears in a new context and a new light with the commodification of the literary work. Like fashion, imitation had its parallel in the new marketing techniques created by a demand for the appearance of status—the desire to emulate and imitate the higher social classes or the more well-known authors. Imitation in fact participates in and replicates a system of fashionable exchange. Thus, when credit or "Exchange Alley" had opened up the literary marketplace in the late seventeenth century and when the notions of "literary property" and property in authorship were being contested, "authorship" was as subject to the metamorphic world of fashion as were clothes (and thus the integrity of the body) in the absence of sumptuary laws.[41] It is not surprising, then, that in observing the extent to which the literary economy was directed by fashion, writers not only would self-consciously write about fashion, but would also fashionably imitate each other's imitations of Ovid.

John Gay, like Alexander Pope in his *Rape of the Lock* (1712–14), wished to write about fashion—clothes, the articles of the toilette, and other commodities that women are so devoted to that they spurn the advances of men and exercise a considerable amount of power in the fashionable world, where appearances are so important.[42] Gay wrote about fashion both to express his anxiety about the new credit economy and to arrest the shape-shifting potential of women through fashion. In 1713, he published a lengthy poem "in three books," entitled *The Fan*. Gay, however, presents this "fan" to women not as a gift to flatter their vanity or to allow them to arm themselves against male violations of their "rites of pride," but to arrest the flight of women from men through shape-shifting by transforming the fan into an emblem of the dangers of metamorphosis.

The poem begins with Corinna disdainfully rejecting the suit of Strephon. Unsuccessful in his use of the mortal skills of singing, flattering, and bribing to win Corinna, he appeals to Venus to fashion him a "bright Toy" to "charm her Sight."[43] Venus ascends to the heavens to attend to the fan's fabrication. Gay pauses in his narration to reflect on the celestial toyshop, wherein various Cupids are busy creating the "glitt'ring Implements of Pride" (I. 114) that women use in their war against men—snuff-boxes, patches, combs, petticoats:

> What force of thought, What numbers can express,
> Th'inconstant Equipage of Female Dress?
> How the strait Stays the slender Waste constrain,
> How to adjust the Manteau's sweeping Train?
> How to adjust the Petticoat surround,
> With the capacious Hoop of Whalebone bound?
>
> Should you the rich Brocaded Suit unfold,
> Where rising Flowers grow stiff with frosted Gold;
> The dazzled Muse would from her subject stray,
> And in a Maze of Fashions lose her Way.
>   (I. 229–234, 241–244)

The world of *The Fan* is so unnatural, so embedded in the denaturing metamorphic structure of the commercial world (where rising "Flowers grow stiff with frosted Gold") that Gay's Muse is entrapped and imprisoned in its Maze. It is like the world of public credit— "the essential shadow of something that is not," something that would only "puzzle," according to Defoe, were we to attempt to explain it.

Corinna, however, ultimately is rescued from the abyss or labyrinth of pleasure and fashion when she receives the fan, heretofor the emblem of fashionable weaponry. Various gods and goddesses, concerned that women wield too many armaments of the fashionable variety, have intervened in the construction of the fan to transform its function. Depicted on the fan are scenes of tragic metamorphoses consequent upon ill nature—pride, jealousy, narcissism. The fan is itself transformed into a tale, a story: willful self-transformation through dress is dangerous self-alienation. Gay exposes the economic origins and interests behind female fashion, and he critiques luxury through fashion. The fan is no longer a fashionable object through which the self is constituted, but a mirror for reading the self and beyond the self—the self inscribed in history. Corinna is brought back to herself after her prideful self-abandonment to fashion. She is prevented from being the woman of fashion that she desires to be. But these desires, Gay suggests, are not intrinsic to women but are cultivated by an economy of desire facilitated by credit. She is, like a wooden fashion doll, animated by the tailor, by desires created in a world of fashion. Women should therefore resist accepting as natural to the female sex the qualities that Defoe had attributed to "Lady Credit." Neither narcissistic self-absorption nor devotion to fashionable commodities empowered women. It was in the interest of men actively promoting or engaged in reaping the benefits of credit and mercantile expansion that women's desires be reconceived in terms of economically useful desires and that the question of there being other desires be put out of consideration. And there were possibilities for the body other than its commercial exploitation—being dressed and ornamented for display.

Gay's poem concludes with Corinna recognizing other desires, desires of the natural body which have been suppressed by her preoccupation with things fashionable: "Why has my Pride against my Heart rebell'd?/She sighing cry'd . . ." (III. 196–197). In being liberated from the fashionable world and the desires created in that labyrinthine realm, she recognizes the true desires of the heart and the body, weds Strephon, and allows her body to be the natural site of generativity and reproduction. We can, of course, see that such a return to apparent self-possession and "natural" desires allows Corinna to be possessed by Strephon and that this natural alternative to the forces of fashion is no doubt equally confining and disempowering. But the battle to determine for women their true interests and desires continued to be waged in works that examined women's fashions, works that were fundamentally concerned with promoting or opposing an economy based on credit.

Alexander Pope wrote to Gay that he admired *The Fan* both as poem and as moral emblem—a fan that, in displaying fashion, defeats its own attempts to subvert nature. He referred to *The Fan* as that "agreeable machine [that] shall play into the Hands of Posterity."[44] The poem, he suggests, will be read and used by posterity. The fan itself consequently will no longer be used by women as a weapon but will encourage generation and posterity. As predicted by Pope, *The Fan* did produce posterity, generate imitations. The next generation of "fans," however, were creatures of fashion, of fashionable imitation. Gay might rescue Corinna from the shape-shifting necessitated by an economy dependent on the perpetual re-dressing of the body, but he could not protect his poem and his reputation from the same commercial forces. In 1716, appeared *The Petticoat* by a "Mr. Gay," *"Cousin-German"* (as he styles himself in his epistle dedicatory to the ladies) to the author of the admired production of *The Fan*. Although Francis Chute, who signs himself either J. or Joseph Gay, insists that he "by no means, desire[s] to Graft a Reputation upon . . . [the] Stock" of John Gay,[45] he reveals, through his image of hybridization, his fashionable conversion of things cultural into nature, and how rooted in fashion is his claim. This Gay-like reader and imitator of *The Fan*, rather than being inspired to resist the endless cycle of fashionable and false transformations that John Gay counsels both the subject of his poem, Chloe, and his reader to avoid, both writes an imitation of Gay's work *and* appropriates Gay's name, transforming himself into a fashionable version of Gay.

The name "Gay," due to John Gay's success with *The Fan, Rural Sports* (1713), and especially *Trivia* (1716), was appropriated as a fashionable commodity by the printer and bookseller Edmund Curll (the same "unspeakable" Curll who engaged a number of writers to rival Samuel Garth's edition of Ovid's *Metamorphoses*), who delegated the name to two of his hack writers, Francis Chute and John Durant Breval. Breval used the name Joseph Gay or J. Gay for at least half of his works; Chute, according to evidence that Curll provided in his apology for his profession, *The Curliad* (1729), was responsible for *The Petticoat* (later reprinted as *The Hoop Petticoat*). Further, Curll, even though he did not own a copyright for any of John Gay's works, endeavored to ensure the eminence and reputation of Gay for the sake of his pseudo-Gays, by bringing out a biography of Gay—*Memoirs of the Life and Writings of Mr. Gay* (1733)—following the death of this very bankable author.[46] Such an attempt to capitalize on Gay opened up a new world of metamorphosis. Pope, in his depiction of scurrilously competitive bookmongers in Book II of *The Dunciad,* depicts Curll desperately trying to grasp the insubstantial nothings that were the products of his press—both the printed page and the authors:

> Curl stretches after Gay, but Gay is gone,
> He grasps an empty Joseph for a John:
> So Proteus, hunted in a nobler shape,
> Became, when seiz'd, a puppy, or an ape.[47]

Pope suggests that Curll cannot ever hope to capture a writer as prestigious and self-respecting as John Gay to perform the scribbling tasks that are demanded of hired hack writers; the most that he can capture (if one can be allowed to capture a protean form) is a pseudonymous hireling author, a Joseph Gay, whose reality and independent existence are in dispute.

Curll, in capturing not Gay but, as Pope reveals, an "empty Joseph"—a joseph being a great-coat as well as a Curll-imposed pseudonym—captures nothing but an identity that inheres in clothes. Behind the name, behind the coat, there is nothing. Pope, moreover, intimates that Curll does not even have the power to exploit fashion effectively: he depicts Curll chasing a fashionable embroidered suit that he deems to be his rightful possession, but which is "by an unpay'd taylor snatch'd away" (II. 110). Pope associates Curll's printed works with sartorial articles of fashion, equally mutable and subject to the marketplace—thereby further revealing the extent to which the economies of fashion and the literary marketplace are ruled by "Credit," or Dulness. And the economies of fashion and credit are characterized by indebtedness: those who are slaves to what is fashionable readily accumulate both financial and, in having appropriated the works and names of other writers, literary debts.

The term "credit" applied to the world of paper currency (paper credit) as well. Such a revolution in the concept of the medium for exchange also had an impact on the other world of paper—the printing industry. Everything appeared to be subject to the fantasy world of fashion. Curll's manifest fictions, the ephemeral paper leaves that he circulated and traded in, were, according to Pope, part of this fantastical world of paper credit. Commenting on the perception that credit, and mobile property in general, allowed the substitution of reality for fantasy and fiction, J. G. A. Pocock observed that the fear of "paper" became rather comprehensive:

> Paper, while produced by the same forces and serving the same functions as gold, is less durable in its physical form and therefore infinitely more liable to subjectivity. There is a danger that all men, and all sublunary things, will now become things of paper, which is worse even than to become things of gold.[48]

The circulation of credit, of paper, can render valueless and insubstantial even that which seeks to establish its fundamental difference from fashion. Surely Gay and Pope wished to distinguish themselves from those who wrote Ovidian narratives that had as their focus the transformation of an author of little or no substance into a contemporary author of some reputation, such as Gay. Joseph Gay and the others who appear in Curll's miscellany compilations of writing on women's fashion[49] do not appear to share the anxieties that Pope and Gay expressed about the transformations of women in response to the dictates of a credit economy.

Whereas Pope depicted Curll and his tribe of hack writers—who published à la mode, writing fleeting *imitations,* with borrowed names, of works on women's fashions—as being confined to the insubstantial and fantastic world of credit, the phantasmagoric neo-

Gays conceived of themselves as being liberated from substance, from the body and from property in authorship (just like the women of fashion that they depict in their own writing) in the world of fashion and imitation. They could attempt to capitalize on the potential, opened up by credit, for an endless succession of transformations. They celebrated their own shape-shifting possibilities opened up by the merging worlds of commodity aesthetics and (paper) credit. Joseph Gay, through his imitation of John Gay (an imitation in name only) eagerly participates in the world of fashionable metamorphosis. Both the various depictions of women's nature and the status of the literary text are brought into conflict on a woman's body, in the field of fashion.

Refashioning himself as Mr. Gay because it is fashionable to imitate and because the imitation has all the exchange value of objects of fashion, Francis Chute (d. 1745), the Curllean Gay, tailors Gay's poem to his own specifications. And in so doing he challenges Gay's assumption that the natural self (either Corinna's or the poet's) can be rescued from the world of fashionable transformation. For John Gay himself, the self-appointed Gay suggests, has rewritten or refashioned Ovid to discuss fashion. Even the venerable Gay has picked up and altered stories of the great poet of change and transformation. In appropriating Gay's name, this would-be Gay has even challenged the existence or substance of a "real" Gay, so protean are his subsequent incarnations. Moreover, Gay's works were not even Gay's property; they were the property of the bookseller or a group of booksellers. For Chute, Gay is not an author, but only a name that can be affixed to a body of writing. In the world of credit and fashion, all that signified was *reputation* (a person's "credit"), the fashionable version of the self. And fashionable identity, residing in dress and reputation, was alienable property, infinitely appropriable. In his poem *The Petticoat* (1716), Chute represents his own freedom to shape-shift by reflecting on women and fashion.

In *The Petticoat,* Chute depicts the deification of a fashionable woman's maid, Betty, for her creation of a hoop-petticoat for her pregnant mistress Chloe, a garment so capacious that it effectively disguises the effects of Chloe's surrender to sexual desire and the body. The hoop-petticoat is used to cover all sorts of natural sins and physical transformations. Fashion is used to conceal and disguise the "lineaments" of the "natural" body, even when the body is itself undergoing a metamorphosis, seeming most emphatically to deny the insubstantiality that the world of fashion confers upon it. The hoop petticoat can once again render the body invisible, allowing the woman to preserve inviolate her reputation, her fashionable self. This instrument of fashion can re-arm the woman and allow her freely to participate in an economy of shape-shifting. She is returned to the realm of fashion. Clearly, this is as much a tale about Joseph Gay's fashionable impersonation of John Gay and the status of imitation as fashionable commodity (through the equally fashionable vehicle of Ovidian metamorphosis) as it is about Chloe. The tale is a mock commentary upon Chute's own activity of disguise. In exposing Chloe's transformation through dress, he self-consciously exposes his own transformations through imitation. Like the woman he depicts, this new Gay is committed to the metamorphic world of fashion and imitation, even in his own appropriation of the name Gay.

Even though writers such as Chute are part of the world of fashion and, as such, are subject to the whims and fancies of "Lady Credit," they hold a certain power over women that ensures that women cannot escape needing the protection of, and thereby driving the economy of, fashion. In appearing fashionable and therefore effeminized, they have disguised their phallic source of power. In ancient times, as is depicted on Betty's thimble,

> CALISTO here without her Quiver's seen,
> Stretch'd at her Ease upon the flow'ry Green;
> Whilst Lustful JOVE assumes DIANA's Shape,
> And in a PETTICOAT conceals his *Rape*.[50]

Gods have cross-dressed as women in petticoats in order to rape them. In modern times, suggests Chute, mortal men have assumed similar disguises. Yet what follows from a rape is not the metamorphoses of women into such things of nature as trees, brooks, or animals as in Ovid; rather, women enter the endlessly shape-shifting realm of fashion. The violation of women's bodies ensures that women will perpetually require the industry and the goods supplied through credit. Fashionable men have not relinquished their desire for the natural body of woman, but their main interest is in ensuring that women abandon that body for their symbolic, fashionable one.

Giles Jacob, another of Curll's writers, depicted just such a transfer of women's interests in a crude imitation of Pope's *Rape of the Lock*, entitled *Rape of the Smock* (1717). Not only does he engage in a symbolic rape of Pope's reputation or symbolic body by imitating him, but he requests of his female audience that they forgive him for "his daring to commit a *Rape* upon a *Part* of their *Furniture*, which ought to be Sacred."[51] He presents a situation in which a woman, Celia offers her actual body to the man who has stolen her most prized possession—her smock—so that she can recover it from him. Her physical body is insignificant and meaningless in comparison with the smock, which she fetishizes as her "Veil so sacred," her "Mystic Veil."[52] This commodity is valued in and of itself, but also for its preservation of her symbolic body, her reputation. She fully is a creature of fashion, devoted both to articles of fashion and to an identity constituted through dress and as credit. In offering up her body to the ravisher of her smock, she recognizes no desires associated with the "natural" body; her body is merely a commodity to be exchanged for the "symbolic" body created by an exchange economy.

Pope's *Rape of the Lock* also depicts another rape of a woman's symbolic body, characterized by a fashionably dressed lock of hair, which is carefully tended for "the destruction of mankind."[53] Like Celia in *The Rape of the Smock*, Belinda would have sacrificed her physical body for the preservation of her adored lock/reputation/fashionable self—"Oh hadst thou, cruel! been content to seize/Hairs less in sight, or any hairs but these!" (IV. 175–176). But the Baron's "fatal engine" (III. 149) closes upon what she most wishes to preserve inviolate: "The meeting points the sacred hair dissever/From the fair head, for ever, and for ever!" (III. 153–154). And to complete the dissociation of Belinda's fashionable and natural selves, Pope ensures that the lock not be the fetishized object of any one person. Belinda's ravished lock, unlike the ravished smock in Jacob's poem, is not returned to her. Instead, the lock is translated or metamorphosed from the realm of fashion into the celestial sphere where it becomes a fixed, guiding star. Belinda is prevented from perpetuating her fashionable self, and a return to the natural body is envisaged. Rather than being a commodity fetishized by Belinda, the lock becomes the non-exclusive property of stargazers.

Pope was critical not only of an economy sustained by mercantile expansion but also of the shape-shifting potential that women gained in such an economy. Belinda initially is depicted as being surrounded by and adorned with the "glitt'ring Spoil" culled from the trade in luxury. Her toilette table reveals an assortment of commodities from the exotic countries that the joint-stock companies, financed by credit, were established to exploit:

> This Casket *India*'s glowing Gems unlocks,
> And all *Arabia* breathes from yonder Box.
> The Tortoise here and Elephant unite,
> Transformed to *Combs*, the speckled and the white.
> Here Files of Pins extend their shining Rows,
> Puffs, Powders, Patches, Bibles, Billet-doux.
>
> (I. 133–138)

Belinda uses the resources of an economy of transformation to undergo the necessary metamorphoses allowed by fashion to escape sexuality, marriage, procreation—those things that Pope has his surrogate "Clarissa" chide Belinda for neglecting because of her vain, narcissistic pursuits. In having denied the body and embraced fashion, in this case the lock of hair that Sylphs (themselves the spirits of deceased fashionable coquettes) ceaselessly protect, Belinda is solely engaged in her devotion to fashion as she performs her "sacred rites of Pride" (I. 128). These rites Pope wishes to disable, thus disrupting the entire credit and fashion system.

Arresting, by means of the rape of the invested self, the power of women narcissistically dedicated to fashion was one of Pope's modes of cancelling credit. He also has recourse to another scheme for halting fashionable metamorphoses. The most frightening and permanently transformative penalty for shape-shifting and devotion to commodities is represented in the famous Cave of Spleen. The spleen or anger vented by a woman following the loss of the objects of her desire causes the transformation of a woman's body into those very objects:

> Unnumber'd Throngs on ev'ry side are seen
> Of Bodies chang'd to various Forms by *Spleen*.
> Here living *Teapots* stand, one Arm held out,

> One bent; the Handle this, and that the Spout:
> A Pipkin there like *Homer's Tripod* walks;
> Here sighs a Jar, and there a Goose-pye talks;
>
> (IV. 47–52)

This is a transformation of the body that, unlike pregnancy, cannot be hidden by dress. Fashion cannot conceal this new commodified version of the body and of the unnatural desire for things. But these images are actually accurate and static emblems of fashion, where the fashionable body is already so denaturalized that it has become a thing. Belinda herself is spared this fate, but the scene remains as a threat and warning.

Ambrose Philips, known for his rivalry with Pope in their writing of pastoral poetry, published a broadside—"The *TEA-POT; or The Lady's Transformation*" (ca. 1730)—depicting a much more horrifying scene of the transformation of women into teapots.[54] It is horrifying because the agency, and therefore the remedy, for such a metamorphosis is not a woman's desire for things (nor her spleen when that desire is frustrated), but a goddess's. Philips offers no critique of a society of transformation; he merely indicts what he supposes to be the innate and intemperate jealousies of women. Elizabeth Thomas (1677–1731), however, provides a larger framework for an indictment of the fashionable activity of tea-drinking among women in order to justify the ultimate transformation of these women's bodies into teacups. Her poem "The Ladies Exercise at Tea . . . Or The Metamorphosis of a Set of Ladies into a Set of China Tea-Cups" was first published ca. 1729 and later, in 1743, added to a work first published in 1730 as *The Metamorphosis of the Town*.[55]

In this latter work, Thomas adopts the perspective of a knight who returns to London after having spent the past forty years in insulated rural retirement. His comments on the transformations of the town since 1690 are standard critiques of the metamorphoses wrought by luxury that were consequent upon the credit or financial revolution beginning in the 1690s. He laments the dissociation between sound and sense in artistic productions of the age: even *The Beggar's Opera* is mere "fustian" (15). But the general malaise of dissociation is most obviously represented in and characterized by the world of fashion or dress. As he and a companion stroll through the park, they come upon women that, according to their apparel, should be country wenches, but who are revealed by an interpreter who knows the fashions of the moment to be ladies of the court. That "Native Innocence" should be expressed as a "Mode" (20) strikes the knight as highly unnatural and incomprehensible. He thus engages in an extended iteration, closely following John Evelyn, of the need to collapse the fashionable distinction between appearance and reality, clothes and the body. Clothes must not "Strain . . . Nature's Excellence" (25). Men appear to be women, and women men. More serious than this gendered transgression of nature however, is the revelation that women have been entirely deprived of their very being. They are animated by the tailor and manipulated as puppets:

> Why, this is worse than all the rest,
> A somewhat! not to be exprest:
> So stiff; so forc'd; as if by Art,
> A Puppet mov'd, and play'd its Part.
>
> (23)

Hence, Thomas provides in this work an extended analysis of a culture of credit that was constantly metamorphosing women into things of fashion. She, like Pope, responds to this commodification of women by taking the process one step further. She reveals the symbolic horrors of commodity fetishism and she attempts to halt the metamorphosis of woman—a metamorphosis that confines rather than liberates—by presenting the transformation of women into teacups.

In examining these works by Thomas, we have to some extent explored the question of how at least one woman has responded to the impact that the credit economy has made on women. Yet the picture may be more complicated. In assuming the voice of a sometimes foolish old man commenting on the decline of English manners, Thomas herself has engaged in some narrative cross-dressing, some shape-shifting that perhaps participates in and perpetuates this fashionable appearance/reality dichotomy. And from what we know of Thomas's life, she actively participated in the world of credit. She is best known for her unauthorized sale of a packet of Pope's letters to the notorious Edmund Curll.[56] All that we can conclude is that Thomas both exploited *and* recognized the dangers of the economy of transformation. Women were clearly caught in the middle, especially when trying to enter the market themselves.

Lady Mary Wortley Montagu (1689–1762), on the other hand, was very clearly an apologist, both in her journalism and in her more personal epistolary reflections on fashion, for a Whig economic structure based on credit. In her *Letters* she refers to the intriguing "metamorphosis of some of [her] acquaintance" through dress, transformations which "appear as wondrous as any in Ovid."[57] Later, as a tourist and expatriate in Venice, Lady Mary is astonished by the delight she experiences at a masquerade ball. In a letter to Lady Pomfret, she reflects upon having been "animated" and enlivened by the Promethean tailor, through dress:

> I can hardly believe it is me dressed up at balls and stalking about at assemblies, and should not be so much surprised at suffering any of Ovid's transformations, having more disposition, as I thought, to harden into stone or timber than to be enlivened into these tumultuary entertainments. . . . [58]

Her transformations are not, she claims "Ovid's transformations." Whereas most women in Ovid are depicted metamorphosing into objects of nature, hardening into trees (timber) or melting into rivers to escape the predatory pursuits of gods and men, Lady Mary experiences the mobility associated with resisting a final form, of assuming a succession of forms. It is this *protean* insubstantiality, facilitated by clothes, that allows her to avoid either being caught or hardening. That Lady Mary rereads her own transformations as *sustaining* life (because of never having to harden into any one shape) also suggests her own political interest and investment in an *economy* of transformation, dependent on luxury.

In vigorously supporting the Whigs and Walpole she was also supporting a credit economy. The difference is that she resisted the allegorical implications of the representations of credit in the treatises of male Whig writers: despite the economic system based on exchange, *she* was not about to be exchanged between men. She perceived it to be an economy that certain women could actively (and consciously) participate in—buying and selling stock and commodities. Lady Mary even arranged to be a broker (for a man,

Nicholas-Francois Rémond) in the sale of South-Sea stock.[59] When his money was lost following the precipitous decline of the value of South Sea stocks in 1720, he threatened her with blackmail. Rémond demanded that she reimburse him for his losses or he would circulate rumors of an affair between them. He retaliated for his loss by threatening to violate her own credit—her reputation, her fashionable body. Anxieties about the loss of her credit began to affect her physical body: "I carry my distemper about me," she laments to her sister, Lady Mar, "in an Anguish of Mind that visibly decays my body every Day."[60] The pleasures of the credit economy were not unalloyed. Women in this economy did not have the freedom that, at other times, Lady Mary is convinced that they have had. Women's bodies may, indeed, be subject to "Ovid's transformations."

Eighteenth-century Ovidian narratives of metamorphosis frequently depicted the possibilities and anxieties created by the shifting world of class, gender, and commerce. Many writers on the subject of fashion, or in writing about their own experiences with fashion, reconstructed Ovidian tales of metamorphosis to account both for fashion and the metamorphosis of women through fashion. Significantly, economic issues, particularly the debate about the new credit economy, were waged on the field of fashion and had as their text the bodies of women.

NOTES

The writing of this chapter was made possible by an ASECS fellowship sponsored by McMaster University Library in the summer of 1988. A previous version was read at the meeting of Midwestern American Society for Eighteenth-Century Studies at Notre Dame, October 1988. I would like to thank James Carson and Abby Zanger for their thoughtful readings of various versions of this paper.

1. Richard Campbell, *The London Tradesman. Being an Historical Account of all the Trades, Professions, Arts . . . now Practised in the Cities of London and Westminster. Calculated for the Instruction of Youth in their Choice of Business,* 3rd ed. (London: Printed by T. Gardner, 1747), title page, and 191.

2. Bernard Mandeville, *The Fable of the Bees,* ed. F. B. Kaye, 2 vols. (Oxford: Clarendon Press, 1924), I. 25.

3. Anthony Ascham, *Of the Confusions and Revolution of Goverments* [sic] . . . (1649), 27. Cited in Michael McKeon, *The Origins of the English Novel* (Baltimore: Johns Hopkins Univ. Press, 1987), 204.

4. Mandeville, I. 130.

5. Mandeville, I. 226.

6. N. B. Harte, "State Control of Dress and Social Change in Pre-Industrial England," in *Trade, Government and Economy in Pre-Industrial England: Essays Presented to F. J. Fisher,* ed. D. C. Coleman and A. H. John (London: Weidenfeld and Nicolson, 1976), 132–165.

7. John Evelyn, *Tyrannus or The Mode: In a Discourse of Sumptuary Lawes* (1661), 2nd ed., ed. J. L. Nevinson (Oxford: Published for the Lutrell Society by Basil Blackwell, 1951), 8.

8. Terry Castle, "The Culture of Travesty: Sexuality and Masquerade in Eighteenth-Century England," in *Sexual Underworlds of the Enlightenment,* ed. G. S. Rousseau and Roy Porter (Manchester: Manchester Univ. Press, 1987), 157.

9. P. G. M. Dickson, *The Financial Revolution in England: A Study in the Development of Public Credit, 1688–1756* (London: Macmillan, 1967).

10. Mandeville, I. 251.

11. J. G. A. Pocock, *The Machiavellian Moment: Florentine Political Thought and the Atlantic Republican Tradition* (Princeton: Princeton Univ. Press, 1975), 459.

12. Harte, 143.

13. Daniel Defoe, *The Review of the State of the British Nation,* VII, No. 116 (Dec. 21, 1710), facsimile rpt. ed. compiled by Arthur W. Secord (New York: Columbia Univ. Press, 1938), XVIII, 461.

14. Defoe, *The Review,* XVII, 225.

15. Defoe, *The Review,* VI, 66.

16. I elaborate upon this in my essay, "Exchange Alley: The Sexual Politics of South Sea Investment," wherein I consider J. G. A. Pocock's observations about the "feminizations of time" in the late seventeenth century—especially his reluctance to pursue the gender implications of credit's feminization by Whig writers: Why masculine minds constantly symbolize the changeable, the unpredictable, and the imaginative as feminine . . . I would rather be excused from explaining" (*Virtue, Commerce, and History: Essays on Political Thought and History, Chiefly in the Eighteenth Century* (Cambridge: Cambridge Univ. Press, 1985), 99.

17. Luce Irigaray, *This Sex Which Is Not One,* trans. Catherine Porter (Ithaca: Cornell Univ. Press, 1985), 177.

18. Irigaray, 180. Italics hers.

19. Nicholas Barbon, *A Discourse Concerning Coining the New Money Lighter* (London, 1696; rpt. Westmead, Eng.: Gregg International Publishers, 1971), 43.

20. The oppositions that Pocock observes in eighteenth-century economic and social theory—between "virtue and passion, land and commerce, republic and empire, value and history" (*Machiavellian Moment,* 462)—were also gender distinctions. For civic humanists, "virtue," accorded a stability guaranteed by land and property, is a masculine quality; the passions, associated with commerce, are deemed feminine qualities.

21. In his poem *To a Lady* (1735)—Epistle II of his *Epistles to Several Persons (Moral Essays)*—Alexander Pope disparagingly refers to the effects of commodity culture and the exchange economy on women. In a culture in which women are "bred to disguise" (1. 203), women are rendered characterless and bodiless; they can only be distinguished by their dress:

> Nothing so true as what you [Martha Blount] once let fall,
> 'Most Women have no Characters at all.'
> Matter too soft a lasting mark to bear,
> And best distinguish'd by black, brown, or fair. (1–4)

Women are thus engaged in eternal shape-shifting: "Arcadia's Countess, here, in ermin'd pride/Is there, Pastora, by a fountain side" (11.7–8). Pope, like other civic humanists (see note 20), believed that virtue was associated with land and that it was a male quality. Lacking a language for describing *female* virtue, he resorts to depicting his friend Martha Blount as a "softer Man" (1. 272). Women of substance, of virtue, thus retain the soft bodies of women, but these bodies are only guaranteed form (a "lasting Mark") by *male* virtue. Whereas men (in this system) take on the symbolic bodies of women when they surrender their identities, women who wish to retain their natural (as opposed to shape-shifting) bodies as well as their character or identity, must acquire virtue, or the character of a man.

I have quoted from Vol. III, ii. of *The Twickenham Edition of the Poems of Alexander Pope,* ed. F. W. Bateson (London: Methuen, 1951).

22. Daniel Defoe, *An Essay on the Public Credit* (London, 1710), 6.

23. In view of Pope's fear of insubstantiality and an economy based on "nothing" in *The Dunciad,* the heavy dose of satirical scatology and the eruption into being of the grotesque body takes on a new significance. Pope

attempts to confer substantiality on the fleeting world of the market and of the creatures that inhabit this world. But the bodies are monstrous— non-natural and non-reproductive (or, if they are capable of breeding, they breed monsters). Many of the male dunces, having surrendered themselves to this new economy, assume (like fops) the bodies of women merely to generate embryo and abortion.

24. Jean Baudrillard, *For a Critique of the Political Economy of the Sign*, trans. Charles Levin (St. Louis: Telos Press, 1981), 94. Roland Barthes makes a similar observation in his *The Fashion System*, trans. Matthew Ward and Richard Howard (London: J. Cape, 1985).

25. *Whipping Tom: Or, a Rod for a Proud Lady. Bundled up in Four Feeling Discourses, Serious and Merry, in order to touch the Fair Sex to the Quick* (London: Printed for James Hoey, 1730), 15.

26. For a discussion of this phenomenon, see Neil McKendrick, "The Commercialization of Fashion," in *The Birth of a Consumer Society: The Commercialization of Eighteenth-Century England*, ed. Neil McKendrick, John Brewer, and J. H. Plumb (London: Europa Publications, 1982), 43–47. McKendrick discusses the history of the fashion doll and consumer demand. At the beginning of the eighteenth century the fashion doll was exported annually to London from Paris. Even war did not present an obstacle to this traffic in fashion dolls. A special pass was granted to the mannequin. The doll was first sent to the English court before being sent to the leading London fashion makers. Variously known as *pandoras*, mannequins, *grand courriers de la mode*, many were lifesize in order that the clothes they were dressed in might immediately be worn. The English fashion doll, on the other hand, appearing in the late 1790s, was a flat model cut out of cardboard, printed by the thousands. Its infinite variety of shapes and designs earned it the contemporary description of "the protean figure." This was fashion directly aimed at the popular market, manipulating and extending consumer demand.

27. Andrew Fletcher, *Discourse of Government with Relation to Militias* (London, 1698), 12.

28. Evelyn, 13–14.

29. Evelyn, 16.

30. Terry Castle, *Masquerade and Civilization: The Carnivalesque in Eighteenth-Century Culture and Fiction* (Stanford: Stanford University Press, 1986).

31. Pocock, *Machiavelliam Moment*, 464.

32. Aileen Ribeiro, in her *Dress and Morality* (New York: Holmes and Meier, 1986), describes the hoop-petticoat: The early full-length hoops, made of can or whale-bone, were fairly modest in dimension, assuming a conical shape. By the 1730s they were round and circular, and in the following decade, vast and square-shaped. By the middle of the century they were no longer worn, except for court...." (97).

33. I have quoted this poem from a work entitled *Poems on Several Occasions* (London, 1728). In this collection, the poem is called "The Hoop-Petticoat." David Foxon in his *English Verse 1701–1750*, 2 vols. (Cambridge: Cambridge Univ. Press, 1975) identifies the poem as "The Farthingale Reviv'd" in his index to first lines.

34. Max Von Boehn, Vol. IV of *Modes and Manners*, trans. Joan Joshua (Philadelphia: J. B. Lippincott, 1932), 224.

35. Margaret Doody, *The Daring Muse: Augustan Poetry Reconsidered* (Cambridge: Cambridge Univ. Press, 1985), 147. In this book, Doody convincingly argues that Augustan poetry is characterized by metamorphosis and "charivari."

36. Sewell had no confidence in his ability to translate; indeed, most of his translations rely heavily on John Dryden's and Joseph Addison's translations (previously printed and later incorporated, with acknowledgments, into the Garth edition). In his introductory epistle to his patron, Barnham Goode, Sewell comments on the excellence of the Garth edition, which he had seen in manuscript, and expresses doubts about his ability to match it. In fact, because he was considered by the booksellers to have been inadequate to the task of translating, he confesses that "the Undertakers [of the project] . . . thought it high time to call in other Hands" ("Dedication," *Ovid's Metamorphoses. In Fifteen Books. A New Translation*, 2 vols. [London, 1717], xvi.). One of these "hands" was John Gay, who took the opportunity to have a revised version of his translation of the story of Arachne (Book VI of Ovid) published. It had previously been printed in 1712 in Lintot's *Miscellany*. Perhaps Gay was not aware that Curll was to be one of the three booksellers publishing this edition. Perhaps he needed the money. However, he could not have anticipated how shoddy the edition would be. Nor could he have anticipated that the work done by individual authors or translators would be so flagrantly disregarded. Whereas in Garth's edition, each author's contribution is clearly identified, in Sewell's edition, not only is this not the case, but Gay is, in passing, incorrectly identified as having translated part of Book VII, rather than Book VI.

37. Preface to Ovid's *Metamorphoses,* ed. Sir Samuel Garth. I am citing from the Amsterdam ed. of this work published in 1732 and rpt. New York: Garland, 1976.

38. George Sandys (1578–1644) published an eminent and widely read translation of Ovid's *Metamorphoses,* 1621–26.

39. Alexander Pope, "Sandys's Ghost," in Vol. I. of *The Twickenham Edition of the Poems of Alexander Pope,* ed. Norman Ault and John Butt (London: Methuen, 1954), 174.

40. *The Humours of the Court: Or, Modern Gallantry.* A New Ballad Opera (London: Printed for W. James, 1732), Preface, iii.

41. There are really two issues here. One concerns the rapid commercial transformation of the book trade in the seventeenth and eighteenth centuries and the other concerns the rights of the author. A group of trading booksellers or wholesalers (congers) emerged, challenging the power of the Stationer's Company to license books and own valuable copyrights. Their interests were, however, essentially the same: to protect their investments, limit competition, and prevent piracy. The expiration of the Licensing Act in 1695 (politicians in the House of Commons, aware of how they could exploit the new vehicle of the press more effectively if it were unrestricted, declined to renew the Act) ensured the rapid expansion of both the number of printers (restricted to twenty previously) and presses. Members of the printing trade were desperate to re-obtain their control of "literary property" and finally managed in 1710 to have some protection for their copies with an Act for the Encouragement of Learning (known as the Copyright Act). Under the guise of protecting the rights of the author— making authors, not booksellers, the proprietors of their own works—the booksellers managed to have the bill passed. But these references to author's rights were actually removed in committee. The Act, as the Licensing Act, was designed to protect the copyowners. However, as the Act did not set up an effective means of detecting copyright infringement, piracies became more common. With booksellers such as Curll trying to exploit the book trade, there were more obvious opportunities for competition in, and exploitation of, property in an author. The author's name was something that both legitimate wholesaling congers and illegitimate pirates could trade in. See John Feather, *A History of British Publishing* (London: Routledge, 1988) and Terry Belanger, "Publishers and Writers in Eighteenth-Century England," in *Books and their Readers in Eighteenth-Century England,* ed. Isabel Rivers (New York: St. Martin's Press, 1982), 5–25.

42. The power that women are shown to exercise, however, is confined to the sphere of fashion. For Mandeville, women are granted the right to exert power over men by resisting men's attempts to have authority over them in the domestic sphere, in relationships. They were allowed to enjoy and fetishize consumer goods, the production of which was fostered by women's pride. Mandeville insists that although women have the power to drive this economy, they must not consciously participate in it.

43. John Gay, *The Fan,* in Vol. I of *John Gay: Poetry and Prose,* ed. Vinton A. Dearing and Charles E. Beckwith (Oxford: Clarendon Press, 1974), II, 229–244.

44. Alexander Pope To John Gay, 23 August 1713, in *The Correspondence of Alexander Pope,* ed. George Sherburn (Oxford: Clarendon Press, 1956), I, 188.

45. [Francis Chute], *The Petticoat: An Heroi-Comical Poem in Two Books.* By Mr. Gay (London: Printed for R. Burleigh, 1716), i.

46. This is merely a compilation by Curll of passages from what he considers to be Gay's best work. There is little narrative or commentary. But Curll certainly intimates that Gay's works are *his* property.

47. Alexander Pope, *The Dunciad* (B), in *The Twickenham Edition of the Poems of Alexander Pope,* ed. James Sutherland (London: Methuen, 1943), II. 127–130. Pope's note on Curll (*Dunciad* A, note 54, 104) further comments on these protean, insubstantial authors: "He possest himself of a command over all authors whatever; he caus'd them to write what he pleas'd; they could not call their very names their own."

48. Pocock, *The Machiavellian Moment,* 451–452.

49. In 1718, Curll edited a collection of such works entitled *The Lady's Miscellany,* which included *The Hoop Petticoat* (1716), by Joseph Gay; *The Rape of the Smock* (1717), by Giles Jacob; *The Art of Dress* (1717), [by John Durant Breval]; and *The Fan.* This latter work is not in fact John Gay's, nor is it even Joseph Gay's. Rather, it consists of a few words on the subject by Francis Atterbury. This collection was later reprinted as *The School for Venus; or The Ladys' Miscellany* and included Francis Hauksbee's *The Patch* (1723).

50. Chute, *The Petticoat,* 17–18.

51. [Giles] Jacob, *The Rape of the Smock: An Heroi-Comical Poem,* 3rd ed., rpt. in *The School of Venus,* 2nd ed. (London, 1739), Preface.

52. *Rape of the Smock,* 18, 22.

53. Alexander Pope, *The Rape of the Lock,* in Vol. II of *The Twickenham Edition of the Poems of Alexander Pope,* ed. Geoffrey Tillotson (London: Methuen, 1940) II. 19.

54. Cited in *The Poems of Ambrose Philips,* ed. M. G. Segar (New York: Russell & Russell, 1937), 163–165. Much was being written about tea in the early eighteenth century. Having been imported to Britain in the late seventeenth century, it became a new focus for critiques of luxury: it was a foreign commodity and upset the balance of British trade. It also generated an industry in tea table commodities, associated with groups of women, and was distinguished from the native British drink, beer, associated with groups of men.

55. In the following year and in subsequent editions, "Metamorphosis" was changed to the plural, Metamorphoses. Elizabeth Thomas, *The Metamorphoses of the Town; or, a View to the present Fashions. A Tale after the Manner of Fontaine.* I am quoting from the 3rd ed., 1731.

56. In 1726, Thomas conveyed to Curll some of Pope's letters to Henry Cromwell. For this, she received from Pope a place in his *Dunciad* (B), II. 69–76):

> Full in the middle way there stood a lake,
> Which Curl's Corinna chanc'd that morn to make,
> (Such was her wont, at early dawn to drop
> Her evening cates before his neighbour's shop.)
> Here fortun'd Curl to slide; loud shout the band,
> And Bernard! Bernard! rings thro' all the Strand.
> Obscene with filth the miscreant lies bewray'd,
> Fal'n in the plash his wickedness had lay'd.

Thomas later argued that these had been letters that had been given to her by Pope, but she had needed to sell them because of the desperate financial straits she was in following the deaths of her mother and fiancé (see *Pylades and Corinna; or, Memoirs of the Lives, Amours, and Writings of Richard Gwinnett Esq. . . . and Mrs. Elizabeth Thomas,* 1731).

57. *The Complete Letters of Lady Mary Wortley Montagu,* ed. Robert Halsband, 3 vols. (Oxford: Clarendon Press, 1965), II, 37.

58. *The Complete Letters of Lady Mary Wortley Montagu,* II, 182.

59. The South Sea Company was set up in the early eighteenth century as a result of the Assiento Treaty with Spain to give Britain the exclusive privilege of trade along the east and south coast of America from

Surinam (now Guyana) and the West Indies up to Canada. The trade to America was confined to supplying the Spanish colonies with slaves, but they were also allowed cargoes of "permission" wares for trading purposes. But it was also established to reimburse the national debt. In 1719, the South Sea Company proposed to take up 33 million pounds of the public debt in transferable stock. This was the beginning of the stock market— and it crashed rather precipitously in 1720 when the stock valued at 1000 pounds fell to the value of 200 pounds, when it was discovered that the number of sellers exceeded that of buyers.

60. *The Complete Letters of Lady Mary Wortley Montagu,* II, 8.

Donald Rackin

7

Mind over Matter:

Sexuality and Where the "body happens to be" in the *Alice* Books

The more closely one considers the representations of sexuality in
the Wonderland and Looking-Glass adventures of Lewis Carroll's
dangerously curious heroine, the curiouser those representations
seem. To begin with, they are curiously submerged: explicit sex
seems to play—at least at the texts' whimsical surface levels—
almost no part in these fantasies so charged with implicit sexual
energy. Despite the free associations of Alice's dynamic dreams,
despite the fact that she begins her subversive adventures with an
impulsive leap down a rabbit-hole "burning with [a] curiosity"
(*W* 8) perhaps best understood as erotic,[1] tangible sexuality remains throughout a well-kept secret, artfully buried in the mad
underground of *Wonderland* and behind the silly mirror-reflections
of *Looking-Glass*. William Empson once remarked that Alice's adventures need only to be retold to "make the dream-story from
which [they were] elaborated seem Freudian" (270–271). In Carroll's
own telling, however, hardly a shred of direct sexual reference
survives the wary dream censor's watchfulness.

In Wonderland, for instance, Alice encounters several creatures
conventionally associated aboveground with sexuality, but in each
case, those associations are purged. The bloodless White Rabbit is
the most obvious example; but the libidinal urges figured in
such creatures as the mad March (i.e., breeding) Hare, the hysterical, decapitating (i.e., castrating) Queen of Hearts, and the (philan-
dering) Knave of Hearts have also gone deeply underground,

transformed in the laughable adventures of Alice's well-insulated dream into de-sexed, hypostatized versions of common verbal expressions, or into flat playing-card counters—abstract, disembodied cartoon-metaphors for grotesque but impotent rudeness, insanity, or rage. So too in matters of gender: many Wonderland creatures are designated by the neuter pronoun "it"; and even those few important figures who are explicitly gendered tend, in this generally neutered context, to become disembodied, generalized forces rather than the sexually specific creatures who embody those forces.

Through the Looking-Glass (1871) exhibits a similar overdetermined sexual reticence. But in this sequel to the *Adventures in Wonderland* (1865)—this more wakeful, conscious effort to recapture the free-flowing spontaneity of the original set of extemporaneous dream adventures—the dream censor seems occasionally to lose control, and Carroll's more conscious censoring hand becomes apparent. For example, his decision to change his original Passion Flower to a Tiger-lily in the final *Looking-Glass* manuscript version of "The Garden of Live Flowers" (chapter 2), ostensibly to avoid the religious connotations of Christ's Passion on the Cross (Gardner 200, note 1), was probably also an attempt, more or less conscious, to expunge all connotations of animal passion. Examples of such excessive verbal fastidiousness occur throughout the waking life of the hyper-respectable Charles Dodgson, alias Lewis Carroll. Nevertheless, the Tiger-lily retains the erotic resonance of its original: like a thinly disguised mirror-reversal of Wonderland's passionate, sexually threatening, but ultimately impotent Queen of Hearts, screaming "Off with [his, or her, or its, or their] heads!" the Tiger-lily (quondam Passion Flower) hysterically screams "Hold *your* tongue!" to the timid Violet, and "Silence, every one of you!" to all the flowers in the "very hard" flower bed, "waving itself passionately from side to side, and trembling with excitement. 'They [the other flowers] know I can't get at them!' it pant[s], bending its quivering head towards Alice, 'or they wouldn't dare to do it!' " (*L* 122).

In the 1870s, few of Dodgson's adult readers (as he surely knew) could have missed in "The Garden of Live Flowers" a witty parody of the talking flowers in Tennyson's openly sensuous *Maud* of 1855, a hotly debated, rather scandalous poem by one of Dodgson's favorite authors.[2] Like Carroll's parodies of Wordsworth's egocentricity and sentimentality, his send-up here of Tennyson's literary affectations and the over-heated sexuality in *Maud* derives from a conflicted mixture of attraction and disapproval. In one of his first reactions to *Maud*, recorded in his diary on September 25, 1855, Dodgson wrote, "Read *Maud* again in the evening [he first read it the day it arrived in the post, August 14, 1855] ... the canto beginning 'I have led her home' is true, passionate poetry.... " (*Diaries* I, 65). The canto Dodgson refers to reads:

> I have led her home, my love, my only friend.
> There is none like her, none.
> And never yet so warmly ran my blood
> And sweetly, on and on
> Calming itself to the long-wished-for end,
> Full to the banks, close on the promised
>   good. (Part I, 11, 599–604)

Tennyson's blatantly erotic garden and impassioned, love-maddened protagonist, who tells of holding close his adored Maud, the two "tranced in long embraces/Mixt with kisses sweeter/Than anything on earth" (Part II, 11, 148–150), must have played for many of the first adult readers of *Looking-Glass* a not-so-secret, steamy counterpoint beneath the respectably desexed, children's "nonsense" surfaces of Carroll's hilarious "Garden of Live Flowers." And despite Carroll's seemingly pious conversion of the Passion Flower to the seemingly innocuous Tiger-lily, for those adult readers "The Garden of Live Flowers" still referred by easy association directly to the notorious "garden of [R]oses/ And [L]ilies" in *Maud*, where at the top of the gate, a lusty ornamental "lion ramps ... claspt by a passion-flower" (Part I, 11, 489–496).

Such literary disguises and displacements, of course, come as no surprise today, well-versed as we now are in the psychological principles of sexual repression and sublimation, particularly as they operate in the dynamics of jokes, fantasies, and dream narratives. Less easily recognized in Carroll's time, these disguises and displacements were probably even more necessary, for respectable middle-class Victorians were often very sexy souls who diligently kept their sexuality under wraps, well clothed and decently upholstered. The celibate Reverend Mr. Charles Lutwidge Dodgson (1832–

1898) is admittedly an extreme example: his shyness, his Grundyism, his elegant verbal evasiveness, his daily triumphs of abstemiousness, his obsessive delicacy and sexual reticence, his completely respectable but curiously amorous relationships with a succession of little-girl friends look today like a Wonderland caricature of Victorian sexual repression. Nevertheless, the ordinary social conventions of mid–nineteenth-century bourgeois England prohibited even the blandest public references to sexuality—certainly in books by a respectable Oxford churchman-don, books carefully fashioned in the first instance for the sheltered daughters of the Dean of Christ Church, Oxford. In the case of Carroll's *Alices,* however, these commonplace Victorian attitudes and psychological mechanisms are, by the concentrated agency of ambivalent dream signification and the peculiar absurd humor of their highly repressed but impassioned creator, distilled and intensified, and at the same time strangely complicated, energizing those comic fantasies with a dynamic, but subtle and elusive tension between overt sexlessness and covert sexiness, between apparent absence and secret presence, which attracts and excites many adult readers even today, long after many of the books' more ostensible comic pleasures and specific relations with their cultural contexts have lost for those readers their original force and immediacy.

Particularly revealing in this connection are Dodgson's principal self-portraits in the *Alices:* the frightened and ineffectual White Rabbit in Wonderland and the aged, impotent White Knight behind the Looking-Glass, two of the most overtly asexual figures in the books' extensive gallery of asexual figures. These characters constitute, among other things, telling burlesques of male celibacy and sexual neutrality. Their whiteness alludes to Victorian ideals of purity, but it also recalls the colorless respectability those ideals often required in the lives of celibate university dons like Charles Dodgson. Both of these comic-pathetic figures appear to have shed all traces of sexual energy, the underlying psychological process caricatured neatly in the White Knight's laughable formulation of the classic mind-body question: " 'What does it matter where my body happens to be?.... My mind goes on working all the same.' " (*L* 186).

In Carroll's narrative—as, I would argue, in Dodgson's life—the Knight's absurd question has a pathetic urgency. It hovers behind both sets of Alice's dream adventures, but it is addressed most directly in "It's My Own Invention," the climactic eighth chapter of *Through the Looking-Glass,* which focuses on the shy, feckless Knight, Dodgson's fullest and frankest published self-portrait.[3] The form of the Knight's question indicates the answer he so urgently desires: the commonplace expression "what does it matter" plays on the term "matter" to assert that the "working" of the mind renders the "matter" of the body irrelevant. In the Knight's empty busyness and in his numerous pointless inventions (similar, in some ways, to the impracticable schemes and contrivances actually invented by the Knight's inventor, Charles Dodgson), matter and the physical principles of the real material world lose their force and application. In the Knight's "invented" world (as in Dodgson's cerebral, looking-glass game-worlds of mathematics, symbolic logic, semiotics, playing cards, chess, and nonsense verse), mind is all.[4]

The poor Knight's hilarious bodily exertions and useless, unworkable material contrivances represent his futile attempt to deny the physical conditions of embodied human life. Within the obviously material world of sitting upon and riding real live horses, he is a thoroughly ridiculous failure, falling off his horse at least twenty-five times in fewer than twelve pages. His persistent but vain attempts to remain atop his horse expose the absurdity of his dogged refusal to recognize gravity, the unavoidable connection between "matter" and where a "body happens to be." He is, however, not simply ridiculous: the chapter is also punctuated by plays on the word "grave" (serious, sober, dignified) which refer simultaneously to gravity, death, and time—interlocking presences that play major roles in both *Alice* books, inescapable forces of physical mortality that provide the impetus for a countervailing human desire for carnal love in order to defy the unremitting pull to earth and the grave.[5]

Critics who apply the apparatus of traditional Freudian dream theory to *Through the Looking-Glass,* interpreting the White Knight's words and deeds as dream/joke/fantasy revelations of Charles Dodgson's displaced and heavily disguised sexuality, are likely to read the Knight as a manifestation of some deep-seated psychosexual dysfunction.[6] In such a reading the impotent Knight's word "working" can be interpreted as Charles Dodgson's unconscious reference to Lewis Carroll's expense of spirit in a waste of non-sense, an irresistible drive of the thwarted id to invent, in fantasy, unworkable phallic gadgets and playthings—a desexed mental onanism. The silly inventions of this inept Knight who cannot stay up on his horse for more than seconds, and certainly cannot ride it, are, like him, impotent and pointless. They are like dreamwork sexual acts, but acts, in the White Knight's case, doubly divorced from the body, completely devoid of their life-affirming dramatic functions and deprived of climactic release in the achievement, even in fantasy, of a natural goal or the possession of a desired, corporeal object—endless mental foreplay, dry rather than wet dreams.

The most obvious parallel between the White Knight and the other principal autobiographical figure of the *Alices,* the equally ineffectual White Rabbit, is the whiteness that connotes both sexual "purity" and absence, as in the proverbial expression "white night," a *sleepless* night. For a man like Dodgson who so treasured the colorful, passionate work of dreams, whose literary fame depends so much on his uncanny ability to communicate the very experience, the palpable feel of dreaming, whose final *Alice* book ends with the sober, perennial question, "Life, what is it but a dream?"; for such a celibate connoisseur of dreams, a night without sleep and hence without dreams might very well induce the same psychic affect as would sudden impotence, at a sexually climactic moment, for a person to whom the body's successful sexual performance (the body's "working") is tantamount to successful living.[7]

In the White Knight, then, Dodgson seems to caricature himself as a pitiable figure self-deprived of the life force. By means of this comic dream-fantasy surrogate, he portrays a real man who has consciously and systematically separated human existence into two isolated, mutually exclusive realms of "mind" and "body," perpetrating upon himself his own ultimate, unworkable *invention*—a permanently wakeful, purely cerebral life devoid of erotic energy. The sad but ridiculous Knight who zealously denies gravity and the natural workings of his body conforms too successfully to the Victorian asexual model of the celibate, "pure" churchman-don's life: by observing too well his culture's rules of conscious self-control and denial, he fails in the game of life. Dodgson was only in his mid-thirties when he composed *Through the Looking-Glass,* but his

White Knight persona is pointedly old, intensifying the sense of impotence and irreversible failure as he sings to his lively young Alice a silly but, as she says, "melancholy" (L 187) ballad about an "Aged, Aged Man" whose inventions are just as ridiculous and unworkable as his own.[8] In the White Knight, Dodgson thus constructs a seriocomic looking-glass reflection of his own futile attempts to liberate mind totally from body, to treat the world—and particularly his own relations with his beloved prepubescent girl friends—as if carnal human nature could be sloughed off, leaving mind completely sovereign and free, "pure" from body and natural bodily desire.

But Dodgson's sexual frustrations and anxieties were not always so deeply buried, so well disguised in dreams, half-dreams, or the fantastic "nonsense" books he invented, ostensibly, for young and innocent children. In several relatively sober non-fiction texts, for example, he exposed in thinly veiled form a distinct fear of the mind's ungovernable sexual energies, even when the mind is, as he liked to think, working free from the body. These anxieties about the dangerous workings of the mind (and, indirectly perhaps, about the psychosexual functions of dreamwork) are graphically revealed in his introductory remarks to one of his own rather unworkable "inventions," the 1893 volume *Curiosa Mathematica, Part II: Pillow Problems, Thought Out During Sleepless Nights.*[9]

In his introductions to several editions of *Pillow Problems*, Dodgson, himself sometimes troubled by sleeplessness, explains that he invented these seventy-two puzzles and mathematical problems, along "with their mentally worked solutions," for himself—"work done in my head," he calls it (*Pillow* xv), to be performed in bed in the dark.[10] With the proper determination, Dodgson claims, the would-be sleeper's mind

can be made to concentrate itself on some intellectual subject (not necessarily mathematics) and thus banish those petty troubles and vexations which most people experience, and which—unless the mind be otherwise occupied—*will* persist in invading the hours of the night.... (Collingwood 321)
... there are mental troubles, much worse than mere worry, for which an absorbing object of thought may serve as a remedy.

There are sceptical thoughts, which seem for the moment to uproot the firmest faith: there are blasphemous thoughts, which dart unbidden into the most reverent souls; there are unholy thoughts, which torture, with their hateful presence, the fancy that would fain be pure. Against all these some real mental *work* is a most helpful ally. That "unclean spirit" of the parable, who brought back with him seven others more wicked than himself, only did so because he found the chamber "swept and garnished," and its owner sitting with folded hands: had he found it all alive with the "busy hum" of active *work,* there would have been scant welcome for him and his seven! (*Pillow* xv)

Throughout Dodgson's letters, diaries and published writings, one can find analogous attempts to control mechanically through what he calls here "real mental *work*" the dangerous, "unholy," "hateful" wanderings of the mind and to deny the uncontrollable, erotic interplay between mind and body. An example that deserves comparison with *Pillow Problems* is the brief essay he composed in his early fifties, "Feeding the Mind" (1884, published 1907). Originally delivered as an informal lecture to instruct the young on the selection of proper reading materials, this essay depends for its serious point, as well as its comic effects, on a whimsical but revealing model of human nature. Throughout the essay, body and mind are conceived as homologous but completely independent, easily controllable mechanisms to be stoked with what Carroll calls their appropriate "foods."

Conceding at the beginning of "Feeding the Mind" that some of the bodily "functions necessary to life [Nature] does for us altogether, leaving us no choice in the matter" ("Feeding" 1071), Carroll nonetheless emphasizes that we are still free to choose what food we eat, and the results of this choice will usually affect our physical health. Similarly, he claims, our mental and moral health can often be rather easily controlled by the kinds of literature we choose to read. "The consequences of neglecting the body can be clearly seen and felt," he declares; "it might be well for some if the mind were equally visible and tangible—if we could take it, say, to the doctor and have its pulse felt" ("Feeding" 1073), so that we could remedy any deficiencies by adjusting our mental diet. Like his own dream-invention, the babyish Humpty Dumpty whom he ridicules mercilessly for believing he can by simple *choice* control completely the meanings of words, making them do his bidding, Carroll expresses here, as he does in *Pillow Problems,* a wistful, mechanistic belief in a human ability to manipulate the psyche by conscious choice, keeping the "mind . . . in first-rate working order" ("Feeding" 1074), preserving the mind so that it can go on working free from all suspect bodily urges and desires. This tacit denial of the ungovernable influence of body on mind in a relatively serious didactic text is especially revealing in light of Carroll's devastating ridicule of the White Knight's impracticable inventions and in light of his own heavy dependence in his compositional practice on unbidden, uncontrollable dreamwork and other products of the unconscious—most notably in the original, extemporaneous, and oral creation of Alice's underground adventures that launched his career as the most successful surrealist in our language.

But we need not look so far afield for parallels to Carroll's wistful allusion in "It's My Own Invention" to the possibilities of mind detached from body, of the head working "all the same" regardless of where the "body happens to be." *Wonderland* abounds with allusions to head/body separations, including several that seriously threaten Alice's existential integrity. The book is haunted by the furious mad Queen of Hearts' continually echoing, wildly impassioned cries of "Off with their heads!" And what Alice herself declares as "the most curious thing [she] ever saw in all [her] life," the Cheshire Cat's "grin without a cat" (*W* 53), is a splendid symbol for Dodgson's lifelong ideal of detached intelligence:[11] the Cat's enigmatic, disembodied, gravity-defying grin hangs delicately, timelessly over the underground dreamwork of a man (born in Cheshire) who persisted throughout his thirty-two-year public career in trying to keep secret the material connection between his two separate selves—the sober, meticulous, wide-awake, asexual mathematician and university don, the Reverend Charles Lutwidge Dodgson; and the wildly irreverent and dangerously inventive dream-author Lewis Carroll, passionate creator of a hidden and disorderly lower world where, as his own Cheshire Cat declares, madness rules.

But what of Alice herself, the heroine and ostensible dreamer of these haunting dream works? And what of the other Alice—the real-life Alice beyond the books' frames, the "[c]hild of the pure unclouded brow" (*L* 103), as Dodgson lovingly addresses his former model Alice Liddell in the first line of the *Looking-Glass* prefatory poem? Do these Alices join him in his White Knight dream-invention of a disembodied game-world "unclouded" by sexuality, an unchanging, incorporeal dream-garden, as the closing poem admits, "[n]ever seen by waking eyes" (*L* 209)? Or do these Alices escape the "pure" but arresting prison-garden that Carroll's de-sexed dream countries would constitute for curious, growing girls like Alice Liddell, and like many another among Dodgson's wide acquaintance of real and plucky little-girl friends whom he loved for their liveliness? How, in other words, does the kinetic, mani-festly physical Alice fit into the fantasy of static asexuality and disembodiment in which Carroll places her? For the two books come to us as Alice's dream adventures, not Charles Dodgson's.

Alice Liddell's middle name, Pleasance, provided Carroll with the grounds for several telling poetic devices and puns, including a crucial one in the final lines of his prefatory poem for *Through the Looking-Glass:* "the shadow of a sigh ... shall not touch, with breath of bale,/The pleasance of our fairy-tale" (*L* 103). "Pleasance" could in Dodgson's day mean, among other things, an enclosed, "secluded part of a garden," a secreted "pleasure-ground" artfully insulated from the demands and troubles of the physical, mortal world outside (*OED* XI, 1028), a place, in fact, much like the charm-ing, secluded Dean's garden inside Christ Church, where the Liddell girls often played and where in 1856 Dodgson first met the lovely four-year-old Alice Pleasance Liddell.

Soon after completing the manuscript *Alice's Adventures under Ground,* the basic core of the published *Alice's Adventures in Won-derland,* Dodgson wrote in his diary (March 13, 1863): "Went into the Broad Walk soon after 11, and met Alice and Edith [her sister] with Miss Prickett [their governess], and had a very pleasant two hours' walking with them round the meadow. I began a poem the other day in which I mean to embody something about Alice [then almost eleven years old] (if I can at all please myself by any de-scription of her) and which I mean to call 'Life's Pleasance'" (*Dia-ries* I, 194); the prefatory poem to *Through the Looking-Glass* was presumably the result of this effort. Dodgson's private (rather piti-able) attempt here in his diary to play suggestive word-games with "pleasant," "please myself," and "pleasance," and with the middle name as well as the person of Alice Liddell, to somehow "embody" part of the real-live child by (dis)embodying her within a cerebral pun in a fixed verbal text is, as Dodgson's rather plaintive words would seem to suggest, a futile dream, but a dream he could not help pursuing. Similarly, the immured and "pure" Alice of the prelapsarian Garden that the impractical White Knight Carroll invented for his already fallen heroine (the "pleasance" of *his* life) was, as the *Alice* books continually demonstrate, a fiction Dodgson could not—even inside his fantastic, punning fictions—make fact. Imprisoning Alice's life in his ultimately sterile "pleasance," like imprisoning life itself in a wit-constructed pleasure-ground, turned out to be an ineffectual verbal trick of mind vainly attempting to work outside inescapable body.

As Alice moves forward through her encounters with the static underground and looking-glass creatures, she displays amazing energy, pluck, and determination to achieve a waking, bodily life. And, despite her ups and downs, she grows larger: first, too large and vital to remain in the restrictive, imprisoning, womb-like Rabbit's House (*W* 27–28); later, too appetitive and eager for mature life to rest content as a mere pawn in someone else's hands, too desirous for the life of a grown-up queen, the most mobile and powerful of all the chess pieces—and in this case infinitely livelier than the childish, fallen White Knight she leaves in her wake. Although she is usually civil to a fault, Alice spends no more than the socially acceptable minimum fraction of her precious youth with the doddering Knight. The comforts of a static, disembodied world, secure from the risks of real tyrants, real sexual desire, and real sexual mutilation ("It's all [the Queen of Heart's] fancy that . . . they never executes nobody, you know" [*W* 74])—that timeless nonsense world cannot satisfy the curiosity, the natural desires of Alice, one of the bravest, most physical, and quickest moving of all the lively heroines and heroes in Victorian fiction.

Alice as we typically remember her—her explicit bodily exertions, her lusty appetite, her inclination to cry hard and laugh with gusto—is by no means a figure deprived of the life force or physical desire. She is always a real, curious child in a world of unreal dream projections. Indeed, among the two-dimensional figures paralyzed in a static verbal medium who populate Carroll's self-contained fantasy worlds, Alice *is* the life force, the sole representative of changing life, of material existence aboveground and on the embodied world's side of the looking-glass. So while Carroll represents his fantasies as Alice's dreamwork,[12] he depicts Alice as a fully embodied child, alive and lively. Moreover, in both books, it is Alice who ends the threatening dreams, breaking out and waking to an unambiguous sexual identity, a full bodily existence. "Carroll's Alice," writes Nina Auerbach, "explodes out of Wonderland hungry and unregenerate" (148).

As Carroll's dreaming surrogate, Alice holds a golden key to his unconscious notions of Eros, of the general life force, the (repressed) libido that struggles against the waiting grave. Most notable in this regard, perhaps, is the fact that this inquisitive dream-child manifests an ambivalent curiosity: an eager, clear-eyed, intellectual curiosity Carroll admired and sometimes equated with life itself; and the dangerous, illicit, "burning" curiosity he struggled to exclude from his works of mind divorced entirely, he wistfully assumed, from the workings of body.

It is worth noting that the words "curious" and "curiosity," used some forty times in the two *Alice* books (mostly in reference to Alice herself), carried several distinctly pejorative connotations for middle-class British readers during the period when the *Alices* were composed and first published (1862–71). For example, in 1867, Dodgson's fellow Oxford don Matthew Arnold states, at the beginning of "Culture and Its Enemies" (published in 1869 as the first chapter, "Sweetness and Light," in *Culture and Anarchy*):

> We English do not, like the foreigners, use this word ["curiosity"] in a good sense as well as in a bad sense. With us the word is always used in a somewhat disapproving sense. . . . the word always conveys a certain notion of frivolous and unedifying activity. . . . there is a curiosity about intellectual matters which is . . . merely a disease. . . . the blind and diseased impulse of the mind . . . we mean to blame when we blame curiosity. (V, 90–91)

In 1864—at just the time Dodgson was completing the conversion of his *under Ground* manuscript into the book *Alice's Adven-*

tures in Wonderland, revising, for instance, the manuscript's opening description of Alice as "full of curiosity" to the first edition's
"burning with curiosity"—Arnold was pointing out that "the word
curiosity, which in other languages is used in a good sense, to
mean, as a high and fine quality of man's free play of the mind on
all subjects, for its own sake ... has in our language no sense of the
kind, no sense but a rather bad and disparaging one" (III, 268).

These statements provide a revealing context for Dodgson's own
declaration, some twenty-one years after publishing his first *Alice*
book, that the Alice of his underground and looking-glass dreams
was perhaps best described as "curious—wildly curious" ("Alice on
the Stage" 283). By the time Dodgson wrote this admiring description of Alice, in fact, the term "curious" had come to mean, among
other things, "[d]esirous of knowing what one has no right to know,
or what does not concern one, prying"; furthermore, the term was
also by this time "used as euphemistic description of erotic or pornographic works" (*OED* III, 145).

Dodgson's Oxford friend, the preeminent critic of art, architecture and society and, from 1869 to 1878, Slade Professor of Art at
Oxford, John Ruskin (like Dodgson, a Christ Church graduate, an
acknowledged eccentric and passionate admirer of prepubescent
girls), delivered two lectures in Manchester in 1864, "Of Kings'
Treasuries" and "Of Queens' Gardens" (published together as part
of *Sesame and Lilies* in 1865). In the first lecture, Ruskin (who was
a close friend of the Liddell family and for a time Alice's private
drawing master) distinguishes between a "noble curiosity"—which
he describes as a "questioning, in the front of danger the source
of ... the River of Life," and what he calls "a mean curiosity, as of
a child opening a forbidden door, or a servant prying into her
master's business" (XVIII, 81).

In *Proserpina: Studies of Wayside Flowers* (1879), Ruskin, fero-
ciously attacking contemporary botanists for "the recent frenzy for
the investigation of ... digestive and reproductive operations in
plants," declares that this ostensibly disinterested and harmless
scientific curiosity actually furnishes "the microscopic malice of
botanists with providentially disgusting reasons, or demonically
nasty necessities, for every possible spur, spike, jag, sting, rent,
blotch, flaw, freckle, filth, or venom" in plants. "But," Ruskin
continues,

with these obscene processes and prurient apparitions the gentle and happy scholar of flowers [as opposed to the professional, scientific botanist] has nothing whatever to do. I am amazed and saddened . . . by finding how much that is abominable may be discovered by an ill-taught curiosity, in the purest things that earth is allowed to produce for us . . . (XXV, 390).[13]

All these contemporary connotations of the word "curiosity," including Arnold's notion of the "free play of the mind," free of material considerations and bodily desire, seem operative, to some degree, in the pun-packed, allusive prose of the ambiguous *Alice* books, secretly inscribed in their ostensibly straightforward, innocent verbal usages. Like the inseparable mind/body amalgam graphically embodied in the shaped, Mouse's "tale"/"tail" of *Wonderland* (*W* 24–25), Alice's natural curiosity can be read as an amalgam of "high and fine" disinterested desires and low and "bad" carnal desires. Her curiosity includes an eager desire to know her dreamlands' "tales"—that is, to know intellectually their explanatory narratives, their working principles; and the desire to know, viscerally, the hidden, bestial "tail" that erotically animates those dreams, a "tail" inescapably linked, after Darwin's *Origin of Species* (1859), with the primitive workings of the lower body. She burns with a devilish curiosity to discover what the impenetrable, asexual surfaces of her adventures seem designed to keep forever secret from her, what her protective White Knight inventor feels she, in the maiden purity and innocence he has imputed to her, has "no right to know": the full answers (including the disturbing Darwinian answers) to her insistent, prying questions about her own worldly nature ("Who in the world am I?" [*W* 15]), about the hidden forces that drive and shape her dream adventures, about her natural erotic impulses and the mature sexual experiences that await her in knowing queenhood. For Auerbach, "Alice's fall is both a punishment for her inveterate curiosity and an alliance with mysterious underground laws that empower her. Like Milton's Eve, the ever-ravenous Alice is a creature of curiosity and appetite" (152).

The erotic implications of Alice's "curiosity" seem safely occulted—as do the erotic implications of Dodgson's ostensibly innocent photographs of nude, pre-pubescent girls.[14] These photographs of children in what Dodgson liked to describe humorously as "their favourite state of 'nothing to wear'" (*Diaries* II, 387), or "Eve's original dress" (*Letters* I, 253), have sometimes been described in modern Carroll scholarship as erotic (e.g., Auerbach 165–168), even pornographic. But Dodgson himself, like most of his contemporaries, would have been horrified by any such allegations. For him, as he told Harry Furniss (illustrator of his *Sylvie and Bruno* books), "naked children are so perfectly pure and lovely" (Lennon 373). After a sketching session in the studio of his friend E. Gertrude Thomson, another of his illustrators (*Three Sunsets and Other Poems*, 1898), he wrote in his diary that the two nude, little-girl models, "Iris and Cynthia . . . were very willing and very patient models, with lovely figures, and yet more lovely innocence. It purifies one to see such purity" (*Letters* II, 987, note 1).

Little boys, however, were another matter. Writing to a dubious mother of two girls (aged eight and nine) who had posed naked for three hours in his Oxford photographic studio, Dodgson explained the difference:

> [t]heir innocent unconsciousness is very beautiful, and gives one a feeling of reverence, as at the presence of something sacred: and if you only had those two girls, I should see no objection (in spite of "Mrs. Grundy") in their repeating the performance, if they wished, next year or even for 2 or 3 years to come. But, for the sake of their little brother, I quite think you may find it desirable to bring such habits [sic] to an end after this summer. A boy's head soon imbibes precocious ideas, which might be a cause of unhappiness in future years, and it is hard to say how soon the danger may not arise. So I shall be quite prepared to find, next year, that they have learned to prefer *dressed* pictures. I am not so selfish as to wish for pictures, however valuable as works of art, the taking of which involved any risk for others. (*Letters* I, 381–382)

In Dodgson's view, apparently, a little boy's head cannot be trusted to go on working free of his body: no matter how carefully his masculine mind is fed, it is nearly impossible to keep *him* from imbibing dangerous ideas. Only the minds of elderly White Knights, it seems, can be trusted in these matters.

Moreover, little boys cannot attain for Dodgson the "purity" of little girls because the bodily manifestations of their sexuality, even in their earliest years, cannot be kept secret, hidden. Hence, for his nude photographs (as opposed to his many conventional photographs of all sorts of subjects, young and old, male and female), Dodgson apparently limited his practice to young girl children: despite the fetching poses he might invent for them, their undeveloped bodies betrayed to his camera's mechanical gaze no indisputable outward signs of sexual function. " . . . I confess I do *not* admire naked *boys* in pictures," he wrote to Miss Thomson. "They always seem to me to need *clothes:* whereas one hardly sees why the lovely forms of girls should *ever* be covered up!" (*Letters* II, 947). As another of Dodgson's female artist friends with whom, in his later years, he shared girl models recalled, "He confessed to me having no interest in boy or grown-up female models, having the 'bad taste' to find more beauty in the undeveloped than the mature form" (E.L.S. 560).

Like the occulted sexuality of Carroll's nude, undeveloped girl models, Alice's sexuality, even in her dreams, remains a secret matter. Despite Carroll's brilliantly realistic portrayals of his heroine's character and motivations, Alice, for all her physicality, is represented at the surface level of the adventures as virtually sexless, a dream-icon of the Romantic cult of childhood innocence that conforms perfectly to the prevailing bourgeois model of prepubescent female purity to which Carroll passionately subscribed.

Thus, Dodgson's strongly marked preference for nude girl models, I would argue, is both a symptom of his repression, his desire to keep the sexual aspects of his love for children completely unconscious, and also the expression of a powerful erotic desire, a desire as occulted as is the sexuality of its objects. Empson puts the matter succinctly:

> [Carroll's] desire to include all sexuality in the girl child, the least obviously sexed of human creatures, the one that keeps its sex in the safest place, was an important part of their fascination for him. . . . So far from its dependence, the child's independence is the important thing, and the theme behind that is the self-centered emotional life imposed by the detached intelligence. (273)

Never apparent at the surface levels of the adventures, Alice's hidden sexuality—like that of the nude girls in Dodgson's photographs—is, however, a driving force of her adventures. When we contrast the Knight's persistent, fruitless, and comical denial of body and bodily sexuality with Alice's energetic physical exertions, her unselfconscious hunger for food, adventure, and forward movement, her passionate, life-affirming, erotic curiosity, and her intimate, unashamed awareness of her own material, bodily nature, we come to the matrix of the sexual-asexual dynamic that animates the *Alice* books. The only character in the adventures with a completely unambiguous bodily identity founded on a physical reality beyond the texts themselves, Alice is surrounded by the silly inventions of a mind working on mind-forged abstractions like mathematics, puzzles, playing cards, chess pieces, games, puns, and nursery rhymes. Alice is the sole figure in the adventures whose "work" is more than an endless, unprogressive, circular reiteration of fruitless and frustrating nonsense gestures; the sole figure who opposes the figures of detachment, mutilation, paralysis, and death produced by the "workings" of the disembodied mind.

The prefatory poem to *Through the Looking Glass,* addressed simultaneously to the real Alice Liddell and to the dream-child Alice of Lewis Carroll's own invention, includes this stanza:

> Come, hearken then, ere voice of dread,
> With bitter tidings laden,
> Shall summon to unwelcome bed
> A melancholy maiden!
> We are but older children, dear,
> Who fret to find our bedtime near. (*L* 103)

Here at the outer edge of the final *Alice* dream adventures, Dodgson voices most overtly his paradoxical attitude towards sexuality. The dreadful "unwelcome bed" that summons the real maiden Alice (now, as he concludes his last *Alice* text, approximately nineteen years old and estranged from him) is for Dodgson/Carroll simultaneously the death bed *and* the marriage bed—an imaginatively fused, "portmanteau" image embodying the complex relationship between sex, death, love, marriage, and life—between reality and dream, things and words, body and mind. For Dodgson, who fretted much about the problems of his bedtime and yet desperately loved the dreams bedtime afforded, the problem is never solved. Left behind as Alice hurries toward her physical and sexual maturity, he remains a childish, impotent, outdated, and anachronistic male protector of maidens, a chaste White Knight forever frozen in his manufactured dreams of a world where a "mind can go on working just the same" without a body. The most ambitious of the White Knight Carroll's ineffectual inventions, the *Alice* books attempt to imprison within their static, asexual dream-worlds (as in Carroll's many wonderful but necessarily static Oxford photographs of little-girl friends) an Alice he loved for her "pure" beauty, but also for her liveliness, her lusty appetite for life, her fervent and dangerous curiosity. The attempted containment fails, of course, and in that failure lies one secret of the books' great and lasting success.

Some twenty-five years after he told Alice Liddell and her sisters his first, extemporaneous tales of Alice's adventures underground, Dodgson attempted a brief analytic description of one of the chief characters in those adventures, the mad Queen of Hearts: "I pictured to myself the Queen of Hearts as a sort of embodiment of ungovernable passion—a blind and aimless Fury" ("Alice on the Stage" 282).[15] In some sense, the Alices of the various dream adventures and Alice Pleasance Liddell herself are also embodiments of what might be called "ungovernable passion." Although their irrepressible curiosity is always thwarted and never satisfied within the adventures, none of them will allow Lewis Carroll to govern the unruly passions that drive them. While Dodgson seemed sometimes to equate sexual passion with madness and the furies, he could not, in his fictions or in his life, impose that vision on the girls he loved.

One of the White Knight's unworkable gravity-defying schemes to save himself from the dynamics of the corporeal state is a plan to keep his hair from falling off, to release himself, that is, from his mortality. Alice, by contrast, rushes eagerly forward toward her impending queenhood and that by no means necessarily "unwelcome" bed which is the destination of her embodied mortality, she leaves the feckless Knight behind, imprisoned in the chapter of a fantastic book his inventor invented for them both. Inspired by Eros, she will live outside the frames of her calculating Pygmalion's invention. As usual, Alice says it best. Speaking for herself (as well as for Alice Pleasance Liddell and for all Dodgson's "pure" little-girl friends), she declares lustily to the pitiable White Knight, "I don't like belonging to another person's dream. . . . I don't want to be anybody's prisoner. I want to be a Queen" (*L* 179, 181).

NOTES

---

1. See the discussion of "curiosity" below, 22–26. In the sixty years since the publication of William Empson's seminal "*Alice in Wonderland:* The Child as Swain," numerous critical studies have followed Empson's example of interpreting Alice's leap down the rabbit-hole in sexual terms.

2. "The entire [Garden of Live Flowers] episode," declares Martin Gardner, "is a parody on the talking flowers in . . . *Maud*" (200, note 1). Compare Empson (285–288) on the close relations between "The Garden of Live Flowers" and *Maud,* a poem even Empson calls "shocking" (285).

3. Many Carroll scholars have, by means of internal and external evidence, convincingly identified the White Rabbit, the Dodo, and the White Knight as Dodgson's intentional self-portraits. In the case of the White Knight, see the recent, conclusive article by Jeffrey Stern.

4. Compare Elizabeth Sewell's celebrated study of Carroll and Lear, *The Field of Nonsense,* a study that depends on the premise that "in nonsense [such as that of the *Alices*] all the world is paper and all the seas are ink. . . . The scope of inquiry is limited to what goes on inside a mind" (17).

5. See Rackin 121–146, where this topic is explored at length.

6. The White Knight has been interpreted in this way by a number of critics and biographers since the 1930s, most extensively by Phyllis Greenacre in *Swift and Carroll: A Psychoanalytic Study of Two Lives.*

7. Dodgson's almost obsessive fascination with dreams and the elusive distinctions between the dreaming and waking state continued until the end of his career. Indeed, one of the saving graces of the generally soporific *Sylvie and Bruno* books (1889, 1893) is the inventive and sometimes powerful narrative strategies they employ to offer eerily accurate representations of the dreaming state as well as of the delicate, problematic transitions between dreaming and wakefulness.

8. In Carroll's original plan for *Through the Looking-Glass,* the discrepancy between Alice's youth and the White Knight's old age was

further intensified in "It's My Own Invention," which ended, not with Alice's farewell to the White Knight, but with her subsequent farewell to the Wasp in a Wig, an even more aged figure whom Alice also treats with solicitude, despite his rude crankiness. See "The Wasp in a Wig."

9. In his second (suddenly produced) edition of *Pillow Problems* (also 1893), Dodgson carefully changed in the title "Sleepless Nights" to "Wakeful Hours," in order, he claimed, to allay his friends' anxieties that he suffered from insomnia, but also, perhaps, to conceal such things as the relations between himself and his dream-figured White Knight. Dodgson was curiously insistent about withdrawing the first edition. As Dennis Crutch reports, " . . . Dodgson wrote to Macmillan [the publisher] that no more copies of the first edition [of *Pillow Problems*] were to be supplied, and that unsold copies in the hands of agents were to be recalled: 'supply, instead of them, copies of the new edition, as soon as you get it.' " Despite the fact that Dodgson claimed to Macmillan that " 'The improvements in the 2nd edition are so important, that any purchaser of the book might reasonably consider he had been very hardly dealt with, if, with the new edition on the point of appearing, he was allowed to buy a copy of the inferior edition,' " Crutch points out that except for the change in the title from "Sleepless Nights" to "Wakeful Hours," the insertion of the three-page "Preface to second edition" (which includes Dodgson's assertion that the "title was not, I fear, wisely chosen" [*Pillow* ix]), and his inordinately lengthy disclaimers about that first title, the "rest of the book is very slightly altered" (Crutch, 182).

10. In another response, perhaps, to sleepless nights, Dodgson invented a device for writing in the dark, the Nyctograph. In her excellent biography of Dodgson, Anne Clarke states that he "invented the Nyctograph to spare himself the unpleasant task of getting out of bed and striking a light when he wanted to commit an idea to paper; but although he found it answered the purpose well, most people would consider it too complicated and far more trouble than getting a light" (Clarke, 254).

11. For Empson, the Cheshire Cat symbolizes Dodgson's ideal, "the detached intelligence." "The famous cat," Empson writes, "is a very direct symbol of this ideal of intellectual detachment; all cats are detached, and since this one grins it is the amused observer. It can disappear because it can abstract itself from its surroundings into a more interesting inner world; it appears only as a head because it is almost a disembodied intelligence, and only as a grin because it can impose an atmosphere without being present" (273).

12. Nina Auerbach emphasizes the fact that the *Alice* books are meant as representations of Alice's dreams and that all their characters and

incidents are dream projections of Alice's anxieties and desires. For example, Auerbach writes: "as she moves more deeply into Wonderland . . . [Alice] is both the croquet game without rules and its violent arbiter, the Queen of Hearts. The sea that almost drowns her is composed of her own tears, and the dream that nearly obliterates her is composed of fragments of her own personality" (133). For a more recent interpretation that also stresses Alice's psyche as the center of all the elements in her dreams, see Mark Conroy's "A Tale of Two Alices in Wonderland."

13. In 1878, according to Colin Gordon, "Ruskin had submitted to Alice [Liddell] a proof of a chapter from his new book on naming plants [*Proserpina*]. . . . " (Gordon, 105).

14. The evidence clearly indicates that there were many such nude photographs, as well as nude drawings, but that all but four were destroyed or returned to the young sitters' parents. In 1978 these four appeared for the first time in *Lewis Carroll's Photographs of Nude Children*, with an introduction by Morton Cohen. They were subsequently published in *Lewis Carroll, Photographer of Children: Four Nude Studies*.

15. In the same essay, Dodgson sums up the autobiographical White Rabbit this way: "For [Alice's] 'youth,' 'audacity,' 'vigour,' and 'swift directness of purpose,' read [for the White Rabbit] 'elderly,' 'timid,' 'feeble,' and 'nervously hilly-shallying'" ("Alice on the Stage," 282).

WORKS CITED

Arnold, Matthew. *The Complete Prose Works of Matthew Arnold.* Ed. R. H. Super. Ann Arbor: University of Michigan Press, 1965: Vol. III, "The Function of Criticism at the Present Time"; Vol. V, *Culture and Anarchy.*

Auerbach, Nina. "Alice and Wonderland: A Curious Child" and "Falling Alice, Fallen Women, and Victorian Dream Children," Chapters 8 and 9 of *Romantic Imprisonment: Women and Other Outcasts.* New York: Columbia University Press, 1986. 130–168.

Carroll, Lewis. "Alice on the Stage" in *The Theatre,* 1887. Rpt. in Gray edition (below) 280–284.

———. *Alice's Adventures in Wonderland* (cited in my text as W) and *Through the Looking-Glass* (cited in my text as L) in *Alice in Wonderland: Authoritative Texts of "Alice's Adventures in Wonderland," "Through the Looking-Glass," "The Hunting of the Snark."* 2nd ed. Ed. Donald Gray. New York: Norton, 1992.

————. *The Diaries of Lewis Carroll.* 2 vols. Ed. Roger Lancelyn Green. New York: Oxford University Press, 1954.

————. "Feeding the Mind," in *The Works of Lewis Carroll.* Ed. Roger Lancelyn Green. Feltham, Middlesex: Spring Books, 1965. 1071–1074.

————. *The Letters of Lewis Carroll.* 2 vols. Ed. Morton N. Cohen. New York: Oxford University Press, 1979.

————. *Lewis Carroll, Photographer of Children: Four Nude Studies.* New York: Clarkson N. Potter, 1979.

————. *Lewis Carroll's Photographs of Nude Children.* Edited and with an introduction by Morton Cohen. Philadelphia: The Philip H. & A. S. W. Rosenbach Foundation, 1978.

————. *Pillow-Problems Thought Out During Wakeful Hours* (signed "Charles L. Dodgson"), fourth edition. rpt. New York: Dover Publications, 1958.

————. *The Wasp in a Wig: The "Suppressed" Episode of "Through the Looking-Glass and What Alice Found There" With a Preface, Introduction and Notes by Martin Gardner.* New York: The Lewis Carroll Society of North America, 1977.

Clark, Anne. *Lewis Carroll A Biography.* New York: Schocken Books, 1979.

Collingwood, Stuart Dodgson. *The Life and Letters of Lewis Carroll (Rev. C. L. Dodgson).* New York: Century Co. 1898.

Conroy, Mark. "A Tale of Two Alice in Wonderlands." *Literature and Psychology* 37, no. 3 (1991): 29–44.

Crutch, Dennis. *The Lewis Carroll Handbook.* Folkstone, Kent and Hamden, Connecticut: Dawson & Sons and Archon Books, 1979.

E. L. S. "Lewis Carroll as Artist. And other Oxford Memories." *Cornhill Magazine* (November 1932): 559–562.

Empson, William. "*Alice in Wonderland:* The Child as Swain," in *Some Versions of the Pastoral.* London: Chatto and Windus, 1935. 253–294.

Gardner, Martin. *The Annotated Alice.* New York: Clarkson N. Potter, 1960.

Gordon, Colin. *Beyond the Looking Glass: Reflections of Alice and Her Family.* New York: Harcourt, Brace, Jovanovich, 1982.

Greenacre, Phyllis. *Swift and Carroll: A Psychoanalytic Study of Two Lives.* New York: International Universities Press, 1955.

L. See above, Carroll, Lewis. *Alice's Adventures.*

Lennon, Florence Becker. *The Life of Lewis Carroll* (new, revised edition of *Victoria through the Looking-Glass*). New York: Collier Books, 1962.

The Oxford English Dictionary, 2nd ed. Oxford: Clarendon Press, 1989, Vols. III and XI. (Cited in my text as *OED.*)

Rackin, Donald. *"Alice's Adventures in Wonderland" and "Through the Looking-Glass": Nonsense, Sense, and Meaning.* New York: Twayne, 1991.

Ruskin, John. *The Works of John Ruskin,* Library Edition. Ed. E. T. Cook and Alexander Wedderburn. London: Longmans, Green, and Co., 1906, Vols. XVIII and XXV.

Sewell, Elizabeth. *The Field of Nonsense.* London: Chatto and Windus, 1952.

Stern, Jeffrey. "Carroll identifies himself at last, or a problem solved, and a problem posed." *Jabberwocky—The Journal of the Lewis Carroll Society* 19 (summer/autumn 1990): 18–19.

Tennyson, Alfred Lord. *Maud* in *Tennyson: A Selected Edition,* Ed. Christopher Ricks. Berkeley and Los Angeles: University of California Press, 1989. 511–582.

W. See above, Carroll, Lewis. *Alice's Adventures.*

8

Oeuvres Intertwined:

Walter Pater and Antoine Watteau

The concept of the body, either as textual or material, has interest-ing implications for Walter Pater studies. His *oeuvre,* maligned for its sensuous caressing of desire, has become entombed in the oft-repeated epithet: "to burn with a hard gemlike flame," and is re-membered selectively through sections from *The History of the Renaissance,* or *Marius the Epicurean.* Such a fate is partly due to a tendency in Victorian aesthetics (and in later schools of criticism) to discard the material body along with its desires and replace it with metaphysical formulations or critical opinions about Pater's texts. In a general sense, the Western paradigm for recognizing the potency of desire is to categorize it, even theorize it out of the text. If desire is to be acknowledged within the body of the text, it is usually refined into metaphors of aesthetic value. In such a cat-egory, textual desire is tamed by exhuming it through ideological or hermeneutic theory. If, on the other hand, desire is understood as an unconscious drive in the subtext, then it is explained away through psychoanalytic (or feminist) theory. But Pater refused to obey any textual or critical formulae for mediating textual desire. He continually gestured toward the materiality of texts through his chimera-like play on desire. Within the theoretical frame of the textual body, it is accurate to say that Pater critics tend to dema-terialize his body, and aestheticize desire out of the text. Pater critics have read his *oeuvre* as always, another, safer text. One instance of such a critical practice is the continued emphasis on "flux" as an aesthetic register in Pater's textuality. Examined in another light, "flux" can be read as Pater's enunciations of the shifting sites of desire, always eluding stabilization, therefore always escaping categorization. I posit a reading of Pater's "A Prince of Court Painters," a portrayal of Antoine Watteau, from *Imaginary Portraits* that is (self-consciously) imitative of his text. I will examine some instances where Pater theatricalizes textuality, offering different sites of representation, revealing a fluidity that we have come to associate with drama, and articulating a polysemic/phonic discourse that is necessary for spectacle.[1]

Pater's "A Prince" is unique in discussions of the materiality of texts. First, it is the only work in which Pater thematizes desire by routing the materiality of pleasure through the narrator, Marie Marguerite's "journal" entries. Second, it is the one portrait in Pater's *oeuvre* which responds to the demands of historical accuracy in documenting Antoine Watteau's life, even though Pater manipulates this very historicity with layers of fiction. With these two procedures Pater interlocks two bodies of information—texts of subjective disclosure and of objective analysis. Finally, under the pretext of recording Watteau's life and art, Pater dramatizes the way in which desire can only be read as a play between fixed/ elusive and material/textual boundaries. In other words, Pater articulates the relationship of the material body (journal writer) to the textual surface (journal), at the same time that he fractures the connection by dislocating Watteau's *oeuvre* from Marie Marguerite's "journal" in precisely those places where she blatantly records her unrequited love for him. These moments of rupture provide Pater with an opportunity to critique Victorian culture which underpins both bodies—the material and the textual. By intertwining *oeuvres,* Watteau's paintings and his own verbal discussions figured through Marie Marguerite's physical/fictional body, Pater reveals a conflict between desire and authority. On the one hand, he holds his text within the margins of an expressive, private discourse, which is saturated with emotional responses, and on the other, he stretches the limits of constraints that Victorian culture imposed on public utterances.

Pater places himself in three simultaneous narrative positions: that of a factual recorder documenting Watteau's biography, that of a cultural decoder suppressing Watteau's *fêtes galantes* as inappropriate for a woman's journal, and that of an inter-subjective encoder signaling homoerotic desire deflected via a woman's body. In other words, Pater situates himself on the margins of historical and fictional moments so as to challenge his reader to acknowledge the eluding dimensions of desire which are woven between three positions of narrative identity. Pater's anomalous stance toward history (subjective, factual, anachronistic, accurate, and ambiguous) is explicated in his "Prosper Merimée"[2] lecture, where he argues that while history must be told as a story of

> the pursuit of exact truth, [it is in reality] a keenness of scent, a peculiar *mental preference. Power* here too again, the *crude power of men and women which mocks, while it makes its use of average human nature:* it was the magic function of history to put one in living contact with that. (*PM* 16–17, *emphasis added*)

History for Pater is not merely a document of facts but a topography of "crude power" and caprices of "human nature." Pater anticipates Michel Foucault's thesis that the myth of history moves its object of study from the status of a "document" to become a reified "monument," always legitimating representations of the body through power.[3] Pater structures his narration as a "journal" with entries that are predicated on the desires of all three participants— Pater (author), Marie Marguerite (narrator), and Watteau (text).

Pater as Factual Recorder

Pater's choice of Antoine Watteau as his figural emblem is not accidental. Watteau mirrors Pater's own *oeuvre,* a body that is a montage of texts, portraits, poetics, and music, all saturated in emotion, all engaged in evoking desire. Yet, Pater arranges Watteau's life in "A Prince" on a mimetic grid of time and space: he left for Paris in 1701 and died in July 1721, and the "journal" retains this parameter for describing the events in Watteau's life and art. Watteau biographers note that the artist himself was presented as an "arabesque" text much like his famous canvases. Thomas E. Crowe, a noted art historian, helps explain the importance of this concept in the painter's technique:

at its most subtle, the arabesque format allowed playful and intriguing layered allegories of desire which could make reference to contemporary experience without being merely imitative of it. It was Watteau's great move in 1712–13 to project the disjunctive strategies of the arabesque on an apparently unified moment in space and time . . . [which] anticipate the procedure and document of contemporary taste for the most *implausible allegories of pleasure.* (64, *emphasis added*)[4]

Watteau is concurrently artist, musician, and muse for literary masters.[5] Art historians see Watteau's genius in reworking Rubens, Giorgione, Titian (to name just a few masters), and in extending the frame of the canvas itself. In his art, the figures of love, dressed in the costumes of the theater, question traditional notions of mimesis and representation. Just as Watteau's masterpiece, "L'Enseigne de Gersaint" (the Shopsign) shows his awareness of art as a representational sign, as a commodity, and as a subject of connoisseurship—the quintessential bourgeois version of desire—similarly, Pater crosses genre lines in "A Prince" when he uses the informal "journal" form to represent his formal treatise on desire, and when he conflates gender boundaries in narrating the "journal" to experiment with categories of signification or representation.

For Pater, Watteau is a sign, signifying in numerous registers, even exceeding signification, to go beyond the canvas to be refigured in literary texts, markedly that of Edmund de Goncourt's *L'Art de XVIII Siècle.*[6] Thus, the historical, material Watteau of the eighteenth century is translated into a nineteenth-century salon figure, who is then circulated by Pater as a literary text. Art historian Norman Bryson makes the connection between Watteau's art and the music of Debussy, Chopin, Mozart, and others (Bryson, 65), and Pater readers can now begin to see the tracings of a similarity between his works and Watteau's art as it was portrayed in the nineteenth century. Pater's own picturesque style, his ear for rhythm in texts, and his attempts at wedding word and harmony make Watteau appealing to his Victorian sensibilities. Pater must have felt a special affinity for the depiction of this nineteenth-century Watteau because he himself attempted a melding of text and music in his works. His famous statement "all art constantly aspires towards the condition of music ... so that the meaning reaches us through ways not distinctly traceable by the understanding ... but seems to pass for a moment into an actual strain of music" (*The Renaissance* 135, 136–137) is asserted in the "Prince," too, where Watteau's murals make the narrator exclaim: "Only, the very walls seem to cry out: - No! to make delicate insinuation, for a music, a conversation, ... with this fairy arrangement—itself like a piece of 'chamber music'" (April 1714). Pater's attraction to Watteau can be seen as his fascination with an eighteenth-century *artist* who has been reconstituted by the Goncourts as an *artifact*. Thus, Pater seems drawn to Watteau by a mirroring of subject portrayals, methods of portrayal, and responses to art, all contained within the Victorian "monument" created to stand for Watteau's art in Pater's day. In comparing Pater to Watteau, specifically in regard to their textual strategies, one can posit the fulcrum of similarity on their intertwined impressions of desire and *ennui*, rather than the verisimilitude of textual persona.

The Goncourts highlight three concurrent fields of aesthetic value in Watteau's art: image, music, and text. In reading Pater's Watteau as portrayed in the "Prince" we can use the same parameters. When the Goncourts reintroduced Watteau's art to the salons of nineteenth-century Paris, it is their reading, perhaps, more accurately, their misreading[7] with its excessive aesthetic judgements, which Pater incorporates in his portrait. Edmund de Goncourt documents Watteau as "embodying and revitalizing the spirit of rococo, ... charm, seductiveness, grace, and play became the catchwords for the movement, which is still the yardstick."[8] This deflection of Watteau and his art through the Decadent lens of the Goncourt brothers allows Pater to position himself in a particular historical moment and to *re*-write history. He layers his portrait of Watteau with a thin veneer of biography/history covering over and revealing the blatant desire of Marie Marguerite for Watteau. Pater creates the illusion of factual representation by treating the "journal" to the highest degree of verisimilitude intended by its author, Marie Marguerite. Pater is *not,* then, proposing a simple resemblance between text (the material object, i.e., "journal") and the referent (historical object, i.e., Watteau). Thus, Pater fabricates the connections between specific social forces (historical events) and the regulated discourse of the "journal" through the hidden motivations of Marie Marguerite's unrequited love. But by not focusing solely on the semi-documentary contents of the discourse (historical factualness) but rather on its conditions of possibility (a fictional, undocumented liaison), Pater, in a Foucauldian way, lays the groundwork for a model for understanding the relationship between *pouvoir*/power (as unconscious desire) and *savoir*/knowledge (its inscription in language).[9]

Consequently, Pater's text will reveal history as the record of political success and failure, always within the manifestation of unconscious desire and cultural power. The Goncourt brothers immortalized Watteau as the "great poet of the eighteenth century," and their eulogy, used in most introductions of Watteau criticism, is that his art "is that fine essence which appears as the smile of a line, the soul of a being, and the spiritual physiognomy of matter."[10] Pater had access to this gallery of myriad, Parisian responses to Watteau's art, framed by these self-conscious intellectuals, all of whom are aware of the fragility of language as a representational sign. Pater's portrayal reconstitutes Watteau as a fictional figure, a palimpsest of personalities—a "consumptive" (Goncourt), "Romantic" (Baudelaire and Banville), and "macabre" hero (Gautier) in this portrait. What is missing in this already mythicized (a)historical figure of Watteau is a delicately refined eroticism, scripted as a *play of desire* that Pater narrates through Marie Marguerite's tale of a fantasized love affair. "A Prince" traverses two genders (male/female), two media (word/image), and two historical eras (eighteenth and nineteenth centuries), making its intertextuality subtle and complex. In it, a discursive identity (Watteau of the diary) pre-exists an individual identity (a double identity, if you will, Pater beneath Marie Marguerite) who comes to fill or enact a historical identity (Antoine Watteau). It is a portrait that fills a space created *by* Watteau's art *via* Goncourts' writings, *through* Marie Marguerite's discourse, *into* which Pater steps to deflect history so that Watteau cannot become "monumental." Thus, historical accuracy is etched in "A Prince" by "trac[ing] like the bloom of a flower" (June 1705) Marie Marguerite's growing awareness of Watteau as the artistic body. It is here that Watteau's *oeuvre* becomes superimposed on Pater's *oeuvre,* with all its attendant imagery of sensuality and decay, and Pater uses history to selectively voice, suppress, and re-route incidents to create Marie Marguerite's desire with its new textual surface and hierarchies.

Marie Marguerite's first entry acknowledges Watteau as her "father's namesake, the apprentice of the M. Metayer [in Paris] for whom he works, labours all day long, . . . Antony is already the most skilful of them" (Dec. 1703). Compte Caylus, Watteau's biographer, records the same details.[11] But even in bustling, fashionable Paris, "[Watteau's] thoughts . . . are not wholly far from home" because he has just finished the "Un Depart de Troupes—Soldiers Departing—one of the scenes of military life, one can study so well here at Valenciennes" (May 1705). However factual this may be, Pater's source is, nonetheless, the essay on Watteau's art by the Goncourt brothers. They admired the "Soldiers on the March" declaring that the heavy lines and dark colors/themes of the scene revealed an inherently "melancholic" Watteau. Marie Marguerite's pleasure in seeing Watteau retain his heritage is a Paterian echo of a nineteenth-century *interpretation* of the painter's life through his art. Even though Pater attempts to position himself as factual recorder of history, he is inadvertently biased by the re-recording of his contemporaries. It is a case where "the crude power of men and women mocks" while revealing "peculiar mental preferences" (*PM* 17).

Similarly, Marie Marguerite pictures Watteau relaxing in the palace gardens of Luxembourg, projecting the 'romantic hero' myth propagated by the Goncourts: "when his long summer-day's work is over, enjoying the cool shade of the stately, broad-foliaged trees . . . almost as if it belonged to that open and unbuilt country beyond, over which the sun is sinking" (Dec. 1703).[12] The sentiment is an extension of her own longing to stroll with him on the "ramparts" at Valenciennes, "walk there and muse" (Oct. 1701). She translates desires from her body to signal the exhaustion of Watteau's body, and fantasizes a consummation by imagining a lovers' stroll in the "ramparts" of Valenciennes. By using a literary-pastoral motif as both a translation from material to textual surface, and as a transference of passion, she not only releases desire from her own body, but also allows it to transcend the textual body through the Romantic metaphor. While Pater remains faithful to the nineteenth-century image of a Romantic Watteau (troping desire through deferral and repression), he still lets the reader glimpse the frustration of that desire that Marie Marguerite records in the privacy of her "journal." Slowly, Pater is moving into the position of cultural decoder (he unravels her thoughts, perceptions and responses), balancing in the textual space created for Marie Marguerite, a shy village belle.

Pater as Cultural Decoder

Pater adopts the camouflage inherent in stepping into Marie Marguerite's position with inordinate grace. He is acutely aware of her place in culture, and veils the journal entries, especially the explicitly sensual ones, carefully. But the reader can trace the fading boundaries of the author's position in the places where Marie Marguerite, as narrator, inadvertently reveals her desire. Thus, when Marie Marguerite reports her perception of events, she deliberately suppresses parts of Watteau's life that cause her embarrassment. The author, however, is consciously manipulating her and letting the reader know that she is embarrassed. She casually remarks that she prefers the work of "Peter Porbus to the hot flesh-tints of the Medicean ladies of the great Peter Paul [Rubens]" (Aug. 1705).[13] It is intriguing to trace Pater's intention behind this reference, for Peiter Porbous, according to the *Encyclopedia of World Art,* married his master's daughter. That is the strategic clue Pater gives his well-informed, nineteenth-century readers, revealing Marie Marguerite's unconscious preference for Porbous's action as represented in his art work. She reads Rubens's voluptuous canvases as a translation of Watteau's life style, revealing her anxiety about Watteau's libidinous desires in Paris. Will Watteau's admiration for Rubens make him want to play with the "Medicean ladies" and forget the village girl? Pater signals the cultural restraint placed on a woman from expressing her desires, and the fact is brought to bear with delicate force by the narrator as she voices her translated sentiments—desire for Watteau via Porbous.

Marie Marguerite catalogues Watteau's "free intercourse with those wealthy lovers of art, M. de Crozat, M. de Julienne, the Abbe de la Roque, the Count de Caylus, and M. Gersaint, the famous dealer in pictures, who are so anxious to lodge him in their fine *hotels,* and to have him of their company at their country houses" (Feb. 1712). Again, she occupies the cultural space Pater creates for her and silences the well-known fact that these "lovers of the arts" spent their free time painting nude women. That, too, was a move away from established cultural conventions of her petty, bourgeois world, and even that of Pater's Victorian world, but certainly not for the eighteenth-century, gentlemanly one of Watteau and his contemporaries. While Watteau and his fellow artist were allowed to circulate erotic art, Pater was punished for signing his name to a passage of purple prose. Seen in the context of eighteenth-century France, Watteau's erotica reflects a defiance of the prevailing sanctimony and dullness of (the later) Louis XIV's court, which in turn, parallels Pater's own rebellion against the dogma and prudishness of the Victorians. Pater chooses to make the culture-specific voice of an eighteenth-century woman translate into partial discourse what was impossible for him to say in the nineteenth century. A good woman does not speak of nudes, but she may allude to them elliptically, perhaps interject a moral note by discussing its value in art. It is, ultimately, such a translation from the materiality of desire into an abstract value that Pater interrogates through his position as cultural decoder.

Another instance of Marie Marguerite's partial fidelity to Watteau's art is her praise of his "Seasons." Ironically, she describes the effect of the canvases on the room as "a sort of *moral* purity; yet, in the *forms* and *colours* of things" (June 1714). Donald Posner points out that it was E. de Goncourt who felt that the " 'Seasons' derives its 'unworldly purity of motives . . . from a chastity both physical and spiritual.' In point of fact, many of the master's *fêtes galantes* [nudes] are primarily about sensual desire and libidinous passions" (34).[14] What Pater (via the narrator) attributes to the "Seasons" is anachronistic, didactic, and is an attempt to portray a sublime painting, when in actuality the "Seasons" ushered in Watteau's fame as a master of nudes in the *fêtes galantes* tradition. Pater shields himself behind Marie Marguerite's acculturated body as *resisting* the sleek, chic lines of Parisian art in its representations of desire. Yet Pater, in the guise of Marie Marguerite, is conscious of such a deflection of history and the entry continues: "Is the actual life of Paris, to which he will soon return, equally pure, that it relishes this kind of thing so strongly?" (June 1714). Not only is Pater deliberately silencing the *fêtes galantes* side of Watteau's *oeuvre*, but through his strategic overcompensation he is forcing the reader to interrogate Marie Marguerite's ideological investment in denying the materiality of pleasure. It seems Pater is offering an evocative *misreading* of Watteau's art. In this instance he distorts history, deliberately creating a gap between Marie Marguerite's record of Watteau's art and his actual *oeuvre*. It is a gap, moreover, that allows Pater to explore the degree to which cultural policing of desire can occur in the name of morality.

Finally, the details of Watteau's fatal illness and death are again only partially true in Marie Marguerite's "journal." She records accurately that Watteau became seriously ill in April–May 1721 and went to rest in Nogent-sur-Marne at Abbé Haranger's house. She records that he died in July 1721, and his biographers concur. But her journal entry reads: "Antony Watteau departed suddenly. . . . At the last moment he had been at work upon a crucifix for the good *curé* of Nogent, liking little the very rude one he possessed. He died with all the sentiments of religion" (July 1721). Marie Marguerite makes it appear as if Watteau came to religion voluntarily. Biographers, however, record that Watteau was forced to repent by the "good *curé*" for his extravaganza in painting voluptuous *nudités*. Pater creates the illusion of abject repentance as a textual ploy to intertwine fictional with historical fact. The Goncourt catalogue mentions Watteau's painting "Crucifixion," which was half-finished at his death, but which has since been lost. Pater uses the strategic suggestion of a pious ending to graft his own *oeuvre* on that of Watteau's. The final scene in "A Prince" echoes the closing of *Marius the Epicurean*. Pater readers are bound to reflect upon the similarity (and dissimilarity) of Watteau dying with a cross clutched in his hands and Marius dying with a wafer between his lips. Both depictions are suggestive of a Christ-like transcendence, but the difference is that while Watteau's death is overtly factual, Marius's is overtly fictional: while Watteau is forced to repent, Marius has no cause to repent. More than establishing a text-text connection inside his own *oeuvre*, Pater creates a new trajectory for desire itself. He intertwines Watteau's fictional body ("journal") with Watteau's art body ("Crucifixion") and his own fictional body of works. In all this braiding together of bodies, the religious metaphors of forgiveness and transcendence are delicately underscored. While the focus in *Marius* is on the young, unblemished hero, in "A Prince" it is upon the reader's judgmental response. Even more haunting than the Marius/Watteau mirroring is the cultural critique that Pater hints at. While it was possible for (earlier) Pater's

Marius to use the economy of the transcendence metaphor, (the later) Pater's Watteau seems lost because the import behind the metaphor is bankrupt. Thus, the "journal's" ending becomes problematic—a simplistic affirmation of faith keeps the portraiture well within the cultural conventions of an uncorrupted, village maiden—but her very discourse has become questionable. Her acquiescence in maintaining the cultural ban on the discourse of desire serves as a reminder of the degree to which this practice was hegemonic.

This is Pater's ideological agenda; he interrogates the sanctions and status that Watteau enjoyed in eighteenth-century France, which seem denied to him by Victorian standards. By positioning himself otherwise, Pater makes the reader aware of the level of repression in Marie Marguerite's entries and grants her cultural authenticity through her textual self-control. This form of control seems to emanate from inside her body, but Pater questions its very origin in history. By pointing to instances where the narrator attempts to control her desires, yet reveals them, he shows how Victorian culture policed the body.

Pater as Intersubjective Encoder

Pater uses Marie Marguerite to signal places in Watteau's art that are programmatically sexual, thus eroticizing desire through her voice.[15] Watteau serves as the artist, the art object and the fictional site of desire, making him a perfectly sculpted candidate for intersubjectivity. In other words, Pater uses Watteau as both the means and the ends of his/Marie Marguerite's "journal." Crowe writes: "Watteau's nudes are characterized by their voluptuousness, the female form arched in supine sensuality, surrendering, relaxed. The nudes are not mythological or biological figures orchestrated with heavy allegorical meaning—but just naked women" (Crowe 54). In much the same way that Watteau experimented with representation to force his viewers to reorient themselves and seek new meaning, so too is Pater's work innovative, voluptuous, and forces the reader to glance anew at the imagery and mood of the text and go beyond pre-existing meaning for usual symbols. The transposition between Pater and Watteau is so systematic and so fast that their identities keep shuttling back and forth such that at points in the text *their difference becomes indiscernible.* The slippage between their identities creates the intersubjective space in which Pater situates himself to trace an individual's encounter with ideology.

One such gesture is the 1701 entry where Marie Marguerite records Watteau's sketch of the Harlequin-Columbine scene. In enunciating the historical fact of Watteau's creating this sketch, the configuration of narrator/author/text silences a more pertinent one. The pretext for the *Commedia dell 'Arte* entry is the ban on Italian theater that King Louis XIV imposed in 1697. Watteau, as all his biographers note, was famous for his portrayal of the *comedie,* both in the Italian style (solid, comic figures), and the lauded, French style (chic, poignant figures). In other words, a historical ban like that on the *Commedia dell 'Arte* was politicized and textualized by Watteau, by simultaneously suppressing and expressing both Italian and French registers in his art, which is then appropriated and re-circulated by a sly Pater in the nineteenth century. Thus, Marie Marguerite glosses over (suppresses) the *comedie* form altogether but emphasizes (expresses) Watteau's "genius." Ironically, Watteau's "genius" lies not in the faithful representation of the theater of the mime, but in his bringing together the satire, the mimicry, the pathos of this form with the joyous love making of the *fêtes galantes.* Posner and Crowe specifically focus on this fusion, arguing that it invaded the cultural domain of the *fêtes* to "parade the rough entertainment of the *danse du corde* (mime) and disrupted established hierarchy of art forms" (Crowe 62). The point in such oppositionality is not merely to recognize one and ignore the other, but to establish a dialogic of one with the other. Crowe, the more post-structural of the two art historians, lauds Watteau for *interrogating* eighteenth-century ideology by his fusion of art forms. Pater, in turn, uses Watteau to question Victorian ideologues for moralizing and demarcating the form and content of artistic expressions.

Thus, to say that the *comedie* genre is completely suppressed in Pater's portrayal would deny the anxiety that Pater himself feels about any form of univocal representation. The first journal entry reads "We had our September Fair in the *Grande Place*" where Watteau through his "marvelous tact of omission . . . made trite old Harlequin, Clown, and Columbine, seem like people in some fairyland; or like infinitely clever tragic actors." They portray, she adds "a sort of comedy which shall be but tragedy seen from the other side" (Sept. 1701). Marie Marguerite repeats in the last few pages of the journal: "I am reminded of the day . . . at the Fair in the *Grande Place;* and I find, throughout the course of his life, something of the essential melancholy of the comedian" (February 1720). Pater's use of the Clown in his journal here is very similar to Watteau's auto-biographical painting, "Gilles" the clown. Critics comment on the sadness of Gilles's visage, the despondence of his posture, and the foregrounding of a single human form thrown into sharp relief by the somber desolation of the background. Such an emblematization of alienation is crucial to Pater in connecting his own discarded body (both textual and material) to Watteau's body (auto-biographical and artistic), again, as a critique of Victorian aesthetics.

Marie Marguerite's casual mention of the "Seasons," the "Swing," and "Manon Lescaut" show how Pater uncovers codes of censorship to reveal connections between sex and power.[16] By mentioning the works but not elaborating upon Watteau's orchestration of the theme of the flesh, Pater deliberately raises the question of who has the authority to speak about sexuality, who draws the margins between sensuality and sexuality, between "good" and "bad" discourse, and between sanctioned desire (aesthetics) and unsanctioned desire (erotica).

The "Seasons" entry is the first in such an intriguing pattern. Even though Marie Marguerite makes special mention of "Summer," she does not dwell on the central figure in the painting. Instead she talks of "the summerlike grace, the freedom and softness . . . a hayfield such as we visited to-day, but boundless, and with the touches of level Italian architecture in the hot, white, elusive distance, and wreaths of flowers, fairy hay-rakes and the like, suspended from tree to tree, with that wonderful lightness which is one of the charms of his work" (June 1714). By discussing the "Seasons," she brings Watteau and Pater into the frame. "Seasons" reflects Watteau's astounding innovation in creating the oval frame which draws the glance of the viewer into the frame in a vortex, sustaining it on the central nude figure. The viewer cannot but confront the significant figure of Ceres in the center of "Summer," a voluptuous woman, her robe in an enticing state of dishabille against her pearly white flesh. Posner writes that "there are in fact, three works by Watteau, generally though to be roughly contemporary with the 'Seasons ... *Cupid Disarmed by Venus* ... *Autumn* and *Jupiter and Antiope*" (*Lady at her Toilet*, 23). Marie Marguerite, instead, discusses the hay on which Ceres is seated, completely failing to mention the figure because it is unutterable, even in the privacy of her own journal. In effect, the excess of repressed desire and displaced signification spill out of the journal. There are at least five competing surfaces here, Watteau's canvas, Pater's text, Marie Marguerite's eager inscription in the journal, her anxiety in denying the erotica of the painting by connecting it to the hayfield, and the reader's growing comprehension of intersecting planes of desire.

Marie Marguerite's journal produces a similar effect when discussing "one particular picture (true *opus magnum*, as he hopes), the *Swing*" (Feb. 1716). Watteau portrays a girl on the swing, the swing, high in the air, with a boy in the foreground. At the bottom of the canvas is a bagpipe, a strewn hat and a miniature Bacchus figure. The bagpipe and the strewn hat, more than the playful figures themselves, have been the art critics' focus for the past three centuries. Watteau is credited with having introduced, in the eighteenth century, the bagpipe as a sign of male sexuality and the strewn object as female compliance. For a girl from Valenciennes, with a sensibility nursed on the heavier lines and solid figures of Flemish/Dutch artists like Gerard Dow and Pieter Porbous, to gloss over the iconographic sexuality of the *Swing* is natural. Marie Marguerite's complete omission of all these details shows how clearly she has *silenced* the erotica in Watteau's art, but not erased it. This becomes a dialogic moment signalling the polemics between desire and authority. Posner remarks on how Watteau managed to change the depiction of nudes from the mythological frame to the social one without making them seem like ladies of pleasure. Marie Marguerite serves as the anachronistic interrogator for sanctions in representation. Even though Pater shrouds himself in Marie Marguerite's discomfort on seeing Watteau's blatantly sexual canvas, he projects himself into the historical space that Watteau occupies. Just as Watteau breaks free of the oppression of King Louis XIV, Pater traces an arc of desire that exceeds the borders of the "journal." The unspoken becomes a deafening reminder to the reader about Pater's ambivalence regarding his own status *vis à vis* the prudish oppressive Victorians and the lascivious Decadents.

Finally, there is the acknowledged, anachronistic reference to *Manon Lescaut*. This is a curious choice for an intertext mainly because it deals over and over again with Manon's illicit and graphic affair with a notiviate, the hero. Marie Marguerite talks of a "new book [Watteau] left behind him—a great favorite of his; . . . the story of poor Manon Lescaut—for whom fidelity is impossible— with an art like Watteau's own, . . . And this is the book those fine ladies in Watteau's 'conversations,' who *look so exquisitely pure,* lay down on the cushion when the children run up to have their laces righted" (Oct. 1717 *emphasis added*).[17] And as if the emotion has been too strong, too sexually explicit, she abruptly concludes the entry with: "at all event, I must read the book no more."

This entry has at least three layers, one historical, one culture specific, and the third narrative, while revealing Pater's technique in combining them through his specific positioning of Marie Marguerite. Pater as historic recorder is influenced by the Goncourts, who compared the canvas "Soldiers On The March" to the narrative Manon Lescaut, and he uses the naive village belle to satirize Victorian prudishness. This accounts, partially at least, for Pater's layered thematic plan in including this specifically anachronistic detail. Marie Marguerite lets the reader know that books like *Manon,* with their fascinating, inexhaustible, libidinous desire, were in common circulation at that time. The erotic nature of the book becomes evident when she herself reaches the limits of titillation and forcefully closes, both the book and her entry. Uncomfortable with the tableau of blatant desire, she attempts two clear diversions. First she talks of respectable "pure" married women who read this novel, attempting to lure the reader into sanctioning such material. In this position she is well within her cultural parameters. Next, she uses allusions to the weather as a transference technique. The analogy between the scorching text and the hot summer is eased by "the thought of cold [which] was a luxury" (Oct. 1717). What she leaves unsaid the reader inscribes as an analogy of fulfillment.

The last position in the Pater/Watteau intertwining is the narrative one. Pater situates himself on the interstices of two works, "The Soldiers on the March" and "Conversation," without ever naming either, both of which were well known to his readers. While the former is a genre painting, the latter is a *fête galante;* while one immortalizes death and pain, the other frames clandestine pleasure. Their systematic clash puts into circulation the gap of desire between the two, as if retelling Manon's story. Just as Marie Marguerite attempts to tame desire by domesticating it, Pater (Watteau) gestures toward the polemical relationship between desire and power. For Marie Marguerite, Manon is a symbol of romantic love whose wish to legitimize her sexuality is continually postponed. For Pater's Watteau, her story becomes the site for locating institutional persecution, symbolically disclosing societal pressures.

And, finally, there is Watteau's most memorable work, the *L'Embarquement pour Cythere*. This painting (with its French syntactic focus on *pour*) has puzzled art critics because of its particular ambiance. Michael Levey writes that it was the French symbol of disillusionment, and contrasts the transient nature of earthly/earthy love to the ideal nature of Biblical/mythological love.[18] The painting is autumnal, the time is late evening, the landscape is washed over with a fine spray of mist, revealing supine, exhausted figures. There is an eerie mood of stillness and *ennui* that makes it difficult to pinpoint whether the people are going to or coming from the island of love. Here the archetypal, Christian, journey metaphor is parlayed in sexual terms. Since this kind of ambivalence is typical of both Pater and Watteau but discomfiting for Marie Marguerite, she does not mention the canvas at all.[19]

While the nineteenth-century Rue de Doyenne group fastened upon another trait in Watteau, that of creating a counter culture, an alternate theater, providing simultaneously "an elevated improving culture for the nobility, and a low marginalized one for the common majority" (Crowe, 52), Pater was not allowed into such arena of discourse. Such moments of rupture in the "journal" call attention to Pater's role as an intersubjective, cultural encoder. A graphic example of this is his inability to mention Watteau's *Cythere*. More than others, this is a Watteau canvas that is redolent with post-coital languor, and Pater is at a loss for words to describe it in Marie Marguerite's "journal." Neither he nor his narrator have the vocabulary to discuss the painting. This *gap* reveals the ban on articulating desire or enunciating a discourse of pleasure. All Pater can do is gesture to the absence of language in Victorian England to speak about such desires. The point at issue here is not the mirror reflection of Watteau-Pater, but the refraction of one another *through* Marie Marguerite as a cultural lens. Crowe's succinct analysis of Watteau becomes particularly pertinent to Pater's *oeuvre:* "Rather than some 'realistic' grounding of the genre, we are dealing here [in Watteau's art] with related artificial systems of representation being maneuvered into productive contact" (Crowe, 57). This is Pater's strategic "tact of mission" (Jan. 1701), simultaneously anxious and exultant about the materiality of pleasure circulated in textual bodies from intersubjective positions.

J. Hillis Miller's analysis of Pater's technique also argues against positing one theoretical paradigm. His argument is not specifically focused on the materiality of Pater's texts, but he too advocates a cultural, semiotic analysis that will take into account the various forces operating in Pater's texts. He writes:

> Alongside those ideas [historic and cultural], overlapping them, folded inextricably into them, contradicting them, and yet necessary to their expression is a notion that is properly literary or semiotic. . . . It can hardly be called a fully developed 'theory.' It is more an implicit assumption in all Pater's practice with words. This 'theory' in all its dimensions involves *categories of difference and discontinuity.* ("Walter Pater: A Partial Portrait," 87)[20]

Pater's preoccupation with desire and the systematic encoding of pleasure is microcosmically represented in "A Prince." Hence, his *oeuvre* would be dismembered if read through a "theory" or assigned a "category." It must instead be read against the grain, as testing the limits of language within a hegemonic culture. In other words, Pater's textual body can be recovered only through reticence, gaps, and elliptical gestures of "discontinuity."

NOTES

I would like to thank Gurudev, Susan Green, and Jessica Munns for all their invaluable suggestions while I wrote this chapter.

1. In the academic frame of recovering bodies, both material and textual, it is ironic that Pater's *oeuvre* is mostly overlooked and discarded

except for *The Renaissance* and *Marius*. Because of his radical theatricalization of material desire through textual surfaces, Pater was left with no legitimate status in the literary *corpus*. For example, the paperback edition of his *Imaginary Portraits,* edited by Eugene J. Brzenk (New York: Harper & Row, 1964) is now out of print. In effect, his textual body is not available for circulation in literature classrooms. The collected *Works of Walter Pater* (New York: Macmillan, 1910) is the only available, definitive edition. The University of California Press is expected to issue the complete edition by the end of this decade. In the biographical frame of rewriting bodies, Pater lost a proctorship at Oxford and his academic standing when he published a signed version of the "Conclusion" to his *Renaissance.* Benjamin Jowett, Matthew Arnold, and other literary stalwarts conveyed their displeasure of Pater's sensual texts by writing him out of the Victorian literary circle. Later, T. S. Eliot condemned Pater for being careless with his literary borrowings, and announced that he was unworthy of study because of his chaotic textuality. Literary criticism till the middle of the twentieth century was focused on proving the extensive, and often unacknowledged use of literary references in Pater's works. It was Ian Fletcher who ushered in Pater scholarship with *Walter Pater* (White Plains: Longman, 1959), where he argued that Pater's so-called unoriginal style was, in fact, a revolutionary technique in the construction of texts.

2. All quotations from Pater works are cited from the standard *New Library Edition of the Works of Walter Pater* (London: Macmillan, 1910). The Prosper Merimée essay is from *Miscellaneous Studies: A Series of Essays* (1895), and "A Prince of Court Painters" from *Imaginary Portraits* (1887). All citations from "A Prince" will be included parenthetically by indicating the dates of these journal entries in the original work.

3. See Michel Foucault's *Archeology of Knowledge,* trans. A. M. Sheridan Smith (New York: Vintage, 1972). Here, Foucault discusses knowledge as *connaissance* and *savoir,* as concepts used in discourse systems to understand and record history. He writes: "By *connaissance* I mean the relation of the subject [writer] to the object [events] and the formal rules that govern it [discourse]. *Savoir* refers to conditions that are necessary in a particular period for this or that type of object to be given *connaissance* and for this enunciation to be formulated" note #2, "The Discourse on Language," 15. But Foucault fails to account for a speaking subject who inscribes such power, coloring the *savoir* of the age with his own particular *connaissance.* In fact, a whole range of twentieth-century scholars belonging to the *"les histoires de mentalités"* tradition were formulating similar paradigms for discussing history as a social discourse.

4. For more on this aspect see, Thomas E. Crowe, *Painters and Public Life in Eighteenth-Century Paris* (New Haven: Yale Univ. Press, 1985).

5. Pater critics like Harold Bloom, J. Hillis Miller, Gerald Monsman, Ian Small, Jay B. Loseley, and others have argued that he blurs strict genre categories in his fictions. Most critics are also familiar with Wolfgang Iser's phenomenological account in *Walter Pater: The Aesthetic Moment* (London: Cambridge Univ. Press, 1987). However, Iser focuses on inner sense impressions of the reader rather than specific male/female play of desires in the text.

6. The Goncourt brothers, to a large degree, helped sharpen Pater's portrayal of Antoine Watteau and, in turn, "catalyze" Pater's writing. To get the connection between Watteau and French nineteenth-century artists, see Norman Bryson's *Word and Image: French Painting of the Ancient Regime* (London: Cambridge Univ. Press, 1981). Bryson writes that Baudelaire, Gautier, Banville, Nerval, "the members of the *rue de Doyenne* group," refashion Watteau to signify and serve as pretext for their own Decadent "extravaganza" (Bryson, 64).

7. The general understanding of misreading can best be explained through Lacan's use of *méconnaissance* from *Four Fundamentals of Psychoanalysis*. There are some scholars who read this term strictly within the parameters of a Freudian Lacan agreeing that it means a misrecognition of the self through error in perceiving the self mirrored on the Other. But Lacan can also be read semiotically, where the Other is put into discourse and the self reaches out metonymically, constantly moving in its signification, continually signalling various differential positions of the self in relation to the other. This suggests a multiple, dynamic, semiotic self that is like the Kristevan subject interrogating its own positionality with reference to the other, calling into question both reading and *mis*reading.

8. See *Encyclopedia of World Art*, Vol. 12, 235. See also Edmond de Goncourt, *French Eighteenth-Century Painters*, trans. R. Ironside (Ithaca: Cornell Univ. Press, 1981).

9. For a clear analysis of the connections between *pouvoir, savoir* and history, see M. Foucault *The Archeology of Knowledge*, and "The Discourse on Language" trans. A. M. Sheridan Smith (New York: 1976), *History of Sexuality*, Vol. I (New York: Vintage, 1978), for an explanation of the materiality of history.

10. "E & J de Goncourts 1859–75" in *The Complete Paintings of Watteau: The Classics of the World's Great Art Series*. Intro. John Sutherland,

catalogue and notes by Ettore Camesasca (New York: H. N. Abrahms Inc, 1968), 9. Pater, in all probability, looked at the manifesto of the Decadent and Symbolist writers, and captured the enigma of Watteau for his "Prince." Bille Jo Inman in *Walter Pater's Readings* (London: Garland, 1981) records that Pater had read Michelet's *Historie*, Vol IV, he must have read a contemporary analysis of Watteau's works. (Inman, 304, 313). Similarly, Baudelaire's *"Les Phares"* praising Watteau's art was in general circulation, and his *Salon de 1846, (Le Portefuelle)* calls attention to Watteau's "marvelous vanishing creatures." Pater also probably read Gautier's sonnet on Watteau that discusses the artist's preoccupation with the grotesque as a *"goût"* for the somber and mournful. Turner paid homage by inscribing Watteau in his "Titian's Workshop" (London, Tate Gallery), and Delacroix notes Watteau's "delicious" colors. It is possible to assume with a fair degree of accuracy that Watteau's art was fashionable, its critical appraisal by nineteenth-century aesthetes commonplace, and that Pater must have heard such comments in conversation with friends.

11. I have used a series of art history texts, and have taken some general statements from the following. Smiche's *Le Romantisme et le goût esthétique du XVIIIe siècle* (Paris: Didier, 1976), *Encyclopedia of World Art*, Vol 12, especially the section on "French Eighteenth Century Painters," Ironside's *Eighteenth Century French Painters* (London: 1968), and *Complete Paintings of Watteau: the Classics of the World's Great Art Series*, intro. John Sutherland (New York: H. N. Abrahms Inc. 1968), *Watteau*, compiled by M. M. Grasselli and Pierre Rosenberg, National Gallery of Art, Washington, 1984.

12. For more information on the influence of Watteau's art on the French Romantic thought see S. Simches' *Le Romantisme et le goût esthétique du XVIIIe siècle* (Paris: Didier, 1976).

13. In fact, there was a minor Flemish painter in the sixteenth century who worked on religious subjects in Northern France, and some of his work survives in remote churches in Northern France. Wright either correctly or incorrectly records that Porbus's work hangs in the *Musée De Beaux Arts* in the Boulevard Watteau in Valenciennes. See Inman's *Walter Pater's Readings*, the section of Wright, 344.

14. Donald Posner, *Lady at her Toilet* (London: Viking, 1973), 34. Posner explains the place of Watteau's nudes in the culture of the time, and shows how he captured natural moments in a lady's toilet that came to be construed as erotica.

15. For a clearer understanding of the connections between sexuality, power, and repression see Michel Foucault's *The History of Sexuality*, Vol.

I (New York: Vintage, 1978), especially the section on "Repressive Hypothesis." Harold Bloom, Gerald Monsman, and others have hinted at a homoerotic register in Walter Pater. Most recently, Richard Dellamora discusses a homosexual tendency in Pater. See Richard Dellamora, *Masculine Desire: The Sexual Politics of Victorian Aesthetics* (Chapel Hill: N. Carolina Univ. Press, 1990). My discussion, however, places Pater in the gaps between homo-hetero-auto erotic desire.

16. Foucault in *The History of Sexuality,* Vol. I, outlines how sex is deployed in discourse in the seventeenth, eighteenth, and nineteenth centuries. He argues that even though sexuality was forbidden in public, and controlled by political, religious, and economic powers to promote a heterosexuality clearly held within the bounds of marriage, there was concurrently, a proliferation of literature about sex and sexual practices. While some of this bordered on "erotic literature" others were validated as scientific literature under such categories as biology, natural sciences, psychopathology.

17. Pater's own note in the 2nd ed. of "A Prince" reads: "Possibly written at this date, but almost certainly not printed till many years later." This suggests that he was conscious of the delicate intertextual ploy at this point.

18. Art critics also compare Watteau's work to Nerval's *Voyage a Cythère* and Banville's in *Le midi,* documented in Donald Posner, *Antoine Watteau* (Ithaca: Cornell Univ. Press, 1984), 286.

19. Crowe writes that Watteau's *Cythère* is an adaptation of Rubens' "Garden of Love." Rubens's painting is mythological, but Watteau's "narrative is projected on to a vastly different pictorial economy. The mood is all irony; the attenuated and self-effacing figures give no purchase to the 'robust allegory' of Rubens, or to the complex of conventional and reassuring meanings it embodies: that is eroticism as resolved and contained in the institution of marriage." Thomas E. Crowe, *Painters and Public Life in Eighteenth-Century Paris* (New Haven: Yale Univ. Press, 1985), 54.

20. For a variety of critical opinions on Pater, see *Walter Pater,* ed. Harold Bloom (New York: Chelsea House, 1985). J. Hillis Miller's essay, "Walter Pater: A Partial Portrait" is in this collection.

9

Florence Nightingale and the Negation of the Body

At the beginning of her enormously popular how-to book *Notes on Nursing,* Florence Nightingale wrote that "every woman is a nurse."[1] She might as easily have stated as her cultural given that every woman is a patient; not, in Nightingale's own account of it, because of any inherent weakness or instability, but rather, she suggests, because bodily incapacity was the only valid apology for exempting women from their social duties.[2] Nightingale herself was both the most celebrated nurse of her time and, shortly after her return from the Crimea in 1856, an invalid who, for more than fifty years scarcely left her invalid's couch. That the Lady with a Lamp spent most of her life in bed tenderly nursed by others seems at first an ironic twist of fate, but any irony lies in the assumption that nurse and patient are opposite roles. In fact, for Nightingale, and I would argue, in the imaginative lives of many Victorian women, they were essentially the same role. For both nurse and patient, the sick body was the mediating term by which the desire to go beyond restrictive gender roles and the cultural imperative to renounce that desire could be reconciled. By occupying themselves with the body in all of its insistent materiality women could affirm the dominant cultural view of their proper role and sphere and at the same time assert their own claims through the particular set of circumstances and privileges that prevailed in the sickroom.

On the opening page of her biography of Nightingale, Cecil Woodham-Smith writes, "It would have been better if Florence had been a boy."[3] Woodham-Smith's remark, in context, relates to the complications attached to the property of Nightingale's father, which, if Florence had been a male, would have remained in the family rather than passing to her aunt and then to her aunt's eldest son. The comment, of course, is true in a more significant way than this, although the descent of property through the male line, and with it the power such property confers, is centrally at issue. From an early age, Nightingale possessed a conviction of her own greatness, but, as a woman, she had no appropriate sphere within which to exercise her powers. Bound by laws excluding women from political and economic life, by conventions limiting them to the performance of social duties and the fulfillment of family obligations, and by the moral rigor with which she judged her own motives and actions in accordance with the terms available to her, she suffered through long years of frustration and distress attempting to discover a vocation that would free her from these checks on her ambition while still satisfying their claims upon her conscience. "Only think of the happiness," she wrote from her ailing grandmother's bedside, "of working, and working successfully too, and with no doubts as to His path, and no alloy of vanity or love of display or glory, but with the ecstasy of single-heartedness."[4] As the site of this remark indicates, she found a temporary respite from her conflicts in the unsolicited urgencies of illness—an overriding duty to which she could gratefully submit without incurring the guilt of self-initiated action. This therapeutic effect of nursing was not an uncommon experience in the lives of middle and upper-class Victorian women. George Eliot found a similar kind of respite from the agonizing conflicts between her own aspirations and her familial duties. Nursing her father in his final illness, she wrote to a friend: "I am enjoying repose strength and ardour in a greater degree than I have ever known and yet I never felt my own insignificance and imperfection so completely."[5] As both quotations indicate, the anxiety that nursing specifically allays is that one's actions or exertions might be imputed to "vainglory"—to self-promotion or assertion— a motive suspect even for men in Nightingale's social milieu, unthinkable for women. Nightingale ultimately translated this temporary respite from her hunger for accomplishment and her family's resistance to it into a clear sense of vocation sanctioned, according to Nightingale, by God Himself. After a protracted struggle with her mother and her sister Parthenope, which the appeal to the higher filial obligation to God helped her to win, she began at the age of thirty-two the career that would send her to Scutari and the embrace of legend.

In becoming a nurse Nightingale was defying not only her family but societal conventions and expectations as well. The wealthy and well-connected Nightingale was expected to make a brilliant social success, to marry well, and to bear children, not to immure herself in the sordid world of hospitals for the destitute or in the battle-fields of the Empire. What was considered the highest role a woman could perform within the home—an act of tenderness, sympathy, and tact—was, outside of the home, and for hire, considered to be menial, degrading, and improper. Nurses belonged to the servant class and, as F. F. Cartwright notes in *A Social History of Medicine,* "when employed in private houses, were regarded as equals of the scullery maid rather than of the upper servants."[6] Although the paid nurse was not always such a reprobate as the popular image of her would have it,[7] nursing, even at the administrative level, was no job for a lady. Drunkenness and promiscuity were common among them, especially those who worked in hospitals where "large supplies of alcohol were available in the wards and the presence of a number of young apprentices and house pupils encouraged prostitution" (Cartwright, 154). For the most part, nurses were un-trained and uneducated—until reforms were instituted for which Nightingale was in part responsible—and were required to work long hours under deplorable conditions without supervision and in difficult, even dangerous, circumstances.

Despite the less than exalted actuality of the nursing profession at mid-century, there existed a concomitant idealization of the nurse figure to which Nightingale responded in her search for a vocation commensurate with her ambitions and to which she greatly con-tributed by her service in the Crimea. There are evident reasons why the idea of nursing might have appealed to her desire to ap-pease social expectations and yet satisfy her ambitions for a wider scope of effect. The nurse's duties outside the home corresponded to the male middle-class ideal of public service and yet could be seen as an extension of a woman's household tasks—she provides food, ensures cleanliness, and sees generally to the needs of those under her care. The nurse, moreover, embodies feminine ideals of compassion and self-abnegation, "doing" for others at the expense of her own vital powers. At the same time that the nurse devotes herself to her patients' needs she is also in control of his or her (but more specifically his) conduct and the disposition of his person. Nursing puts her in a position of authority, in other words, which may be openly exercised under the aegis of a uniquely feminine power. "Nursing," Nightingale wrote, "is the only case, queens not excepted, where a woman is really in charge of men."[8] There is also an at least implicit intimacy in this charge of men's bodies and their sickbed confidences, an intimacy kept in check by the restraint of debility and at the same time made obligatory by it. When Nightingale wrote of the incessant daydreaming indulged in by idle young women, she included among the romantic encounters that characterize such dreams "the nursing of some new friend in sickness" (*Cassandra*, 27). It is perhaps that awareness of how closely linked, indeed, how precariously vulnerable such physical intimacy and tenderness of address is to sexual desire that led Nightingale later to emphasize chastity in her description of the good nurse. She should be "1) Chaste, in the sense of the Sermon on the Mount; a good nurse should be the Sermon on the Mount in herself" (*Selected Writings*, 351). At some level, even more appealing for women of the leisured classes, was the overt, even publicly acknowledged sense in which lives, specifically male lives, depended on the execution of female duties which in the ordinary course of events were, according to Nightingale, mere "conventional frivolities" if not "bad habits" (*Cassandra*, 37).

For Nightingale, a combination of privilege, ruling-class connections, and fortuitous historical circumstances permitted her to become nurse-in-chief to the British Army at war. The spectacular nature of her accomplishments, her social rank, the drama of wartime, and the voluntary status of her work was more than sufficient to overcome the opprobrium attached to nursing and to the exercise of female authority in the public domain. Like Joan of Arc, to whom she was repeatedly compared, Nightingale became a heroine rather than a model that might provide a precedent for reexamining the capacities of women to work in fields from which they had been excluded. She could be conveniently considered *sui generis*. Still, Nightingale, in the popular representation of her as ministering angel to the troops, enduring incalculable hardship in a wholly masculine terrain to the acclaim of her nation and government, incarnated the shared fantasies and concrete aspirations of millions of women, who, like Dorothea Brooke in *Middlemarch,* wished for more than to have "lived faithfully a hidden life and [to] rest in unvisited tombs."[9]

Something very like the shape of her career informed the plots of novels written both before and after the Crimean War. In these novels a woman leaves home (a necessary component of the story), often explicitly having broken communal and kinship ties, and ends up ministering to multitudes, usually in a foreign land. In *Romola,* for instance, George Eliot's heroine, who has allowed herself to be defined by the various men in her life in ways that negate her being and stifle her capacities for knowledge and achievement, becomes, providentially, the heroic nurse of a village decimated by plague. Her activities there redeem by example a society plagued by corruption and intrigue, and earn her the reverence of the villagers (who at first believe her to be the Virgin Mary). In Elizabeth Gaskell's *Ruth,* the seamstress seduced, impregnated, and abandoned by her upper-class lover expiates her sin by single-handedly nursing a hospital full of typhus patients, becoming in the process a saintly figure who helps to heal social divisions. Harriet Martineau's *The Sickness and Health of the People of Blaeburn* recounts in fictional form the story of Mary Pickard, an American woman who nursed an English village stricken with fever, becoming known to the villagers as "The Good Lady" and leaving behind a legacy of moral and hygienic probity. Nursing in these novels and in Nightingale's life does not extend the range of vocational possibilities for women, but rather expands the apparent significance of the nurse's functions in the construction of a just society or, at the very least, extends the benefits of a woman's salutary powers beyond the home. Significantly, each of these heroines, having exhausted herself in the service of others, becomes a patient in turn, thus assuring her return to the dependency and incapacity that mark her as female and initiating her return to private life and familial obligations. The interim period of convalescence, however, is not without its attractions. The ailing Romola, for instance, lies on a "delicious bed" being fed "honey, fresh cakes, eggs and polenta" by the villagers.[10] The members of Ruth's adoptive family "vied with the other in the tenderest cares."[11] Indeed, the transformation of nurse to patient in these fictions indicates what I take to be the originating impulse of the heroic-nurse narrative—the desire to construct a self that can simultaneously command others and submit to them, effect a form of solidarity in isolation from society, authorize self-indulgence and yet exact self-denial, and all within the sphere deemed suitable to women. Being a patient achieves this reconciliation of opposed desires as, or even more, effectively than being a nurse. No longer required to attend to the bodies of others, one must be attended to according to one's own specifications. "A patient wants according to his wants," in Nightingale's words (*Selected Writings*, 352). If we change the pronoun to "her" such a statement could only be an exhilarating license to women who were taught to want according to the wants of others. Through physical debility, the patient asserts the fact of self—her claim to attention and recognition—without incurring the guilt or risking the dangers inherent in self-promotion. She is, moreover, able to separate herself from her ordinary duties and social relations and determine the structure of her social and physical environment for herself. For Victorian women the sickroom was sometimes the only available "room of one's own." In Nightingale's *Notes on Nursing,* she sets standards for the regulation of everything from the height of the bed to the appropriate modes of consolation. Other works of the period, such as Mrs. Leslie Stephen's *Notes from Sick Rooms* and Harriet Martineau's *Life in the Sick-Room,* share this concern for the arrangement and management of the sickroom environment according to the needs and sensitivities of the patient. Martineau specifies where the bed should be placed, what sort of view from the window should be afforded the sufferer, what sorts of pictures placed on the wall, and like Nightingale, what forms of consolation should be tendered in deference to the anxieties of the patient concerning his or her recovery. Each of these books cites as well the special properties of social relations within the boundaries of the sickroom, in particular the release from restraining proprieties on intimacy of speech and subject matter. Julia Stephen writes that "the ordinary relations between the sick and the well are far easier and pleasanter than between the well and the well. . . . in illness we can afford to ignore the details which in health make familiar intercourse difficult."[12] And Martineau declares the sickroom to be "a sanctuary of confidence. It is a natural confessional, where the spontaneous revelations are perhaps as ample as any enforced disclosures from disciple to priest, and without any of the mischiefs of enforcement."[13]

Like her fictional counterparts, and in apparent recognition of what Martineau called "the gains and sweets of invalidism," (*Life*, 197), Nightingale returned from the Crimea in shattered health and within two years of her return had settled into the life of the confirmed valetudinarian surrounded by a chosen few who ministered to her wants—both professional and companionate. It is generally supposed that Nightingale had no organic disease. Though from time to time her doctors concurred that she was on the very brink of death, she not only lived until the age of ninety but continued to work indefatigably for, among other things, the reformation of the Royal Army Medical Services in England and then in India. Whatever the actual nature of her physiological condition might have been, and that she felt herself to be suffering is clear, she managed to work for her reformist aims more effectively through her status as perpetual patient than she ever did as physically active nurse and administrator. After a brief period of public celebrity, then, she imposed upon herself an obscurity made all the more hermetic through the exemptions and prescriptions of ill health. To be the icon of public piety borne through the streets and presented at innumerable dinners and social occasions would have essentially returned her to the life she had struggled so hard to extricate herself from, to have her energies dissipated, a prey to constant interruption. As she put it in a private note, "there are hundreds of human beings always crying after ladies" (W-S, 28). In Nightingale's view of it, the role of the leisured middle- and upper-class woman was to circulate continuously, to be occupied endlessly, doing nothing in particular. Invalidism permitted the inversion of this sentence imposed by her gender and class by permitting her to sequester and immobilize herself while laboring prodigiously on projects of both national and imperial importance. "Our bodies," she wrote of the common view of women, "are the only things of any consequence" (*Cassandra*, 42). As nurse and then as patient Nightingale used this cultural assumption to reverse what were for her its more onerous consequences. Just as her divine calling to nurse had superseded the authority of family by asserting a more exalted form of filial subordination and locating ambition in self-sacrifice, so the claims of her own sick body provided a set of emotional and physical imperatives that overrode more mundane familial and social obligations and left her free to pursue her own aims, still in the acceptable form of commitment to others at the expense of her own well-being.

The assertion of the materiality of the body through organic illness, in other words, negated the social body and its customary or cultural dispositions. In the place of those bonds constituted by the coercions of blood and marriage, nursing and illness permitted her to construct a physical tie with others that was as voluntary as friendship and as essential as survival itself. The soldiers became her family, her children, her beloved, and through a process of identification which seems to me at the heart of her experience as nurse and patient, they became, quite simply, herself—the self whose needs she could not directly serve. In a letter to Sidney Herbert, she wrote, " 'Us' means in my language the troops and me" (Cook, I:52). Their suffering, their victimization were hers; the neglect of their needs by the authorities whom they loyally served and upon whom they were dependent was the neglect she suffered at the hands of a family and a society that thwarted her at every step. She never relented in her disdain for the notion of the prior or superior claims of kinship. In a private note of 1857, she wrote:

> The real fathers and mothers of the human race are not the fathers and mothers according to the flesh. . . . What is 'Motherhood in the Flesh?' A pretty girl meets a man and they are married. . . . The children come without their consent even having been asked because it can't be helped. . . . For every one of my 18,000 children, for every one of these poor tiresome Harley Street creatures [her patients in the Institution for the care of Sick Gentlewomen in Distressed Circumstances] I have expended more motherly feeling and action in a week than my mother has expended for me in 37 years. (W-S, 212)

It was only, in fact, when her mother, Fanny, became enfeebled by age, a patient whom Florence could nurse, that she began to relent in this sweeping condemnation: "I don't think my dear mother was ever more touching and interesting to me than she is now in her state of dilapidation" (W-S, 289).

On her return from the Crimea she replaced her mother and sister (who were officially declared bad for her health) with devoted attendants, most notably Arthur Clough and his mother-in-law, Nightingale's Aunt Mai, who left her own husband and children to become Nightingale's nurse-companion. An intense affection grew up between Nightingale and her aunt, who referred to her as "my child, my friend, my guide . . . my dearest one on earth or in heaven." "We were like two lovers," Nightingale wrote later (W-S, 212). (It is characteristic of Nightingale's demands upon people and her lack of appreciation for familial obligation that when Aunt Mai returned to her husband and family after three years of uninterrupted service Nightingale cut off any contact with her for twenty years.) In addition to those who cared for her there were the men who submitted to be guided by her zeal for sanitary reform (the "band of brothers" as they called themselves), who visited her daily and wrote to her as often and whose widow she claimed to be at each of their deaths. Among them was Sidney Herbert, whose high governmental positions (including Secretary of State for War) assured her influence in the administration of the Army Medical Services. Even these select few were continually subject to recrimination for their several failures of devotion to the causes for which she exerted herself.

And exert herself she most certainly did. The impression given by all the various sources—memoirs, correspondence, biography— is of almost superhuman activity, days and nights of urgent work amassing, analyzing, and presenting immense collections of data, thousands of pages of notes, millions upon millions of words. And along with this ceaseless effort of marshalling and organizing facts and coaching her representatives there was the immensity of the task itself—each hospital with its supplies, its uniforms, its furniture, its personnel, its bodies, to be itemized, cleaned, and arranged. The entire subcontinent of India to be put in order, to be ventilated, to be drained. Nightingale's biographer, Cecil Woodham-Smith, confesses to be wearied by the mere contemplation of the work Nightingale performed from her sickbed. "Work always loomed ahead of her, mountains of it, endless labor, endless toil which somehow must be struggled through" (225). All this frantic activity, urgent, momentous, unlimited in scope, incalculable in effect kept her as insulated from the common concerns of life, the dreadful pull of the mundane chores and mere milling about that she associated with the life of the idle and ornamental woman of her class as did the invalid life in which she immured herself. It is commonly conceded that she became ill in order to work, but there is something to be said for the notion, however paradoxical it may seem, that both the interminable work and the threat of terminal illness were expressive of a supervening desire for absolute control over the disposition of her own time and body.

While bodily suffering exempted her from the intrusions of female duties, it also testified to the enormity of the sacrifice her more "masculine" work entailed, thus clearly distinguishing it from such proscribed motives as self-fulfillment or professional ambition. Her prostration and self-imposed obscurity called more attention to the burden than the glory of such work. She frequently referred in her letters to her sufferings, most often in conjunction with her overwork, and insisted as each of her fellows failed in health that her sufferings were greater, her sacrifice more severe. There is something almost savage in her repeated insistence on the primacy of her own exertions and the suffering they caused her. Though she made obscurity a requisite of those exertions, among her co-workers and well-wishers there was to be no mistake that this work of hers was imperative and that it was costing her her life.

Finally, like her nursing, her disability mandated her confinement, thus keeping her well within the sphere where women could legitimately hold sway while still officially dependent on the power and mobility of men. The importance of this assertion of dependency in the very teeth of its defiance can, perhaps, be most vividly seen in her peremptory, indeed dictatorial demands on the time and dedication of Sidney Herbert and her continual reference to him after his death as her "Master." More concretely, it can be traced in her continuing resistance to the enfranchisement of women, and to the certification of nurses. These changes would declare on the one hand the possibility of direct participation in government rather than the oblique "influence" that she practised with such skill and determination, and on the other the professionalization of the work which she continued to wish to be considered "a calling"— a matter of character, not of knowledge. What made a good nurse, as she delineated the qualifications, were honesty, truthfulness, quietness, cheerfulness, cleanliness, calm, and chastity. Again, she herself was the model from which she drew the likeness, and only strong character and grueling experience had made her what she was. Medical knowledge and certifiable standards of performance would make nurses merely inferior doctors unable to claim, at whatever price in nominal subordination, the uniqueness of nursing and its particularly feminine character.

The doubleness of her self-image—indomitable yet frail, leader of men and loving disciple—and her image of nursing—autonomous yet subordinate, authoritative yet obedient—had its counterpart in her ambivalent attitude toward her own sex. *Cassandra,* her moving protest against the oppression and enforced idleness of women, gave way to diatribes against agitators for women's rights and contempt for women in general. ". . . Women crave *for being loved,* not for loving. They scream at you for sympathy all day long, they are incapable of giving *any in* return. . . . They cannot state a fact accurately to another, nor can that other attend to it accurately enough for it to become information" (W-S, 260). At the same time, she insisted that women were uniquely suited for nursing and she delighted in the company of the young nurses from the Nightingale Training School. She condemned women who wished to be doctors, on the grounds that they had "only tried to be 'men' and they have succeeded only in being third rate men" (W-S, 311). Yet she referred to herself as a man and wrote of her relations to Herbert and Clough: "Sidney Herbert and I were together exactly like two men—exactly like him and Gladstone. And as for Clough, oh Jonathan, my brother Jonathan, my love for thee was very great, Passing the love of women" (W-S, 260). Such ambivalence is hardly surprising in an age when character and capacity were so stringently grounded in sexual difference, in such notions of masculine vigor and feminine sensitivity. Men and women had to encounter with this meager vocabulary of gender the full range of their experience and potential. Nightingale's complex and punitive relation to her own sex surely contributed to her encasing of her femaleness in forms of seclusion and denial.

Nightingale's obsession with dirt, foul air and disease-bearing emanations from the body is a striking attribute of her writings even given the fact that she was a sanitary reformer and necessarily concerned with hygiene, and may also be linked both to the sequestration that characterized her life and to the tyranny of gender roles. Even a cursory glance over her voluminous notes reveals an attention to the danger of infection from the environment that goes far beyond the conclusions of the zymotic theory of disease to which she stubbornly clung long after the germ theory was generally accepted. (Zymosis is a process something like fermentation by which, it was once thought, diseases were produced and which required as a disease prevention measure the constant cleaning and ventilation of the dirt and effluvia from which disease arose.) Nightingale wrote endless accounts of the poisonous odors and noxious exhalations that pervade the average household, breeding in the carpets, clinging to the curtains, stored up in porous brick walls and wood flooring. "A dirty carpet literally infects the room," she wrote in *Notes on Nursing;* mattresses are "saturated with organic matter," and cupboards in the large private houses where disease lingers "were always reservoirs of foul air" (50, 45, 18). But the real danger arose from the body. In her paper on sick-nursing and health-nursing she designated "the body the main source of defilement of the air" (*Selected Writings,* 372.) It should be noted in this connection that for six years of her invalidism she remained in one room only and even on frequent occasions had her visitors (among them her personal physician) send notes to her from an adjoining room. She believed moreover, apropos of such extreme seclusion, that the interruption of other thoughts upon one's own mental activity decomposed nervous matter and could do positive injury to the brain.

Nightingale's profound sense of the invasiveness of bodies, their intrusion on time, on health, on the very air she breathed, may, I am suggesting, have been the primary determinant of Nightingale's decision to be, as both nurse and patient, one who controls and limits that invasiveness. It also refers on the most general level to a peculiarly female experience—the feeling of exposure to the demands and constructions of others; the painful awareness that a woman's body (I quote Nightingale again) "is the only thing of consequence." Mary Poovey has asserted that Nightingale's hygienic concerns and principles helped underwrite the ethos of empire.[14] Yet by interring her body in a series of secluded sickrooms, declaring it, in effect, to be no body insofar as its customary functions were concerned, and by dedicating her life to the institution of hygienic procedures on a global scale, Nightingale enacted a familiar narrative of subjection as well. Her resistance to the disabling conditions of gender merely reconstituted those conditions under her own very efficient, very exacting, auspices.

NOTES

1. Florence Nightingale, *Notes on Nursing: What It is and What It is Not* (London: Harrison, 1860), Preface.

2. ———, *Cassandra* (New York: The Feminist Press, 1979), 30.

3. Cecil Woodham-Smith, *Florence Nightingale* (New York: McGraw-Hill, 1951), 28. Further references, cited as *W-S*, will be incorporated parenthetically in the text.

4. Sir Edward Cook, *The Life of Florence Nightingale* (London: Macmillan, 1913), I:52.

5. *The George Eliot Letters*, ed. Gordon S. Haight (New Haven: Yale Univ. Press, 1954–56) 1:262.

6. F. F. Cartwright, *A Social History of Medicine* (London: Longman, 1977), 154.

7. See Anne Summers's discussion of the hired nurse in "The Mysterious Demise of Sarah Gamp: The Domiciliary Nurse and Her Detractors c. 1830–1860," in *Victorian Studies:* 32 (Spring 1989).

8. *Selected Writings of Florence Nightingale*, compiled by Lucy Ridgley Seymer (New York: Macmillan Company, 1954), 351.

9. George Eliot, *Middlemarch* (Boston: Houghton Mifflin, 1956), 613.

10. ———, *Romola* (Harmondsworth: Penguin, 1980), 649.

11. Elizabeth Gaskell, *Ruth* (Oxford: Oxford Univ. Press, 1985), 430.

12. Mrs. Leslie Stephen, *Notes from Sick Rooms* (Orono, Maine: Puckerbrush Press, 1980) repr. [London: Smith, Elder & Co., 1883.]

13. Harriet Martineau, *Life in the Sick-room: Essays by an Invalid.* 2nd ed. (London: Edward Moxon, 1844), 211.

14. Mary Poovey, *Uneven Developments: The Ideological Work of Gender in Mid-Victorian England.* (Chicago: Univ. of Chicago Press, 1988), 195.

Freddie Rokem

10

Slapping Women:
Ibsen's Nora, Strindberg's Julie, and Freud's Dora

> O that this too too solid flesh would melt
>
> Hamlet

There are many striking similarities among Henrik Ibsen's *A Doll's House* (1879), August Strindberg's *Miss Julie* (1888), and Sigmund Freud's *Fragment of an Analysis of a Case of Hysteria,* usually referred to as the case history of *Dora* (written in 1901 but published in 1905). This paper will discuss and analyze some of the elements constituting the psyche as well as behavior of the heroines in these texts authored by men. For Ibsen this was his second realistic play, for Strindberg it meant a deepened probing into the depths of his own psyche and the conflicts he found there, as well as in his gradually disintegrating marriage with Siri von Essen, and for Freud this was his first in-depth psychoanalysis of an individual, excluding his own self-analysis.

Ibsen, Strindberg, and Freud are the authors/authorities with regard to their heroines as well as the texts in which they are embedded. What these women re-present is not only a male view of the feminine in the specific context of the fin-de-siècle European bourgeois society and its overt and hidden norms, but also an emblematic, and for our culture almost archetypal, situation of men not only creating fictional women characters but also watching them (Mulvey; Metz). This gaze has been institutionalized by the theatre as well as the cinema, and *A Doll's House* and *Miss Julie* are plays written to be performed on the stage, but which can easily be transferred to the screen. Psychoanalysis too is a "scene" where the texts generated by Dora and re-created by Freud in his case history reproduce an intricate network of stories about the masculine gaze.

The interpretation of physical action in the textual medium is a prerequisite for the performative praxis of theatre (as well as film and television): for returning the text to the physical medium of the actor's body. Performance is the process of interpreting the text on stage by "translating" the text back to visible bodily behavior. Through this process the actor's body is transformed into an artistic sign that carries aesthetic significance. The human body as an artistic sign is the intentional aesthetic extension of the body as it appears and functions in its everyday social and psychological contexts. This process creates a hierarchical model of performance comparable to Roman Jakobson's understanding of the literary text, where the attention/set (Einstellung) toward the poetic function of language has a dominant position. In performance there is a similar emphasis of the aesthetic function of the human body. Every production of a play (and consequently every performance of it) is a concrete bodily realization of the presence of the human body in the dramatic text that draws our attention to the cultural and aesthetic codes of bodily behaviour.

The texts of Freud and other psychoanalytic theoreticians function as a point of departure for the clinical practice of psychoanalysis. The presence of the human body is perhaps even more prominent in psychoanalysis than in literature. As a form of treatment it involves the performative aspect of "saying" a text directly involving the body of the speaker (Felman). Dora's body, as it has been "fixed" textually by Freud in his case study, continues to transmit meaning in psychoanalytic discourse and practice, particularly regarding transference, which can be understood as the "body language" of communication, that is, as the physical subtext of psychoanalytic practice. Here I wish to focus on the textual embeddedness of physical actions: the manner in which they are, metaphorically speaking, textually inscribed, thereby drawing attention to the body and its various functions as well as the body as an interpretative focus in the narratives.

The three texts analyzed here depict their respective authors' understanding of physical and psychological processes revealing certain intimate details about the life of the three women: Nora, Julie, and Dora. Ibsen, Strindberg, and Freud, as well as Racine, Flaubert, and Tolstoy (among others) before them, publicly probe the private and even secret regions of their heroines. At a critical point in the process of exposure in these texts, however, there is a growing tension between the female protagonists and their male-dominated surroundings, which culminates in the termination of their exposure, and ends with the sudden and abrupt departure of the women. In the cases of Nora and Dora this complex process is expressed in a growing opposition toward their surroundings. Julie, by contrast, even though she is more independent in her confrontation with male authority and physical power, is finally more submissive. She leaves Jean and her father to put an end to her life, while Nora and Dora leave to make a new start.

The female characters are authored in this way. The different departures are textually inscribed by the male authors in the written fictionalizations of the three women. Resistance and independence mutually condition each other in the characterizations of Nora and Dora, two female figures who have become archetypal for our understanding of a modern liberated woman, and had been adopted as models by some women's liberation movements. But even as Nora and Dora step out of the arena of action, by "departing" from the text as an action of revolt, they are at the same time effectively expelled from the texts by their respective male authors/authorities. It is men who have written departures which, however strong their liberating effect, are profoundly ambivalent, not only from the women's point of view, but also for their male textual partners and authors. This ambivalence concerning the so-called "final departure" constitutes an important component in the project of writing the life of a literary character, in creating a text inhabitated by a fictional person. Departure and death are integral elements in the ritual of writing.

Here I shall analyze the male authoring of some female bodily and behavioral patterns in *A Doll's House, Miss Julie,* and *Dora.* I wish to suggest that the bodily behavioral patterns ending in the departure of the women from the scene of action belong to a larger pattern of physical and erotic attraction between men and women as it has been fictionally expressed in the different media of modern culture. One central theme of each of these texts is actually the conditions under which the heroine will submit her body and/or soul to the male gaze. The bodily gestures I shall concentrate on here lead either to or away from such a possible submission, a submission that does of course not have to be realized (as in the case of Julie) in order to be an important element in these texts.

The sudden departures of Nora and Dora are for both the last stage in a behavioral chain that starts with both of them surrounded and observed by men: Nora primarily by her husband Torvald Helmer, the family friend Dr. Rank, and the villain Mr. Krogstad, from whom she borrowed money on the basis of her father's forged signature on a promissory note. Dora is surrounded by her own father as well as Herr K., her father's friend and the husband of his mistress, who has tried to seduce her at least twice. And through her treatment on the couch she becomes observed by Freud himself, who becomes an important agent in the case history as well as its author. Julie is much more assertive in her initial exposure to the male gaze, and her behavior leads to sexual intercourse during the actual stage-action, which even if it does not take place on the stage itself, is quite unusual in drama.

The final departures in all of these texts are profoundly ambivalent. They represent the ultimate choice following a series of alternative possibilities presented in each of these texts. Nora would probably not have considered her final exit had her husband shown her some kind of pure love, something she had explicitly asked for when her forgery had been discovered. Strindberg makes his couple consider a flight together to the semi-mythological world of Swiss hotels. And Freud presents a number of different alternatives of action while Dora surprises him with the one he thought about least of all. Ida Bauer, the real person whom Freud gave the name of Dora in his case study, left, while Dora remains Freud's forever.

In the scene where Nora shows Dr. Rank her silk stockings in *A Doll's House,* his gaze leads to physical attraction, as well as a very clearly expressed erotic tension between them. The kiss between Dora and Herr K. by the lake in Freud's case history presents a similar pattern of erotic arousal. In both texts the erotic tension ends or nearly ends, abruptly, at the same time that it reaches a climax as the women slap the men across the face. Their final departures are an extension of this slap. Julie not only slaps Jean's face several times, but in their case there are other bodily approaches as well, like the dancing, all of which serve as a prelude to sexual relations. But here too the process ends with a departure—Julie's suicide. The slap across the face establishes direct physical contact between the women and the men. It is an extreme and clearly distinguishable form of behavior which is observed and interpreted by the men in and outside of the texts, and by the readers/spectators, the professional gazers, as well.

In each of these texts death is proximate to expressions of these heroines' ambivalently felt sexuality. The erotic aspect of Nora's relationship with Dr. Rank is aroused immediately after Dr. Rank has announced to her that he is soon going to die, the victim of his "father's gay subaltern life" (Ibsen).[1] These bitter words indicate that he suffers from syphilis. Eros and Thanatos are clearly related in this scene. It is important that Dora's father also suffered from syphilis. The deep ambivalence on the part of the women toward sexuality in Ibsen's as well as Freud's texts is the result of what Sander Gilman has termed "syphilophobia": a fear of the illness with an "ability to destroy across generations [which] made it one of the late nineteenth-century paradigms for degenerate sexuality" (Gilman, 211). Nora's husband Torvald has also been ill, and she forged her father's signature to get money for a trip in order to save her husband's life.

In the scene between Nora and Rank there is a moment of embarrassment as a result of the erotic arousal, during which both of them smile and laugh. After having discussed what will happen after Rank dies, Nora tries to comfort him by saying:

Now Dr. Rank, cheer up. You'll see tomorrow how nicely I can dance. And you can pretend I'm doing it just for you—and for Torvald as well of course. [She takes various things out of the box.] Come here, Dr. Rank. I want to show you something. (47)

She shows him a pair of silk stockings and exclaims:

Flesh-coloured! Aren't they lovely! Of course, it's dark here now, but tomorrow. . . . No, no, no, you can only look at the feet. Oh well, you might as well see a bit higher up, too. [. . .] Why are you looking so critical? Don't you think they'll fit? (47)

Rank answers that he "couldn't possibly offer any informed opinion about that," and Nora (according to Ibsen's stage directions) after looking "at him for a moment," exclaims "shame on you," and "hits him lightly across the ear with the stockings," after which she "folds them up again" (47).

Dr. Rank confesses his love for Nora just after this playful and erotically charged slap, while Nora's stocking as well as her hand and arm serve as metaphorical substitutes for her leg. It was impossible at the time to expose these parts of the body because of the Victorian norms of the theatre and of bourgeois social life. This confession, however, causes Nora to break the erotic magic of the situation, fully aware of her intentions. She gets up abruptly, walks away to the door leading to the hall, the same door through which she will leave her husband at the end of the play, and calls for the maid to bring in the lamp. This is a signal that the darkness which she had earlier characterized as comforting has become threatening. In the same way, the slap which previously was playful has at this point become a slap of rejection. When the erotic attraction becomes explicit Nora clearly rejects it.

Similarly, Hedda Gabler, the heroine of a later Ibsen play (1890) and her "Dionysian" childhood friend Eilert Lovborg recall an erotically charged scene from their youth, which had also been interrupted by a similar reluctance on the part of the heroine. And here, too, fear made it impossible, or at least very difficult, for the heroine to experience her body erotically by having intercourse with a man or becoming a mother. Nora leaves the "duties" of motherhood being warned about infecting the house with the germs of deception; Hedda rejects them in advance, "departing" through her suicide.

Freud's description of the scene at the lake between Dora and Herr K., his kiss and her reaction, is similar to the "stocking scene" in *A Doll's House*. There are, however, important differences in the textual and rhetorical strategies: Herr K. denied the existence of the seduction scene with fervor, while Dora's father for different reasons had accepted Herr K.'s version of the incident. Since the testimonies of both men contradict Dora's version, Freud's first task in his treatment of Dora is to ascertain if she is telling the truth. Freud reaches the conclusion that the scene by the lake actually did take place. However, there is an expression of ambivalence in Freud's description of the scene which neither he nor we have witnessed, as opposed to the stocking scene which is shown on stage. Freud concludes that:

> No sooner had she grasped Herr K.'s intention than, without letting him finish what he had to say, she had given him a slap in the face and hurried away. Her behavior must have seemed as incomprehensible to the man after she had left him as to us, for he must long before have gathered from innumerable small signs that he was secure of the girl's affections. (Freud, 79)[2]

It is significant how close Freud's perspective is to Herr K.'s (Lacan, 100; Gearhart, 121). Just as the slap in the face is incomprehensible to Freud during the analysis, it was, he concludes, not understood by Herr K. Freud's inability to understand his own identification with Herr K. became one of the major stumbling-blocks of the treatment; Freud failed to recognize his own counter-transference: the physical attraction of the analyst to his patient. When Dora announces that she is going to leave Freud, with an abruptness similar to her sudden departure after the kiss at the lake, he naturally (but too late according to Freud's subsequent thinking on transference) returns to the interpretation of the slap in the face.

During their last session, Dora adds some significant details to the case and informs Freud that Herr K. had tried previously to seduce the governess, while uttering the same words—"I get nothing out of my wife" (138; 146–147)—that he had said to Dora at the lake. From the fact that Herr K. had used the same phrase in his attempted seduction of both young women, Freud draws the following conclusion, which he immediately communicates to Dora with great self-assurance:

> Now I know your motive for the slap in the face with which you answered Herr K.'s proposal. It was not that you were offended at his suggestions; you were actuated by jealousy and revenge. [. . .] 'Does he dare,' you said to yourself, 'treat me like a governess, like a servant?' Wounded pride added to jealousy and to the common motives of common sense—it was too much. (147)

Servants are sources of sexual information in the three texts discussed here. Just after Nora has asked the servant to bring in the lamp—usually an expression of rationality and afterthought in Ibsen's plays—and half playfully scolds Dr. Rank for being too explicit about their sympathy, love, and even sexual attraction, which were evident by their common but hitherto silent communication, Nora adds that:

> When I was a girl at home, I loved Daddy best, of course. But I also thought it great fun if I could slip into the maids' room. For one thing they never preached at me. And they always talked about such exciting things. (50)

Dr. Rank answers by wondering if it is the servants' role that he has taken over. Dora is assigned a similar middle position in the K. household: Herr K. talks to her as he talked to the servant and at one point, though she was a family friend, Dora had taken care of Herr and Frau K.'s children, like the governess. Dora is assigned to the position of servant, and she functions as a source of sexual information for Freud, who is the last in the row of her suitors. Freud also comments that Dora gave notice to him, her analyst, just as servants give notice to their employer. The network of abstract sexual information and erotic possibilities are two sides of the same coin. What both Ibsen's and Freud's texts show, however, is that the "abstract" knowledge does not necessarily lead to a satisfying physical experience. The slap in the face—the short moment of physical contact—with all of its different reverberations, interrupts the process where knowledge and action have a possibility of becoming unified.

In *Miss Julie,* the servant Jean serves as the direct tool as well as object of Julie's sexual experience. She is not content with getting the relevant abstract information from him so she uses him to get the experience itself. In this play, as I shall point out later in more detail, the slaps in the face initiate direct physical contact, whereas in Ibsen's and Freud's texts they only hint at a possibility which does not become real.

Freud draws attention to the fact that Herr K. made the same comment to the two young women that Dora's father had made to him about his own wife, that is, that he gets nothing out of her

(57). This further underlines the juxtaposition of sexual frustration and female aggressiveness in the texts discussed here. Freud describes this as an "incapacity for meeting a *real* erotic demand" (151) on the part of the women, concluding that "the slap Dora gave him by no means signified a final 'No' on her part" (151). The men in Ibsen's and Freud's texts suffer twice as a result of these female bodily messages: they endure both physical pain and frustration and mental anguish as the victims not only of a slap, but of their own unsuccessful interpretation of events. In Freud's case this is further complicated by his own unsuccessful counter-transference, that is, his inability to understand and cope with his feelings for the woman he called "Dora." He feels hurt as well as puzzled by the fact that Ida Bauer, alias Dora, also leaves him without prior notice. This, as I implied above, is the slap across Freud's face.

In the texts by Ibsen and Freud the slap in the face, playful as well as serious, a sign of attraction as well as rejection, is a female gesture. The male characters understand the slap as the end of a process instead of as the beginning of another one, even if the texts imply this alternative. On the level of the plot in both of these texts the slap across the face foreshadows the final departure. It is thus very difficult to apply one specific meaning to the slap across the face, and the gesture remains deeply ambivalent, a gesture of attraction as well as of defiance.

I would even like to offer the conjecture that one of the reasons why the slap has become such a strong focal point in the texts dealt with here, as well as in culture in general, is that by hitting the men in the face, by stretching out and aggressively attacking the men in their face, the "scopic" center and the source of their gaze, with a member of their bodies, the arm and the hand, the women are performing what I figuratively call a "phallic gesture." By "phallic gesture" I mean a bodily activity that in some way gives the women a masculine force; an aggressiveness through which they reach out from their bodily limits. Although the human body is not primarily a cultural or symbolic sign, psychoanalytic theory has drawn our attention to the cultural significances of the physiological differences between the male and the female body. By slapping the men across the face, the women have assumed the position of the other sex, activating a whole series of new relationships and possibilities.

The slap across the face has played an important cultural role from Jesus to the whole tradition of flagellation, as well as in sports and contests. When Jesus asks his disciples to turn the other cheek he refers to Agape--the lovingkindness of loving one's neighbor—and not to Eros. The slap must be distinguished from a friendly handshake, a gesture where the hands of two individuals are stretched out in mutual support and recognition. The slap is rather a form of bodily aggression intended to upset the balance of the person attacked. This is accomplished when the slapped person tries to move away from the approaching hand, and when the slap hits, the balance is upset again by the contact between the attacker's hand and the victim's chin. This is in effect a metonymic reenactment, through the use of the body, of the tragic fall.[3] The fall for which a woman is responsible also echoes Eve's seduction of Adam in the Garden of Eden when she stretches out her hand with the forbidden fruit. This gesture leads both to the expulsion and the fall. In the narratives dealt with here only the women are expelled from the text, while the authorative men are not.

The slap is directed against the face, the scopic center of the respective male observers, the source of their piercing gaze. The vulnerability of this scopic center is most clearly exemplified by the confession Nora's husband Torvald makes after they return home from the Christmas party (where she has worn her silk stockings and danced the Tarantella for all to watch)—just before she makes her final decision to leave her home:

> You know, whenever I'm out at a party with you ... do you know why I never talk to you very much, why I always stand away from you and only steal a quick glance at you now and then ... do you know why I do that? It's because I'm pretending we are secretly in love, secretly in love and [...] that I am taking you to our new home for the first time ... to be alone with you for the first time [...] And as I watched you darting and swaying in the tarantella my blood was on fire ... I couldn't bear it any longer ... and that's why I brought you down here with me so early.... (70)

Nora's response to this confession is like a slap in the face:

Go away, Torvald! Please leave me alone. I won't have it. (70)

In *Miss Julie* the same materials of bodily communication and confrontation are used but with very different consequences. Jean, the servant, is also obsessed with observing Julie, the daughter of the Count, in different situations. He tells her the story of how he, as a child, used to watch her secretly in the beautiful garden of her family estate. After they have intercourse, however, Jean tells Julie that he has invented parts of the story on the basis of newspaper articles and stories he has heard. Strindberg thus emphasizes how strongly the "scopic drive" is connected to a fictional, imagined, and even clichéd dimension of the male perception of women.

In the first scene of *Miss Julie,* Jean tells Kristin, the other servant, that he has witnessed Julie's break-up with her fiancé, in which she tries to upset his balance:

They were on the barnyard one evening and she was training him as she called it—do you know what she did? Yes, she made him jump over the horsewhip! Like when you teach a dog to jump. He ran twice and was hit every time; but the third he took the horsewhip, broke it into a thousand pieces; and then he left. (Strindberg, 120)[4]

Obviously, Julie struck her fiancé, but in this case it was he who left the scene while she was left behind to bear the humiliation of having been deserted, as opposed to the women who deserted the men they slapped in *A Doll's House* and *Dora.*

Recent textual research done in preparation of the new national edition of Strindberg's works has revealed that, according to Strindberg's own original manuscript, he had intended Julie to have a scar on her chin, presumably as a result of the horsewhip encounter with her fiancé. She tried to hide the scar with her makeup, but, after her sexual encounter with Jean, the scar gradually reappears. Furthermore, originally, Strindberg meant for Julie to suffer from some form of epilepsy or what was usually called falling disease. In his production of *Miss Julie* at the Royal Swedish National Theatre in 1986, Ingmar Bergman brought these textual details to bear on the stage, with Julie's scar as a shameful reminder of her victimization by her former fiancé. After Jean's and Julie's exit from his chamber, she has an attack of her inherited disease as a result of her despair and humiliation. Julie's scar on her chin points to a reversal of the traditional female role as it appears in Ibsen's and Freud's texts. She has become a "fallen woman" both literally and figuratively, even if she has initiated the physical encounters intended to set the men off balance.

The woman slapping the man on the face and her attack on his scopic center are however also present in Strindberg's text in exactly the same manner as in *A Doll's House* and *Dora*. In *Miss Julie* the concrete results of this attack are quite different. Here the erotic dimensions of the slap on the face are fully realized by the sexual intercourse between Jean and Julie. After having danced with each other twice, Julie invites Jean for a walk in the park. She gives him her arm and suddenly Jean reaches out with his hand to cover his eye. She asks him to show her what he has in his eye, and when he says that it is only a bit of dirt she insists that it was the sleeve of her dress that brushed against his eye, and that she must help him to get the dirt out. The erotic undertones of the situation are explicit, and she tells him,

> Be quiet now; completely quiet! [Hits him on his hand.] So, do as I say! I think he is trembling, the big grownup man! [Feels his upper arm.] With such arms! (136)

Julie's sleeve has hurt Jean, but at the same time she is impressed by his strong arms which are going to "hurt" her. The scene continues with Julie's repeated demand that Jean kiss her hand, while he warns her in French, the language which, significantly enough, he has learned in the theatre: "—Attention! Je ne suis qu'un homme!" (136), a warning that she completely disregards. Or perhaps she is actually enticed by the warning, through the kind of ambivalence appropriate to this kind of situation.

Julie's insistence that Jean kiss her is followed by Strindberg's stage direction that he goes "courageously up to her, grabs her around the waist in order to kiss her" (138), and Julie, as in the situations discussed above, "gives him a slap in the face" (138). As a result of this aggressive reaction Jean immediately decides to clean the boots of the Count in order to diffuse the situation. But Julie, as opposed to Nora, insists on continuing down the road she has taken by starting a discussion about the women Jean has loved, again asking for erotic information from a servant, which leads to his possibly fictitious account, referred to above, of how he secretly watched her as a young boy.

The pattern of the man being slapped across the face by the woman he has dared to gaze at is illuminated further by a small detail in the first scene of *Miss Julie*. Just after Julie has arrived in order to find her disappearing dancing partner and to check the brew Kristin has been preparing to give her little dog Diana to prevent her from running away with the gate-keeper's male dog, a small "preparatory" slap in the face has been inserted in the play. After Jean inquisitively asks if the women are involved in some secret business, which he actually already knows about, Julie gives him a slap in the face with her violet-scented handkerchief. This gesture is a bodily gesture which serves to introduce the whole process of seduction in the play.

Also, the gesture of the raised arm/hand at the end of *Miss Julie* is highly charged with meaning. After Jean has killed the bird Julie wants to take along with her, and after Kristin has warned them she will make sure that no horses are to be removed from the stable before the Count returns, Jean is busy shaving. Julie asks him what he would do in her situation. He "takes the razor and makes a gesture" (186) and says "Like this?" (186). Strindberg's text does not specify what Jean shows her with the knife, but in this scene, Jean usually indicates his throat, showing Julie that she must commit suicide. In their game of changing roles, carried out in an almost hypnotic state, Julie asks Jean to play the Count while she plays him. Julie begs Jean to tell her to become a broom, which is actually the razor, and to sweep the floor. When she becomes ecstatic she imagines that he is a stove looking like a

> man dressed in black with a high hat—and your eyes glow
> like coal when the fire is extinguished—and your face is white
> like the ashes—. (189)

The light from the rising sun has reached Jean, and Julie rubs her hands in front of him in order to warm them.

The hands, together with their aggressive extension—the razor—the head, and the eyes are all present in the symbolic metamorphosis the individuals have undergone in the final scene of *Miss Julie*. But here they are consumed by the burning sun, the fire, which is an important element of redemption in Strindberg's works.[5] The erotic, bodily, encounter between man and woman is only one step on the road to this redemption. Instead of the exits of Nora and Dora out into the world, presumably to start a new life, Julie is now, through her own ritualistic expulsion, making an exit into what she hopes, and perhaps for a short moment even believes, is the next one. The consummation through sexual intercourse of the physical/erotic attraction between man and woman is portrayed as a necessary condition of spiritual redemption.

This essay has concerned itself with two literary texts and one psychoanalytic text. I would like to make a few remarks concerning the relationship between these two textual systems in order to clarify further the notion of "men writing women." The literary qualities of Freud's text and in particular his extremely conscious use of fictional rhetorical strategies to present the psychoanalytic material have contributed to the great importance of this case study in psychoanalytic as well as literary theory. The symbolic-fictional dimension of *Dora* as a text is no less prominent than its empirical aspect as a description of a particular woman. However, my comparison between drama and psychoanalytic writing must take into account the differences in form between the two kinds of texts. In spite of these differences, Steven Marcus has aptly remarked that:

> In content what Freud has written is in part like a play by Ibsen. [. . .] There is, however, this difference. In this Ibsen-like drama Freud is not only Ibsen, the creator and playwright; he is also and directly one of the characters in the action and in the end suffers in a way that is comparable to the suffering of the others. (64–65)

Yet Marcus does not explore the consequence of his remark. Freud's dependence on literary sources for some of the most important concepts in psychoanalytic theory are well known, as the name "Oedipus" reminds us. Freud writes in *Dora* that:

I have shown at length elsewhere *[Interpretation of Dreams]* at what an early age sexual attraction makes itself felt between parents and children, and I have explained that the legend of Oedipus is probably to be regarded as a poetical rendering of what is typical in these legends. (90–91)

Literary texts continue to play a major role in the development of psychoanalytic theory. Rebecca West, the heroine of Ibsen's play *Rosmersholm* (1886), is discussed in a 1916 article by Freud. He remarks that Ibsen deals with this fictional character "as if she were a living person and not a creation of Ibsen's imagination" (313). Freud is always aware of literary technique in his presentation of psychoanalytic material. His report on the treatment of Ida Bauer, the young woman who was fictionalized as "Dora" in the written case history, uses irony to differentiate between himself and the writer of fiction:

I must now turn to consider a further complication to which I should certainly give no space if I were a man of letters engaged upon the creation of a mental state like this for a short story, instead of being a medical man engaged upon its dissection. The element to which I must now allude can only serve to obscure and efface the outlines of the fine poetic conflict which we have been able to ascribe to Dora. (94)

Freud also defends himself against the expected reactions of some of his readers by ascribing a "literary" status to his work:

I am aware that—in this city, at least—there are many physicians who (revolting though it may seem) choose to read a case history of this kind not as a contribution to the psychology of neuroses, but as a *roman à cléf* designed for their private delectation. (37)

Literature has a psychoanalytic aspect and psychoanalysis has a literary one. Literature and psychoanalysis intermingle quite freely; there is a deep resonance between them. A letter from Jung to Freud (October 10, 1907), only two years after the publication of *Dora*, bears witness to the mental universe of discourse in which the founding fathers of psychoanalysis felt at home. In this letter Jung mentions the literary "qualities" revealed through the praxis of psychoanalysis, adding that his current analysis of a young woman is "giving me much enjoyment" because:

> Every properly analysable case has something aesthetically beautiful about it, particularily this one, which is an exact copy of Ibsen's *Lady from the Sea*. The build up of drama and the thickening of the plot are identical with Ibsen's; unfortunately the denoument and the solution lead not to the freeing of libido but to the twilight of antieroticism. (92)

The double irony of this comment derives from the fact that in Ibsen's 1888 drama a husband/doctor cures his wife, Ellida Wangel, from her fears of having to submit to the threats of her former lover. This lover claims his "rights" by using a method in fact very similar to what was later to be called psychoanalysis. The fact that the treatment is effective is revealed to us by her choice, once given the freedom to do as she wants and feels, not to leave her husband and run away with the stranger. In this way the "cured" Ellida Wangel chooses not to run away with the stranger, when she chooses *not* to exit from her author's text as Nora, Julie, and Dora do.

Men writing women, and men writing men *observing* women, results in textual ambivalence which is the expression of a deep cultural ambivalence. Are the women able to free themselves from the possessive gaze of their male observers, and what is the price they have to pay for their independence? The bodies of the three women function as the central focus of these issues on all textual levels. The presence of the female body in these texts (as well as in others too, of course) serves as a source of social as well as symbolic meaning. The larger hermeneutic issue at stake, however, is the relationship between the social and the textual-symbolic dimensions of these meanings. The analysis of these texts indicates that different aspects of the organization of the various materials of male-female relations (the slap in the face, sexual relations, and the departure of the women) take place on a symbolic level separate from any empirical knowledge we might have about the world and its social and psychological relations. These patterns of behavior

may of course conform to as well as confirm what we "know" about
the behavior of women during the Victorian period in Europe.

The textual organization of the material serves as an independent symbolic system of bodily behavior which can of course be
"quoted" in or from the social world, but in the texts analyzed here
the human body serves as an independent symbolic system which
may function as an "archetype" of physical behavior in the real
world. The separation between social behavior and symbolic cultural systems in turn makes it necessary to regard the body of the
actor as an artistic sign when he has taken the role of a fictive
character in the performance. At the same time however, the realistic theatre and a large portion of the modern performance tradition have been striving toward erasing the borderline between the
social and symbolic dimensions of the human body, at least from
the point of view of the spectator.

The texts discussed here are no exception to this symbolic use of
the female body. It is enough to mention Nora's forceful entry with
the Christmas tree in the very beginning of *A Doll's House* and the
fact that she remains on stage throughout the play until her dramatic exit (except for the scene where she dances the Tarantella at
the party upstairs and two of the minor characters are present).
This extended presence makes her departure even more forceful.
But as a result of this presence—until her final departure through
the same door but empty-handed—she is turned into an almost
archetypal cultural symbol of *Woman*.

Even more directly, in *Dora*, Freud has called the physical signs
emitted by the body "symptomatic acts," and he claims that the
patient, when questioned, usually denies that these signs have any
special significance. For Freud, interpreter and author, they are
"most valuable and instructive as being manifestations of the unconscious which have been able to come to the surface" (113). Dora's
"reticule," or little bag, is very easily interpreted, according to Freud.
His extreme self-assurance is no doubt suspicious in the eyes of a
present-day reader, but as a cultural attitude, regarding the body
as a map of the unconscious, it is important for the understanding
of Freud's method of "authoring" female behavior:

Dora's reticule, which came apart at the top in the usual way,
was nothing but a representation of the genitals, and her

playing with it, her opening it and putting her finger in it, was an entirely unembarrassed yet unmistakable pantomimic announcement of what she would like to do with them—namely, to masturbate. (113–114)

Freud goes on to comment that there is "a great deal of symbolism of this kind in life," and a person,

that has eyes to see and ears to hear may convince himself that no mortal can keep a secret. If his lips are silent he speaks with his finger-tips; betrayal oozes out of him at every pore. (114)

In the theatre too there is an overdetermination in the meaning of signs. What seems to be a coincidence on stage, in actors' movement-patterns, diction, or any of the other theatrical sign-systems, is an *intentional* coincidence, serving as an aesthetic sign. On the psychoanalytical couch, from the point of view of the analyst, everything that happens is expressive. There are, according to Freud, *no* secrets, and a denial only confirms that which is contradicted. Freud is quoted having said, discussing the possibilities of the analyst to interpret the sincerity of a patient's statements, "Heads I win, tails you lose."[6] Freud's coin has only one side, that of the winner. The other side has been authored out of existence by his creative imagination.

In an incident related by Jung in his autobiographical writings regarding his psychoanalytic practice, some of the threads developed here—male authority vs. female bodily behavior—are brought together in a somewhat surprising manner. Jung writes, and this narrative hardly needs any further comment:

Once a lady of the aristocracy came to me who was in the habit of slapping her employees—including her doctors. She suffered from a compulsion neurosis and had been under treatment in a sanatorium. Naturally, she had soon dispensed the obligatory slap to the head physician. In her eyes, after all, he was only a superior *valet de chambre*. She was paying the bills, wasn't she? This doctor sent her on to another institution and there the same scene was repeated. Since the lady was not really insane, but evidently had to be handled with kid gloves, the hapless doctor sent her on to me.

She was a very stately and imposing person, six feet tall—and there was power behind her slaps, I can tell you! She came, then, and we had a very good talk. Then came the moment when I had to say something unpleasant to her. Furious, she sprang to her feet and threatened to slap me. I, too, jumped up, and said to her, "Very well, you are the lady. You hit first—ladies first! But then I hit back!" And I meant it. She fell back into her chair and deflated before my eyes. "No one has ever said that to me before!" she protested. From that moment on, the therapy began to succeed.

What this patient needed was a masculine reaction. [. . .] (140–141)

As the last step in my discussion of Nora, Dora, and Julie I would like to analyze their final exits in a more comprehensive context, not only as reactions on plot-level, to the behavior on the part of the different men. As I tried to ascertain the status of women in these texts, I was struck by the fact that the additional female figures have much less prominent roles than the males. For some reason, which the text does not tell us, Nora has not been brought up by her own mother. She tells the nursemaid, Ann Marie, that "you were a good mother to me when I was little," and the nursemaid answers by saying that, "my poor little Nora never had any other mother but me." Ann Marie serves as well as the nurse-maid of Nora's own children, and when Nora wonders aloud "if my little ones only had you, I know you would . . . " (36). All of this is a suicidal reaction to the threats from Krogstad, and a possible question in this context is whether Nora will disappear just like her mother did. It also indicates a hidden intention to commit suicide, which of course is a much more dramatic way of exiting than Nora ultimately chooses. Julie, too, is motherless in more than one respect. First of all, her mother is dead. In addition, Julie's mother had educated her daughter according to a masculine understanding of her psychology and her social roles, turning Julie into what in the play is described as a "half-woman." Kristin, the other female character in *Miss Julie,* also reveals a masculine aspect by behaving like a moralistic priest, according to Strindberg's own preface to his play.

In Freud's text, too, the absence of women other than the heroine is striking. Dora's mother has been assigned a minor role. Freud was presented with only the following clues, which

> led [me] to imagine her as an uncultivated woman and above all as a foolish one who had concentrated all her interests upon domestic affairs [. . .] She presented the picture, in fact, of what might be called the "housewife" psychosis. (49)

Frau K., Herr K.'s wife and Dora's father's mistress, is not given the opportunity to speak directly in Freud's text, despite her importance to Dora. Freud has been severely castigated by feminist critics for not bringing out the female presence in *Dora,* in particular if it is true, as some of these critics (following Freud's suggestion) claim, that the major emotional tie on Dora's part is actually her lesbian love for Mrs. K.[7] This critique stresses that the psychoanalytic treatment was undoubtedly based on different strategies, unconsciously intended, on Freud's part, to prevent her from reaching this insight.

But the absence of women in Ibsen's and Freud's texts goes even deeper. As I have indicated several times, the most striking similarity between Ibsen's and Freud's heroines is that both of them simply leave the scene of action on very short notice: Nora abandons her husband after what for him at least was a very successful Christmas party at their neighbors' home. Nora's motives are very complex, but from her husband's point of view, she simply returns her wedding ring and walks out the door. And December 31, 1900 (what the closeness of the dates means I do not know) was also the date that Dora announced, during one of her regular analytic sessions, that this would be the last one of them. Neither Torvald nor Freud was able to read any of the signs pointing to Nora's and Dora's decision. Julie also leaves the scene of action (on midsummer night's eve), though under different circumstances.

The texts end (or force their authors to end them?) when the women leave. Despite this fact, all of the texts have "postscripts":

Dora with Freud's description of her return fifteen months after her dramatic exit (significantly enough with aphonia, as if *she* had received a slap in the face); *A Doll's House* with its alternative ending, to which Ibsen agreed passively as part of the German translation of the play. In this addition, Torvald forces Nora to take a last look at their children before she leaves. As a result of this melodramatic confrontation her famous final exit is made impossible. Torvald exclaims: "Tomorrow, when they wake up and call for their mother, they will be—motherless [. . .] As you once were" (87).[8] In Nora's case, there were also a number of sequels written to Ibsen's original play exploring Nora's possible future. Similarly, there has been considerable interest among psychoanalysts regarding the fate of Ida Bauer, Dora's model, after she left treatment (Deutsch, 35–43). For obvious reasons, the authors themselves cannot follow their heroines into the world once they have left. Also Strindberg's *Miss Julie* has a "postscript" of sorts. It was first performed in Copenhagen on March 14, 1889, when the implicit subject of the play, Strindberg's estranged wife, the actress Siri von Essen, played the role of Julie. It is difficult to find a more sophisticated way to "direct" the course of reality through symbolic means. The performance was a complete failure and contributed to Strindberg's and von Essen's divorce.

A deep sense of mother-deprivation emanates from the three texts analyzed in this paper. All of the heroines compulsively repeat this deprivation by "leaving" their respective texts. Yet, after all, this absence of significant female figures has been inscribed in the texts by their male authors. The issue at stake is why the male authoring process follows a pattern in which female protagonists, as well as their respective mothers, are either absent from, leave, or are, in keeping with a ritualistic approach, on a certain level actually expelled from the texts. Nora, Julie, and Dora begin to constitute a threat when they raise their hands to slap the men, approaching them erotically through a masculine gesture which at the same time "tells" the men to go away. This threat has to be manipulated out of the text, or *written out* of it, in the same way as the female figures were initially *inscribed* in the text. Women who raise their hands with the ambivalent gesture of attraction and aggression have in the end no place in texts where *men* have been writing *women*.

NOTES

An earlier version of this chapter was first presented at the symposium on women in Israeli and American literature at the Tel Aviv University, 1989. Since then I have made extensive additions and revisions. I especially want to thank Galit Hasan-Rokem, Lori Lefkovitz, and David Titelman for their constructive comments and criticism and Mimi Ash for her editorial assistance.

1. All quotations cited from Henrik Ibsen, *A Doll's House*, trans. James McFarlane (London: Oxford University Press, 1961).

2. All quotations cited from Sigmund Freud, *Fragment of an Analysis of a Case of Hysteria*. (Harmondsworth: Pelican Freud Library [1905], 1977), vol. VIII.

3. As I have tried to show in my research on the art of acting in the theatre, the loss of balance on the stage holds a strong expressive potential. The most extreme form of losing balance is falling, letting go of the body completely, relying on the stage-floor to restablish the balance which has been lost. See Freddie Rokem.

4. All quotations cited from August Strindberg, *Preface to Miss Julie and Miss Julie, Samlade Verk*. (Stockholm: Almqvist & Wiksell, 1984), vol. 27. My translation.

5. The most obvious example of this appears in the final scene of *A Dream Play*, where all the characters are burning their worldly possessions just before Indra's daughter returns to the heavenly spheres.

6. Quoted from Peter Gay, *Freud: A Life for our Time* (New York and London: W. W. Norton & Co., 250n).

7. For a feminist critique of *Dora* see several of the articles in Bernheimer/Kahane.

8. See also a letter from Henrik Ibsen to a Danish newspaper on 17/ 2 1880, where he tries to excuse the alternative ending, "for the use in an emergency [. . .] If it is used, it is therefore completely against my wishes; but I cherish the hope that it will not be used in very many German theatres." Quoted from *Henrik Ibsen: A Critical Anthology*, 90–91.

WORKS CITED

Bernheimer, Charles, and Claire Kahane, eds. *In Dora's Case: Freud— Hysteria—Feminism* New York: Columbia Univ. Press, 1985.

Deutsch, Felix. "A Footnote to Freud's 'Fragment of an Analysis of a Case of Hysteria,'" in Bernheimer/Kahane, 35–43.

Felman, Shoshana. *Jacques Lacan and the Adventure of Insight: Psychoanalysis in Contemporary Culture*. Cambridge, Mass. and London: Harvard Univ. Press, 1987.

Freud, Sigmund. *Fragment of an Analysis of a Case of Hysteria*. Harmondsworth: Pelican Freud Library (1905), 1977, vol. VIII.

Freud, Sigmund. "Some character-types met with in psychoanalytic work." Harmondsworth: Pelican Freud Library (1916), 1985, vol. XIV.

The Freud-Jung Letters. Ed. W. McGuire. Princeton: Princeton Univ. Press, 1974.

Gay, Peter. *Freud: A Life for our Time*. New York and London: W. W. Norton & Co., 1988.

Gearhart, Suzanne. "The Scene of Psychoanalysis," in Bernheimer/Kahane, 105–127.

Gilman, Sander. *Difference and Pathology*. Ithaca and London: Cornell Univ. Press, 1985.

Ibsen, Henrik. *A Doll's House*. Trans. James McFarlane. London: Oxford Univ. Press, 1961.

Henrik Ibsen: A Critical Anthology. Ed. James McFarlane. Harmondsworth: Penguin, 1970.

Jakobson, Roman. "Concluding Statement: Linguistics and Poetics," in *Style in Language*. Ed. T. A. Sebeck. Cambridge: Harvard Univ. Press, 1960, 350–377.

Jung, C. G. *Memories, Dreams, Reflections*. London: Collins and Routledge & Kegan Paul, 1963.

Lacan, Jaques. "Intervention on Transference," in Bernheimer/Kahane, 92–104.

Marcus, Steven. "Freud and Dora: Story, History, Case History," in Bernheimer/Kahane, 56–91.

Metz, Christian. *The Imaginary Signifier*. Bloomington: Indiana Univ. Press, 1982.

Mulvey, Laura. "Visual Pleasure and Narrative Cinema." *Screen* 16:3 (1976): 6–18.

Rokem, Freddie. "A Meeting between two Worlds: Some Methodological Problems in the Empirical Research of Gesturality in Acting." Paper presented at the XIth congress of IFTR, Stockholm, 1989 (Unpublished manuscript).

Martina Sciolino

11

The 'Mutilating Body' and the Decomposing Text:

Recovery in Kathy Acker's *Great Expectations*

"Do you know anything good I can say over your mother's mutilating body?" (Acker 109)

Kathy Acker's *Great Expectations* is several stories folded together, "enveloped" in a structure that gives the effect of continuous narration without the linear logic inherent in that conventional form. The fiction travels very deliberately from a first part entitled "I Recall My Childhood," to the third and final part, "The End." While the narrative is open at either end—beginning with a revision of Dickens's introduction to *Great Expectations* and ending with a comma—the overall effect produced in reading the text is sequential; the reader is led from one event to another without quite understanding how it all holds together. Analogous situations and repeated themes work against the text's disjunctive elements, creating a discourse that vacillates between expressive coherence and disarticulation.

Great Expectations is fragmented in that it is several stories in one, and these are conflated with texts ranging from *Á la recherche du temps perdu* to *The Story of O*. In addition, this montage has

more than one beginning: the first paragraph introduces a protagonist named Peter, but the next paragraph gives us *another* protagonist who is mourning her mother and whose name the reader does
not know. We do not have time to wonder about the displacement
of the first protagonist because more problems await us as the
second speaker develops her narrative by slipping back and forth
in time and in between fantasy and memory. Her story takes us
through Part Two, "I Journey To Receive My Fortune," as she travels in a taxi from New York City to Egypt. On her return to the city,
Acker cuts to a darkly burlesqued situation-comedy dialogue between a "Hubbie" and a "Wife" that ends when "Hubbie" shoots
down a four-year old girl from his window. In the manner of *Candide*,
the tone of this fragment is utterly incommensurate with its content, yet it has serious implications. As if she has been searching
for truth in this quasi-television fantasy, the female narrator comments: "Is there anything else? Is there anything else? What is it
to know?" To which the male protagonist returns to answer: "I,
Peter, don't know..." (23).

From here, Acker launches into an epistolary section beginning
with a letter to Peter from Rosa. Could Rosa be the young woman
who was speaking before? Acker does nothing more to warrant our
inferences in the matter. Rosa travels through "The Underworlds of
The World," and her adventures include meeting Egyptian terror-
ists and being incarnated as O, in whose body she experiences
sexual terrorism.

Part Two of *Great Expectations* describes the experiences of Sarah,
a young woman whose infatuation with the memory of her dead
mother involves her in the mystery surrounding her mother's al-
leged suicide. Sarah believes it was a murder. While tracking the
murderer, Sarah meets her father for the first time. Part Two continues with a subsection entitled "The First Days of Romance,"
where Acker parodies the Gothic novel by continuing the story of
Sarah, who has now married her father's friend, Clifford. This
subsection is followed by the story of two artists and their love/hate
relationship, "Seattle Art Society"; inexplicably, all of the characters here have the names of fifteenth-century French nobility. Are
these allegorical figures? It seems not to matter any more what the
names of the characters are; rather, one responds to a tentative
coherence by attending to the repetition between the artists' love

affair, the implicit analogy to a love affair at the French court, and those that have preceded them in the text. Acker explicates this section with still another analogy and what might be an autobiographic aside: "Historical Example: Peter fell madly in love with Kathy . . ." (81).

Part Two closes with a dialogue between Clifford and Sarah that is written like a play. Soon, the typographical arrangement of the dialogue mutates so that the characters' names are removed from before the colons that precede their lines, so that the dialogue stands without reference to specific characters. At this moment, Acker provides a "skeleton key" to her text: as in Beckett, it does not matter who is speaking. A plethora of characters and their stories are analogous, which suggests that they may all be extensions of the writer and her experiences. Yet, like Beckett, Acker wavers between the need to confess and the need to retain her privacy, writing herself out of the work by creating a *series* of hypothetical personas, suggesting that "her story" cannot be reduced to a single version as in autobiography. The texts that compose Acker's *oeuvre* mark the stages in an imaginary journey wherein a writer reads her culture and herself. The reader of *Great Expectations* accompanies Acker on her quest to answer the following questions: how does a woman interrupt the intertextual weave of her own identity? How can she "think back through her mothers" when her own mother only leaves a legacy of masochism and suicide? When will she be done mourning the loss of that mother? How can she extricate herself from the melancholy and desire that propel her into a series of self-destructive relationships?

Like its formidable namesake, Kathy Acker's *Great Expectations* is inaugurated at an orphan's self-naming before his parents' graves. The first section of Acker's text is called "Plagiarism," and appropriately, its first lines are lifted from Dickens's introduction, though not quite verbatim: in Acker's text, the orphan knows only his father's name, given him by "the authority of his tombstone and [the orphan's] sister—Mrs. Joe Gargery, who married the blacksmith" (1). In Dickens's version Pip reads his mother's name on that tombstone, but Acker erases the inscription, *"Also Georgianna Wife of the Above,"* making the mother nameless in death. While Acker's intentions are obscure, the effects of this erasure are not: this conspicuous omission in the twentieth-century *Great Expectations* highlights the nineteenth-century practice of Civil Death, suffered by the orphan's sister in Dickens's text, who has lost her name in marriage and is known throughout Dickens's novel as "Mrs. Joe." Acker's introduction exaggerates this convention; her revisions indicate that her protagonist's self-naming will occur in a masculine register—in a world where naming has been appropriated by patriarchs; thus, we should not be surprised that her speaker designates himself male: he would be male through the very process of designation reproduced. "To be" in discourse is to be male.

So, opening the book is opening two books, Acker's and Dickens's, and in that double opening, we are introduced into a patriarchal field. At the outset, by gendering a protagonist male, both Acker and Dickens fulfill the expectations associated with *Bildungsroman,* traditionally a male genre. Moreover, in the "original" book, the father's name inscribed in stone is mutated from Pirrip to Pip (or "seed"), a slippage through which Dickens suggests that, by naming himself, Pip creates himself, enjoying a brief moment of self-determination. Acker continues the slippage. Her speaker revises once more to name himself "Peter"—a name with colloquial, phallic connotations. Is this a feminist commentary upon Dickens's text? Here, at the beginning, at the source, one might ask whether Acker's *Great Expectations* actuates a dissemination or an interruption of literary patrimony?

It seems that Acker appropriates discourse to assuage women's disenfranchisement before the Canon, before the Word. As Hélène Cixous asserts, woman's "right to herself has been extorted at the same time as her name" (Medusa, 258). Acker's theft, or extended citation at the dual site of naming *and* loss, of naming and death, disrupts what Cixous calls "the realm of the proper." Patriarchal economy is governed by exchange, driven by possession. As Cixous and others point out, the proper name is a rhetorical mechanism that initiates all offspring—be they naturally reproduced (children) or culturally produced (books)—into this economy. Moreover, naming under patrilinear custom disassociates maternity from (re)production. Patriarchal metaphors for literary creation appropriate the female power of conception by describing the author as a man who conceives; an author then *legitimates* his book by affixing his signature to it. Acker's plagiarism performs a feminist critique in that it strips the value of possessive signing and cuts the *man*-made umbilical cord between author and book. By breaking the laws the govern textual legitimacy through plagiarism, Acker disassociates herself from patriarchal literary tradition. By challenging the concept of creative originality, she refuses the part of father-god: her fictions do not spring whole and hapless like Athena from the head of Zeus.[1]

The procedure of naming and Acker's apparent "debt" to a literary forefather may suggest continuing operations of patriarchal economies. But plagiarism is not the same thing as allusion; theft does not acknowledge debt. Purposeful plagiarism exploits the distance between the author's signature and the work; through Acker's illegal revision, Dickens's work becomes a text, overrunning its margins and reappearing elsewhere, under another's name. The very fact that "Acker's" text begins within another illustrates a confounding of origins. The conflation challenges patriarchal modes of literary possession and performs a commentary about the impossibilities of "making it new" in such a way that the very Oedipal "anxiety of influence" can have no bearing here. Moreover, by burying the moment of a text's origin within a text over one hundred years old, Acker also burlesques the impulse that drives a hero through a *Bildungsroman:* the desire to be fully autonomous, to name oneself, to create one's own identity in speech.

In all of her fictions, Acker returns to the places where identity and gender intersect. The second paragraph of *Great Expectations* comments upon the Dickensian opening and its father/son relationship by presenting still another introduction. Again, Peter's speech is immediately followed by that of an *unnamed* young girl; she introduces herself by recalling her mother's suicide and her grandmother's death a year later. This second protagonist "thinks back through her mothers," points of reference that are sites of loss. While she recalls her mother in explicit detail which includes a descriptive catalogue of the mother's body, she never speaks her mother's name and, unlike Peter, she never tells us her own. Because she is never named, the speaker might be any, or all, of a number of female protagonists who will subsequently appear in the text; she may even take on a male persona. Unnamed, "her" identity is as plastic as Acker's writing.

Great Expectations typifies writing that overflows monological systems of interpretation, and with them, the traditions of literary naming. Through intertextuality, Acker disputes the law that governs canon-formation by challenging genre distinctions (the term "novel" does not fit Acker's text) and disturbing the idea of authority as mastery. Literary thefts in *Great Expectations* also include the *pornographic Bildungsroman, Story of O;* the conflation of Dickens's "corpus"—enshrined in the canon—with a pornographic text—far too corporeal for literary immortality—disturbs the borders by which critics keep "high literature" from contamination. In Cixous's words, Acker's writing turns "propriety upside down" (Medusa 258).[2] Subversions such as these "mark" Acker's text as postmodern, comparable, for instance, to William Burroughs's or Robert Coover's fictions. But is there not a particularly feminist imperative in operation here, a gendered re-marking that undoes the work of conventional signification *with* an object, toward a purpose? It seems, in texts "signed" by Kathy Acker, *l'écriture* is *l'écriture feminine.*[3]

This feminist imperative is inscribed at the bounds of the symbolic order where, as Jacques Lacan infamously observes, "woman is not All"; she will never see her reflection in the mythical Subject of discourse. One of the narrative's "heroines" dis-articulates this estrangement: "I can't help myself anymore I really can't I'm just a girl I didn't ask to be born a girl. When I think, I know totally realistically I'm an alien existent" (117).

The intertextual nature of this fiction disrupts the monologism that feminist critics frequently associate with the mechanisms of patriarchy; several "logics" are at work in Acker's text without subordination. As Cixous puts it, the hegemonic opposition that structures phallogocentric writing is effectively undone when the writer invents "the concert of personalizations called I" (Sorties, 97). In *Great Expectations,* this concert is conducted in such a way that it is impossible to ground the text through autobiographical criticism.

Certain details of the narrative do appear to be autobiographical, such as the reference to a young woman who distributes copies of *Semiotext(e)* at the request of her lover. (Acker has been romantically linked to an editor of this journal—in gossip, if not in fact.) Other bits of information are familiar to Acker's readers: the story of an initiate into the world of pornography, whose mother had committed suicide, whose father had raped her—the reoccurrence of these events throughout her fiction suggest a biographical "core" beneath all of the Acker's work. Yet, within these *autoplagiarisms* (retellings of her own life story) and all of other repossessions in this text, where would we find the real corpus? Which *speaks* for Kathy Acker? When we wonder about the autobiographical nature of her fiction and attempt to fix a correspondence between narrator and writer, the presence of several protagonists and the multiple "authors" quoted without permission create an abundance of sources that criticism can rarely tolerate. Looking for a single source, we find ourselves back at the impasse of authority undone: the "author" of this fiction is, like the character Compeyson in Dickens's "original," a forger who writes "one hundred hands." Which, among them, is Acker's?

Truly, one cannot paraphrase a text like Kathy Acker's *Great Expectations* without stabilizing features within the narrative that the writing sets in motion. At the risk of creating a fiction about the text, one could say that it is the story of a girl's education, perhaps Acker's. Writing through male and female narrators, a typical Acker strategy, demonstrates Cixous's assertion that: "... there is no *invention* possible, whether it be philosophical or poetic, without the presence in the inventing subject of an abundance of the other" (97). While Acker seems to recognize this "abundance," its effects are neither "poetic" nor reassuring. The Acker-protagonist reads the texts that constitute her identity in such a way that she identifies with male heroes, internalizes their speech and adopts it as her own, and then, uncannily, she discovers that, by the dubious virtue of her gender, she is "other" in the discourses of men. The heroines with whom she identifies are involved in various degrees of masochism, themselves victims of internalization! The dynamic nature of the text in general indicates that identity is a work in progress, constituted both beyond and by the speaker.

The becoming of the Acker-protagonist involves crucial confrontations with the memories of her mother's death, a loss that seems to have initiated the daughter's own vertiginous journeys through sado-masochistic relationships that are interpolated here like the adventures of a questing hero (a motif that Acker adopts explicitly in her *Don Quixote*). Appropriately, these modern, psycho-sexual exploits are propelled by a desire impossible to satisfy and equally impossible to name.

As for desire, why juxtapose Victorian coming-of-age (inherent in the extended allusion to Dickens) with a young woman's initiation into absolute prostitution? Although *The Story of O* and Dickens's *Great Expectations* are only two semiotic bits within a complex mosaic, tracing the vacillation between these texts alone could generate a voluminous study of gender and writing.

One might recall that *The Story of O* sparked a famous debate regarding the unknown sex of its author. Many critics were tricked into arguing for either gender through "textual evidence," assuming, for instance, that only a woman would be so attentive to the description of O's clothing. Those remarks told more about the readers than the hypothetical author. The ambiguity of the signature—a female pseudonym—engaged many readers in a naive practice of rhetorico-biological essentialism, a lesson for us all. If both men and women are not users of discourse but also constituted by discourse written by both men and women, then how can one tell whether unsigned or pseudonymic writing is produced by a man or a woman? Any able student may learn the conventions of masculine writing, including the pornograph, or, as the texts of Roland Barthes illustrate, a man may write discourse that is theoretically "feminine" and disruptive of phallogocentricity. Saying that Acker's fiction shares in the operations of *l'écriture feminine* is not to say that only a woman may write through desire and the body. And it is equally misguided to assume that the writing of desire and the body are specifically female capacities. This only repositions the dangerous and age-old hegemony of mind/body, male/female, this time privileging the latter terms in each set.

In fact, Acker's writing is disturbing because she shows us how women can learn to think through male desire and demonstrates that more than one gender may operate in a discourse. O's initiation is "borrowed" by Acker to describe a character's coming of age. The intersection conflates a girl's school with a brothel where the evolving female prepares for ultimate exploitation. Here, the student learns how to be a commodity in order "to be" at all: "this work is creating an image which men will strongly crave. This image has to be composed (partly) of your strong points and has to picture something some men beyond rationality want. You have to keep up this image to survive. . . . You are a perfect whore so you're not human" (48).

Most of Acker's writing struggles within the *specular* reality of patriarchal economy; she literally exploits pornography as a means toward speculating an*other* order where women are free of their appearance as evaluated by male desire, where they will no longer be seen—and see themselves—as the displacement of a mythically male essence. But Cixous warns against a utopic feminism with a remark that could easily be applied to *Great Expectations:* " . . . we are still floundering about—with certain exceptions—in the Old order" (97). Acker also cautions us against great expectations in a world where women are still domesticated by the male gaze, produced according to the other's values which are internalized *in abundance* by the female subject/object. Through writing that reflects this gaze and refracts it back upon itself, Acker reproduces this feminine process of internalization.

Often, this project appalls women readers who mistake consciousness raising for a transcendence that enacts little struggle. For these readers, Acker seems to affront without cause, to deliberately repel, to imprison the reader's psyche within the very contexts she would like to escape. Yet, all too often, the assumption that consciousness raising is an easy, celebratory activity seems nothing more than wishful thinking, a feminism that is only imaginary. The way that Acker represents the process, and engages the reader in it, is definitely not transcendent. Revelations are hard-won and certify little in themselves. In fact, "consciousness *raising*" might be the wrong term for describing Acker's feminist texts. Acker does not nurture; she provokes. She does not let us rise above patriarchal economies, but buries us within them for the duration of our reading; she would interrupt them by working through them. Therefore, her "plots" lead through recognitions that many of us desire to avoid. But ironically, such avoidance often leads to more repression and further burial of the very codes that need to be unearthed.

The pornographic plot is certainly one that utopic feminists would resist. However, pornography exaggerates normative values, and it "perversely" grants Acker a poetic license, a concise way of representing women's psycho-social being. The heroine who finds herself in *The Story of O* learns some harsh lessons about "a man's world." For a woman, success in this economy is possession by the other. Prostitutes caricature the female quest to be attractive, to belong to a man. But a possessed woman cannot subjectively exist. Acker represents O as a metaphysical sign signifying the negation of being. O's absent essence is inscribed in her improper name and emblematized by the prostitutes, "the HOLES who DON'T EXIST" (52).

Therefore, the dynamics of possession are inextricable from the very dynamics of being and non-being postulated as Woman, the epitome of abjection, and the lever that makes metaphysical negation of the supreme subject possible. "The 'master' was never referred to by the name of woman. . . . Who was the dark origin of all this nonsense?" (16). There is always a metaphysical struggle in this fiction that wants to be outside of the Hegelian master-slave dialectic, neither master nor slave. "I want: every part changes (the meaning of) every other part so there's no absolute/heroic/dictatorial/S&M meaning/part" (8).

Amplifying the dialectic between slave and master, sadist and masochist, Acker links orgasm and war—a confusion of love with violence—in order to make us recognize hegemonic relations that need dismantling. So provoked, we are haplessly forced to analyze the classical marriage of Venus and Mars, and the psychoanalytic coupling of Eros and Thanatos. At particular moments in Part One, we find Acker's heroine abruptly shifted to a battlefield within her own imagination. Her war fantasies are expressed in decomposed rhetoric, a collage on the verge of falling apart, a rhetorical mess teeming with violence, debris, and sex. The earliest depicts a young girl's sexual initiation on the battlefield. While it seems that she is raped, her own desire mirrors that of the soldier who takes her. Through rape, through bliss, "the young girl [is] RECOVERED," (15). By emphasizing the word with capital letters, but leaving the sentence unfinished through a floating comma, Acker writes a recovery that is significantly ambiguous. Does the young girl recover from her rape fantasy, or is she re-covered through the violation of her body? In any case, why should she have such masochistic fantasies? And, are all soldiers sadists? Is sadism masculine?

Great Expectations reproduces the way patriarchal society recovers the female body in order to drive itself. Rape is the most violent form of appropriation; O is a prostitute raped to the core of her dubious being. Amidst these extremes, Acker considers some "legitimate" appropriations of woman, and accentuates the convoluted desires *of women* that sustain their absence as subjects from the "sight" of subjectivity: "She's turning around and catching his eyes staring at her as if he loves her. . . . He is saying that he is the perfect mirror of her real desire and she is making him that way" (40). Since one must *become* an object, the object is not passive, but complicitous in her own negation from subjectivity. The successful "prostitute" actively maintains the *appearance* of passivity.

By conflating canonical and underground texts, overturning propriety, Acker recovers the subversive subtexts of mainstream culture. She illustrates how women are initiated according to conventional sign systems, and how these semiologies camouflage the institutionalization of masochism. The following lines appear in her revised *Story of O:* "I'm a masochist. This is a real revolution." The passage goes on to "raise" the reader's consciousness by domesticating the gifts that Sir Stephen exchanges for O's body: "He's giving you a ring, a collar, and two diamond bracelets instead of chains and irons" (53). Yet the exchange only continues a burial that O has instigated through her desires: " . . . she feels she's caught in quicksand so her body is her quicksand" (54).

This focus upon masochism is not so much a fuelling of a dangerous stereotype about the female psyche as a demonstration of how all binary opposition is only arbitrarily fixed. For instance, Freud himself had difficulty separating sadism from masochism. He linked each term of that couple to other binaries—active/passive, male/female—in order to keep them apart, yet Freud also insisted upon the coeval nature of these pairs. Acker uses these oppositions in order to con-fuse them, to blur their difference. By writing through both genders, Acker avoids caricaturing the "war between the sexes," a thesis that depends on the stabilization of difference. One sex is not the unproblematic victor (active subject) and the other, the obvious victim (passive object). One character confesses: "I made a list of human characteristics: every time I had one characteristic I had its opposite" (19). To illustrate, Acker portrays both genders as caught between binary forces, including the libidinal economy of sadomasochism. In addition, neither gender has full recourse to (mythical) subjectivity. Never the master of discourse but submitted to it, each character performs poststructuralist subjectivity, each becomes the "I" re-covered by language. Acker's "poetic language"—constituted by profanity and other disruptive stylistics—displaces mastery through rhetorical *jouissance*.[4]

Yet bliss produces a virginal script; because visceral ecstasy is "properly" untranslatable, its transposition to text would seem to result in a blank page: "Purity is always. There's no duality so purity is phenomena. But (relations): a story. A story plus a story plus a . . . makes . . . a tapestry. Human perception (relation) makes more perception. How can purity be a story?" (79–80).[5] If one attempted to write this story anew, the paper would remain untouched; as constituted by relations—intersecting discourses—the subject cannot be written originally, but requires weaving *a priori* strands into text. The writer is careful not to propose a pure subject, an essential self that can escape being constituted in language. Therefore, even if a heroine confronts her masochistic desires, she has not uncovered her authentic self, just another internalized legend. For instance, the O character demonstrates a struggle with illusory essence before she prostitutes herself: "She realizes that she is . . . a little girl absolutely pure nothing wrong just what she wants, and this unnameable dirt this thing. This is not a possible situation. This identity doesn't exist" (44). This "pure" self, untouched by the filthy practices of degraded sexuality, merely continues a clichéd mind/body split and indicates the operations of hegemonic opposition, the "Old order." The mind escapes, but the body is possessed: a familiar tale.

As demonstrated in *Great Expectations* through purposeful decomposition, *jouissance* disrupts the myth of recovery. Since there is no essential self, a subject cannot be essentially male nor essentially female. In addition, consciousness is diffuse, but not *totally* alterior to all operations of language. According to this text, "self-reflective consciousness is narrational" (58). But its narratability presupposes a discourse free from the demands of traditional narration; "story" telling is homologous to masculine libidinal economy—building action, climax, denouement, as well as other gender-rhetorics. By replacing propriety with uncensored relationship, sustaining a method that works through constellation rather than thetic organization, *Great Expectations* demonstrates *l'écriture*, a linguistic operation more precisely able to express the state of being *in between* states:

There is just moving and there are different ways of moving. Or: there is moving all over at the same time and there is moving linearly. If everything is moving-all-over-the-place-no-time, anything is everything. If so, how can I differentiate? How can there be stories? Consciousness just is: no time. But any emotion presupposes differentiation. Differentiation presumes time, at least BEFORE and NOW. A narrative is an emotional moving. (58)[6]

We are presented with narrational alternatives to conventional story-telling. Another initiate, Sarah, prefers a state of diffuse bliss to directly channelled *affect:* "Constant unendable sensuousness—not passion, which destroys—allows neither time nor memory" (73). Such a state of being cannot be chronologically duplicated. In parallel to Sarah's sensibility, Acker's narrative is not modeled according to cause and effect: ". . . I have never yet been able to perceive how anything can be known for truth by consecutive reasoning" (68). This female protagonist speaks of a passion whose "focus" does not reduce the field of representation, but delivers it up in all of its polyphonia: "Do I care? Do I care more than I reflect? Do I love madly? Get as deep as possible. The more focus, the more the narrative breaks, the more memories fade: the least meaning" (61). Although traditional aesthetics requires an "arrest," a symbolic stasis that would yield the resonance of universal truth, this character's reflective penetration does not provide an absolute focus; rather, it catalyses an explosion that interrupts remembrance and significance. A single protagonist allows an author to develop narrative unity through point-of-view, but Acker never uses this organizational device. While it would seem that all of her fiction is a ruthless introspection, a ceaseless meditation on one life, the deeper Acker's penetration, the more the focus shifts. As one voice puts it: "To me, real moving is discovering" (59).

And real moving is orgasmic; it violates typical syntax, as a love scene/rape scene emphasizes. The following lines occur during the young girl's violent sexual initiation on the debris-strewn battlefield—apparently, at the climactic point: " . . . that's why one text must subvert (the meaning of) another text until there's only background music like reggae: the inextricability of relation-textures the organic (not meaning) recovered. . ." (15). Reading *Great Expectations* places us in between two narratives, each claiming priority: one masculine in procedure, one feminine. Together, these gendered, rhetorical forces attract and repel each other, placing the reader on the very cusp between composition and decomposition.

Acker's *l'écriture* resembles the operations of feminine libidinal economies: "Women's sexuality isn't goal-oriented, is all-over. Women will do anything, not for sex, but for love, because sex isn't a thing to them, it's all over undefined, every movement motion to them is a sexual oh" (49–50). One protagonist's spiritual initiation encompasses her baptism into the utopic flow of *l'écriture feminine:*

> And "she was given the real names of things" means she really perceived, she saw the real. That's it. If everything is living, it's not a name but moving. And without this living there is nothing; this living is the only matter that matters. The thing itself. This isn't an expression of a real thing: this is the thing itself. Of course the thing itself and the thing itself is never the same. This is how aestheticism can be so much fun. . . . This is the thing itself because I'm finding out about it it is me." (63)

Twentieth-century critics often equate linguistic innovation and "the feminine." While continuing a project that seems authentically feminist, Acker consciously places herself within the high formalist aesthetic disseminated through modernism. Or perhaps she demonstrates how feminism ambiguously engages formal experiment, with writing impelled by a political recognition but repelled by the idea of authorial mastery. Here, Acker's text presents the kinds of innovations that have contributed to postmodern discourse—dialogism and interrelationship:

> Cezanne allowed simultaneous viewpoints, and thereby destroyed forever in art the possibility of a static representation or portrait. The cubists went further. They found the means of making the forms of all objects similar. If everything was rendered in the same terms, it became possible to paint the interactions between them. These interactions became so much more interesting than that which was being portrayed that the concepts of portraiture and therefore of reality were undermined or transferred. (81–82)

But how does gender operate within this general compendium of postmodern strategies? Postmodern literature continues the vacillations, the ambivalence, of modernist art. In *Great Expectations,* all protagonists are ambivalent about their relations to desire. Since both *l'écriture* and *l'écriture feminine* are launched by desire, Acker's text resembles *Portrait of the Artist as A Young Man:* each discourse is constituted by inherited semiologies; each desires transcendence of the very libidinal economies that drive it. But neither text can transcend *itself.* The wish to escape these economies is not, in itself, gendered, but socially-derived gender makes the escape a feminist imperative and induces a certain craving that can only be metaphysical: for women, possession intersects with being.

Libidinal economies operate this writing, not only feminine, not only masculine, and never androgynous. Gender competes here: primal, violent. We are forced to take sides, and then when sides dissolve, we are abruptly displaced by fresh conflict. Yet there is pattern here, in fact, too much pattern: Acker's texts seem organized through obsessive insistence and repetition compulsion, in other words, in motif undisguised by plot. Amplifying this driven fiction, each character speaks of desire that, by definition, postpones fulfillment. This desire pushes the narrative beyond resolution by multiplying the guises of a pursued other hopelessly lost to discourse.

At the risk of violating the texture of this fiction, let us separate the feminine narrative from the masculine narrative and chart their different quests. The former is driven by desire for the mater imago:

> My image of my mother is the source of my creativity. I prefer consciousness. My image of my hateful mother is blocking consciousness. To obtain a different picture of my mother, I have to forgive my mother for rejecting me and committing suicide. The picture of love, found in one of the clusters, is forgiveness that transforms need into desire. (6)

This desiring protagonist is propelled along imagistic "clusters" of a tarot deck that is frequently reshuffled and re-placed. The reading of her fortunes begins on the first page of *Great Expectations.* What causes the shifts that displace her pursuit? How does mourning her mother relate to her heterosexual experience? What occurs *in between* her desire for the mother and her desire for an other?

> The mistake is in believing that indulgence in desire a decision to follow desire isn't possibly painful. Desire drives everything away: the sky, each building, the enjoyment of a cup of cappucino. Desire makes the whole body-mind turn on itself and hate itself.
> Desire is Master and Lord.
> The trick is to figure out how to get along with someone apart from desire if that's at all possible. (70)

The feminine economy is recognizable by certain "clusters" that might be traceable to masochism. A desire for the mater imago drives *this* narrative, and early gynocentrism admits no others to consciousness: "The whole world and consciousness revolves around my mother" (14). Men are therefore intruders in/to the girl's imagination: "I'm running away from men who are trying to damage me permanently. I love mommy" (15). Violated by *her own* desire for men, the evolving woman transfers the mater imago unto the new love object: "I do everything for sexual love. What a life it's like I no longer exist cause no one loves me" (109). An uncanny recognition poses the threat that the initiate may end up like the mother who commits suicide in a hotel room—because she is lonely. In the course of masochism, there is no being without the other. The economy of masochism is not all that different from melancholia, at least not in its narrative effects. Both cycles manifest futile substitutions. Until the bereaved works through mourning, her love relationships will be self-destructive.

And how does Acker imagine masculine economies? What kind of consciousness/discourse is governed by this other form of desiring? Her male protagonist tells us: "I, Peter . . . obsessively adore my father" (23):

> My mother is a . . . complete jellyfish. . . . My worst night-mare is that I'll have some of that jellyfish in me. . . . I think talking to humans, acting in this world, and hurting other humans are magical acts. I fall in love with humans who I see do these things. . . . (24)

The knowledge of relationship, of connection, is submerged with "the jellyfish," *la medusa*—the prototypical symbol of castration. Fearing his link to this *abundantly* phallic mother, Peter will fear all coupling. Peter confuses violence with all relations to others; "talking to humans" and "hurting other humans" are both "magical acts," inspired by an alchemy out of his control. For the sadist, the most profound relationships are violent.

This is an existentialism different than that expressed by Peter's girlfriend, Rosa. While Peter disowns his imaginary mother and *externalizes* his fear through violence, Rosa *internalizes* her fears about individuation and separation through a fantasy wherein she is victimized. The link between Rosa and her pater imago is violently "forged" like O's iron ring, a circle made of iron and fire, recalling Pip, the blacksmith's apprentice: "Nightmare: her body mirrors/becomes her father's desire. . . . O had to either deny her father's sex and have no father or fuck her father and have a father" (54). Pip's surrogate father, Magwitch, first appears in irons, and suggests, in the context of Acker's text, the iron ring that binds O to her master; the imagery of handling iron and fire saturates Dickens's *Great Expectations* and indicates imprisonment born of passion.

Rosa and Peter are locked together in a desire that operates amidst their mutual blindness. They exist in negative relation. Each desires from the other what seems absent in the self. Finally, the other will help each realize a certain relationship to power. Moreover, Rosa and Peter are bound in discourse, in Rosa's letters, in Peter's story, imprisoned within literary entropy—a trope of desire. Their love affair is plotted through the following cycle: need, satisfaction, rejection, and (again) pursuit. Therefore, the fiction is itself the transitional object between lovers as each cathects the memory of the fundamentally atopic (imaginary) maternal body in his and her own ways.

Maternity is another text, a myth with nurturing, sensitivity, at its center. Legends about women's emotions (an issue to which *Great Expectations* repeatedly returns) project the full burden of direct human feeling and its secret passages into Woman who "enfolds" the secret of relationship. At one point, Acker parodies popularized feminism in a dialogue between Cynthia and Barbarella: "Men don't like sex. They like being powerful and when you have good sex you lose all power" (111). But whores are trained to submit: "Their knowledge of how vulnerable each of them is defines their ways of talking to each other and creates a bond, the strongest interfemale bond women know, between them" (49). "Feminine psychology" is burdened by a knowledge of interrelationship which remains a mystery to "masculine psychology." As always, power drives the wedge between discourses, making them appear mutually exclusive. In a small detective plot, an artist—who discovers that her mother might not have committed suicide but been murdered—is reunited with her long-lost father, a murderer. Her story puts both masculine and feminine economies into play without resolving their conflicts. No crime, no matricide exists except through association.

Therefore, we find clues to a "gender crime" that is itself a fictional, rather than a historical, event. Moreover, a plethora of clues provide no solution to this mysterious matricide. To "know" relations is to recover object relations, to plunge into a blank space before language, to submit to the nothingness postulated alongside being. To understand *conjugation,* one (anyone, of any gender) must submit to what has so long been described as feminine: the gap, the abyss, the hole. One must recognize an initial link to the maternal body un(re)covered by discourse, a relationship that is never overcome because it is atemporal: "I realize that all my life is endings. Not endings, those are just events; but holes. For instance when my mother died, the 'I' I had always known dropped out. All my history went away" (64).

The risk of contamination by this maternal corpus is represented by an open door that "closes" *Great Expectations.* On the threshold, there is no personhood *per se,* but consciousness in motion as if in a constant, diffused state of bliss:

> At the Door's Edge:
> We shall define sexuality as that which can't be satisfied and therefore as that which transforms the person.
> (Stylistically: simultaneous contrasts, extravagancies, incoherences, half-formed misshapen thoughts, lousy spelling, what signifies what? What is the secret of this chaos?
> (Since there's no possibility, there's play. Elegance and completely filthy sex fit together. Expectations that aren't satiated.)
> Questioning is our mode. (107)

Here, Cynthia encourages her lover, Propertius, to "go over": "Here's the hole the window we can climb through to the place we can fuck in. Holes" (105). Sex seems to be the only link uniting this couple for Cynthia's lover, named for a Roman elegist, antagonistically opposes her sensibility. "Propertius On the Nature of Art: 'I know I'm a macho pig why the hell shouldn't I be why should I be something I'm not I care about Writing. Their emotions and hysterics are all second-class existents'" (121).

Propertius's "proper" philosophy enables him to bypass hysteria and articulate an elegy lamenting the absence that is Woman. Comically, his dedication lacks all lyrical qualities, all subtlety, all grace: "This is my poem to your cunt door" (108).

In order to remain the stable margin of his discourse, to give his elegy an absence around which it can form, Cynthia is asked to circle back into herself, to hollow herself out: "The thoughts that have to be imaginings must make you victim eat you, hole" (126). For the elegist, she would become the very figure of self-conscious absence. *But Cynthia, as such, does not exist;* as a capitalized line asserts: "PROPERTIUS TALKS TO CYNTHIA WHO ISN'T IN FRONT OF HIM" (127). Elsewhere, Cynthia recalls her mother's funeral and refers to the beginnings of *Great Expectations,* where a young woman mourns her mother: "... preacher or rabbi asks me 'Do you know anything good I can say over your mother's mutilating body?'" (109).

The imaginary maternal body is the site of longing, the futile object that inaugurates an epic discourse, spreading over a dozen of Acker's fictions: "I'm going to go after you, aching sore" (118). This corpus is not proper: "The threshold is here. Commit yourself to not knowing" (113). Maternal absence contaminates character with desire (for connection, full-fill-ment) and decomposes the text. Significantly, the "true story" of a mourning daughter remains untold. It is as if *Great Expectations* only *prepared* her to mourn. In retrospect, the narrative seems to have been working through melancholia toward a place from which a recovery could begin, a place outside of the text. The daughter will do her mourning where it cannot be appropriated by discourse—in an utter privacy that may only be postulated beyond the symbolic, as these, the text's final lines (and their indeterminate punctuation) suggest:

My mother committed suicide and I ran away. My mother
committed suicide in a hotel room because she was lonely and
there was no one else in the world but her, wants go so deep
there is no way of getting them out of the body, no surgery
other than death, the body will hurt . . . I ran away from pain.
What is, is. No fantasy. Pain. Just the details. . . . I know the
only anguish comes from running away. Dear mother, (127)

The ability to write this letter that the reader will never see,
addressed to a real mother, has not been easy to obtain. Nor does
Acker write easily. Her writing is a suture that always presupposes
an imaginary wound. She will not provide for us what Proust provides for Sarah: "I had moments of happiness (non-self-reflective-
ness) when I read books" (69). Acker forces her reader, whoever will
stay with her, to *work through* the horrors of socio-psychological
womanhood. But this working through is not without moments of
laughter. In *Great Expectations,* these take the form of silly letters
or burlesqued situation comedy—dialogues that translate domestic
spats as infantile and gruesome. Her gallows humor is much like
Kurt Vonnegut's dark slapstick, but it is always aimed at
deconstructing the war between the sexes which has been internalized as a war between the selves, like two genders inscribed within
one name.

Returning to the initial site of loss and the theft of Dickens's
masterpiece "completes" our passage through *Great Expectations.*
Both openings accentuate inscription in relation to an absent other,
launching an elegiac discourse which soon becomes guilt-ridden,
confessional. In each case, we have an education novel beginning
in loss, with a protagonist seeking attenuation through language
and the recording of memory—each incapable of recapturing the
mother's "decomposing" body. Both the classic and the recent narratives are remembrances of a speaker whose inner conflicts are
manifest in ironic distancing and affective break-downs. *Great
Expectations* is perhaps Dickens's greatest innovation within the
area of psychological realism. By relating to that book and placing
it in unexpected relation to others, Acker demonstrates that consciousness is a rhetorical medium, and further, that "coming to
be"—full of gaps and folds—is a process that often resembles
*de*composition.

NOTES

1. Several contemporary critics have explored a history of paraliterary tropes that implicitly compare artistic creativity to procreativity. See, for instance, Sandra M. Gilbert's "Literary Paternity" and Susan Stanford Friedman's comprehensive "Creativity and the Childbirth Metaphor: Gender Difference and Literary Discourse."

2. There are multitudinous echoes between Acker's fiction and Hélène Cixous's texts on *l'écriture feminine*. However, the writings of these two are ambiguously related. Sometimes the differences between their conceptions are crucial. While *Great Expectations* illustrates "a fiction that produces irreducible effects of femininity," it flatly contradicts Cixous's assertion that "we don't fawn around the supreme hole" (Medusa 253, 255). Cixous's all-inclusive "we" is troublesome, especially in the context of Acker's fiction: working through negation is its *modus operandi*.

3. For an in-depth discussion of these important issues, see Craig Owens, "The Discourse of Others: Feminists and Postmodernism."

4. Julia Kristeva posits her unique definition of "poetic language" in "From One Identity to Another." Poetic language is linked to the semiotic, to preoedipal consciousness, and falls within the imaginary rather than the symbolic register.

5. Susan Gubar discusses virginity and its value within patriarchy and relates the attendant issues of authority and legitimacy to women's writing. See "The Blank Page and Issues of Female Creativity."

6. In *Gertrude Stein's America,* the author proposes a rather utopic text that proceeds without any linkage. Here, Stein quotes a fictional speaker: "Language should move, 'not just moving in relation to anything, not moving in relationship to itself but just moving'" (91). On the other hand, Acker exploits the differences between terms in order to initiate linguistic movement. This contrast between Acker and Stein is crucial when one considers the former's project; Acker represents feminine identity as bound by relationship.

WORKS CITED

Acker, Kathy. *Great Expectations*. New York: Grove, 1982.
———. *Don Quixote*. New York: Grove, 1986.

Cixous, Hélène. "Sorties." Trans. Claudia Reeder. *New French Feminisms.* Eds. Elaine Marks and Isabelle de Courtivron. New York: Schocken, 1981. 90–98.

———. "The Laugh of the Medusa." Trans. Keith Cohen and Paula Cohen. *New French Feminisms.* Eds. Elaine Marks and Isabelle de Courtivron. New York: Schocken, 1981. 245–264.

Friedman, Susan Stanford. "Creativity and the Childbirth Metaphor: Gender Difference in Literary Discourse." *Feminist Studies* 13:1 (Spring 1987): 49–82.

Gilbert, Sandra M. "Literary Paternity." *Cornell Review* 6 (Summer 1979): 54–65.

Gubar, Susan. " 'The Blank Page' and the Issue of Female Creativity." *New Feminist Criticism.* Ed. Elaine Showalter. New York: Pantheon, 1975. 292–313.

Kristeva, Julia. "From One Identity to Another." Trans. Thomas Gora, Alice Jardin, and Leon Roudiez. *Desire in Language: A Semiotic Approach to Art.* Ed. Leon S. Roudiez. New York: Columbia Univ. Press, 1980. 124–147.

Owens, Craig. "The Discourse of Others: Feminists and Postmodernism." *The Anti-Aesthetic: Essays on Postmodern Culture.* Ed. Hal Foster. Port Townsend, Wash.: Bay-Press, 1983. 57–82.

Stein, Gertrude. *Gertrude Stein's America.* Ed. Gilbert A. Harrison. New York: Liveright, 1965.

CONTRIBUTORS

MIRIAM BAILIN is an associate professor of English at Washington University in St. Louis. Author of *The Sickroom in Victorian Fiction: The Art of Being Ill* (Cambridge Univ. Press, 1994), she has also published articles on Charlotte Brontë and Ford Madox Ford and is currently working on sentimentality and culture in nineteenth-century Britain.

ROBERT CON DAVIS teaches in the English Department at the University of Oklahoma. He has published widely in cultural studies, literary criticism, psychoanalysis, and American Studies. His most recent books are *Criticism and Culture: The Role of Critique in Modern Literary Theory* (with Ronald Schliefer; Longman, 1991); *The Paternal Romance: Reading God-the Father in Early Western Culture* (Illinois, 1992); and *Culture and Cognition: The Boundaries of Scientific and Literary Meaning* (with Ronald Schleifer and Nancy Mergler; Cornell, 1992).

SHEILA DELANY is professor of English at Simon Fraser University near Vancouver. Educated at Wellesley, Berkeley, and Columbia, she has published widely in late medieval cultural studies, gender studies and Chaucer. Her most recent books are a collection of her essays called *Medieval Literary Politics: Shapes of Ideology* (Manchester, 1990); *Telling Hours and Other Journal Stories* (Vancouver, 1991); a translation of Osbern Bokenham's *Legend of the Holy Women* (University of Notre Dame, 1992); and *The Naked Text. Chaucer's Legend of Good Women: The Production of a Medieval English Fiction* (University of California, 1994). The essay printed here is excerpted from her forthcoming study of Bokenham, *Patronage, Politics and Augustinian Poetics in Fifteenth-Century*

England. Professor Delany currently holds the Killam Senior Research Fellowship.

PAGE DuBOIS is Professor of Classics and Comparative Literature in the Department of Literature at the University of California at San Diego. She received her Ph.D. at the University of California at Berkeley. She is the author of *History, Rhetorical Description and the Epic* (1982), *Centaurs and Amazons* (1982), *Sowing the Body* (1988), and *Torture and Truth* (1991). She is working on a book on Sappho and contemporary theory.

DEBORAH LAYCOCK is an associate professor of English at Kenyon College. The essay published here is part of a larger project on "Gender and Metamorphosis in the Eighteenth Century." She currently is completing her book on the "urban pastoral" in the Restoration and the eighteenth century.

LORI HOPE LEFKOVITZ is an associate professor of English at Kenyon College where she teaches literary theory and Victorian literature. She is the author of *The Character of Beauty in the Victorian Novel* and articles on fiction, critical theory, and feminism and Judaism. She is currently on the faculty of the Reconstructionist Rabbinical College and a fellow at the Philadelphia Association for Psychoanalysis. Her book project is about the representation of biological sisters.

DONALD RACKIN is a professor of English at Temple University. Since his 1966 *PMLA* prize-winning essay, "Alice's Journey to the End of the Night," he has published extensively on Lewis Carroll's fictions and is generally considered one of the world's leading Carroll critics. His book, *"Alice's Adventures in Wonderland" and "Through the Looking-Glass": Nonsense, Sense, and Meaning,* was published in 1991.

GITA RAJAN teaches Victorian literature, postcolonial discourse, and cultural studies at Fairfield University in Fairfield, Ct. She was an Andrew Mellon Fellow in the Humanities at the University of Pennsylvania and a Fellow at the Center for British Art at Yale University. She is the co-editor of *A Cultural Studies Reader: History, Theory, Practice* (Longman, 1995); *Postcolonial Discourse and Changing Cultural Contexts: Theory and Criticism* (Greenwood,

1995); and *English Postcoloniality: Literatures from Around the World* (Greenwood, 1996). She is currently working on a project that examines the pleasure of play in Indian aesthetic traditions. She is also published in the areas of Postcolonial theory and fiction, Victorian Studies, and Film and Cultural Studies.

RICHARD RAMBUSS is Associate Professor of English at Emory University. He is the author of *Spenser's Secret Career* (Cambridge University Press), essays on Chaucer, Spenser, Donne, Herbert, Crashaw, as well as essays on metaphysical poetry, and gay pornography. He is currently at work on "Pleasure and Devotion: The Early Modern Prayer Closet," a book-length study of seventeenth-century religious subjectivity and the performance of gender, sexuality, and embodiment in the prayer closet.

FREDDIE ROKEM is a senior lecturer in the Department of Theater Arts at the Tel Aviv University in Israel. He has published two books, one on the Swedish theater at the time of the First World War (in Swedish, *Tradition och Fornyelse*) and one called *Theatrical Space in Ibsen, Chekhov, and Strindberg: Public Forms of Privacy* (UMI Research Press). He has published articles on modern European and Israeli theater, and he is a translator.

MARTINA SCIOLINO is an Associate Professor of English at the University of Southern Mississippi. Her articles on postmodern fiction have appeared in *College English, Revue Delta, The Review of Contemporary Fiction,* and *Post-modern Fiction: A Bio-Bibliographical Guide.* She is currently working on a book about women's self-representation in twentieth-century American fiction.

INDEX

Printed in Great Britain
by Amazon

21944933R00175